Structures of Our Time

Structures of Our Time

31 Buildings That Changed Modern Life

Roger Shepherd

McGraw-Hill

New York   Chicago   San Francisco   Lisbon   London   Madrid
Mexico City   Milan   New Delhi   San Juan   Seoul
Singapore   Sydney   Toronto

McGraw-Hill

*A Division of The **McGraw·Hill** Companies*

Anecdote of the Jar ©1954 by Wallace Stevens. Used by permission from Alfred A. Knopf, a division of Random House, Inc.

They All Laughed ©1936 by George and Ira Gershwin. Used by permission from WB Music Corp.

1 2 3 4 5 6 7 8 9 0 DOC/DOC 0 9 8 7 6 5 4 3 2 1

ISBN 0-07-136969-4

The sponsoring editor for this book was Scott Grillo, the editing supervisor was David E. Fogarty, and the production supervisor was Pamela A. Pelton.
This book was designed by its author, Roger Shepherd.
Text was set in Optima; sidebars were set in Futura Book Oblique; chapter titles were set in Helvetica.

Printed and bound by R. R. Donnelley & Sons Company.

This book was printed on acid-free paper.

McGraw-Hill books are available at special quantity discounts to use as premiums and sales promotions, or for use in corporate training programs. For more information, please write to the Director of Special Sales, Professional Publishing, McGraw-Hill, Two Penn Plaza, New York, NY 10121-2298. Or contact your local bookstore.

For the Twin Towers
and all who perished in them.

"I believe that architecture has little to do with the invention of interesting forms or with personal inclinations. True architecture is always objective and is the expression of the inner structure of our time, from which it stems."[1]

— *Ludwig Mies van der Rohe*

Since 1969, the American Institute of Architects has celebrated the enduring power of architecture through its annual 25-Year Award. This award honors a structure that is 25 to 35 years old and is widely recognized to be of special significance and broad influence. The buildings that have recieved this tribute span an important period in recent history.

Some of the award recipients are well known, if only through photographs: Seagram Building, Farnsworth House, Johnson Wax, Gateway Arch, the Guggenheim Museum. Some are less well known: Haystack Mountain School of Crafts, Sea Ranch Condominium, Crow Island School. Some are known, but are remote or difficult to see: General Motors Technical Center, Price Tower, the U.S. Air Force Academy Cadet Chapel. Whether familiar, unfamiliar, or rarely seen, none of these structures may be taken for granted.

This book celebrates the 31 buildings that have been honored thus far.[1] But it goes further than that. In hopes of stimulating greater understanding of architecture's power to shape our lives, it asks the difficult question—what makes a building successful? We'll look at where these structures came from. We'll see how they affect the people who live and work in them. We'll explore how these structures in particular, and architecture in general, transformed the United States, and ultimately the world, in the four decades that followed the Depression.

The present work doesn't pretend to be comprehensive. The spaces between 31 buildings as disparate as these are vast indeed. As a result, the book may strike some as if it were one of those vases that archaeologists painstakingly piece together, filling the lacunae with plaster. We often wonder, how did they decide to put that little fragment over here and that one way over there? The hope here is that as you read, the various and sundry shards will start to add up. At the very least, they make for interesting comparisons, shed a little additional light on the subject, show unusual—and in many cases—never before seen angles, and bring in other than the usual voices. In the end, everything that is included is meant to provoke questions and to lead the reader to other resources. After all, it is hoped that the reader will look further. This book is really an invitation to look at architecture.

There isn't just *one* architecture, and there isn't just *one* story to be told. The Bavinger House represents the past century no less than the Seagram Building, though there are arguably a great many more poor imitations of the Seagram Building in the world. As much as possible, the intention here is to let the structures come forth and show themselves for what they are.

There are many factors that go into these stories: the exchange of ideas here and abroad, what architects say about their practice, what they say about each other, what others say about them—in books, magazines, and exhibitions. The book places particular emphasis on the many different individuals responsible for the enterprise of architecture.

The 31 structures are grouped by affinity into eight chapters. Since buildings are complex and multi-dimensional, these chapters are not meant to pigeon-hole their significance. In fact, each building could easily fit into more than one section. Instead, the chapters are meant to reflect some of the more important concerns of 20th Century architecture as reflected in these particular structures: planning a humane urban environment, improving the work experience; searching for collective identity; enhancing our lives through good design; customizing living in a standardized world; expressing corporate meaning responsibly; pushing new materials and methods beyond mere technological innovation.

Since these buildings were at least 25 years old when they received the award, they wind up spanning a period from 1930 to 1970, which takes us from an international depression to a postwar euphoria. It coincides with the emergence of a full-fledged modernism and—if not its final eclipse—the beginning of the end of its monolithic authority. This book, therefore, is undeniably a testament to the virtues of modernism (with occasional and necessary glimpses at its failings).

This is a book for anyone who is interested in architecture; for those who are curious to know more about the built environment, as well as those who are more familiar with architecture and its history. It is hoped that the former will find observations in clear language, and that the latter will find an unorthodox perspective born from the desire to measure architecture's successes in human terms.

As with any project of this magnitude, there are many people to thank for their assistance and kind generosity. I sincerely hope I haven't forgotten anyone.

Kevin Fry deserves first mention as this was initially his project—an ambitious exhibition that may still happen someday.

I am especially thankful for Robert A. Ivy's faith in me, which he has shown on all projects related to ARCHITECTURAL RECORD.

It was an honor to meet Edward Larrabee Barnes, Dan Kiley, and Jay Henderson Barr, and to get first-hand insights into a number of the projects in this book.

I would like to extend particular appreciation to all those who shared their special places and their enthusiasm for them with me, including: Carla Ashe, SEAGRAM BUILDING; Eames Demitrios, EAMES HOUSE; Sheila Fisher, LAKE SHORE DRIVE APARTMENTS; Mark Granada, LEVER HOUSE; Beth Hebert, CROW ISLAND SCHOOL; Stuart Kestenbaum, HAYSTACK MOUNTAIN; Paul Knedler, JOHN DEERE; Chuck Licari, GENERAL MOTORS TECHNICAL CENTER; Carol Littlefield, SMITH HOUSE; Bob Moore, GATEWAY ARCH; Stephen Parks, YALE UNIVERSITY; Therese Van Ryne, JOHNSON WAX; Randy Stansik, JOHN HANCOCK CENTER; Jacquelyn H. Thomas, PHILIPS EXETER ACADEMY LIBRARY; Hobart Wagener, SALK INSTITUTE; and Dorothy Fue Wong, BALDWIN HILLS VILLAGE.

I thank Carol Highsmith for her fine supplemental photography, which captures aspects of many of these structures that haven't been shown before.

For research assistance I would like to thank Mark Coir of the Cranbrook Archives. I am grateful to my research assistants Jennifer Strohfeld and Tanishka Kachru for their patient detective work. Without my able picture researchers Barbara Hatfield and Peter Kelly this book would be nowhere near as good looking—thank you. I greatly appreciate the time my good friend David Teich spent looking over my writing. And, many thanks to my indexer, Barry Koffler.

A special thanks to Susannah Shepherd, a most capable associate designer. I'm not sure what I would have done without the aid of her discerning eye and her quick and talented hands.

And last, but not least, I thank Ann Ledy for her love and emotional support.

"... a building which is truly a work of art (and I consider none other) is in its nature, essence and physical being an emotional expression. This being so, and I feel deeply that it is so, it must have, almost literally, a life."[1]

— Louis H. Sullivan

Architecture is the longest ongoing human practice with the largest, lasting impact on us all. It can make or break political and economic systems as easily as anything else; even war is respectful or disrespectful of architecture before people.[2] We may revere or revile it. Most of the time, we simply ignore it—unless, of course, it doesn't work.

Architecture's outermost features vary according to time, place, and the circumstances of its making, but its essential qualities transcend appearance. If this were not true, people wouldn't travel great distances to see Stonehenge, the Parthenon, or the Taj Mahal. Structures such as these are sought out as if they were natural wonders; for many, they are more significant than nature itself.

Architecture can draw people to places where they might otherwise have no reason to be. Whatever else may distinguish St. Louis architecturally, we can't think of that city now without the image of the Gateway Arch springing to mind (page 210). Certainly, few make a pilgrimage to Racine, Wisconsin unless it's to see Frank Lloyd Wright's singularly magnificent buildings (page 38).

A structure can symbolize an entire group; the Eiffel Tower *is* France, the Empire State Building *is* New York City. A building of significance has a personality; it can be idealized, caricatured, or turned into kitsch.

Even a seemingly ordinary structure can inform us as to who we are, where we've been, and where we're going. If architecture is that important, then we must ask two critical questions: what makes a building successful? And, can architecture truly change our lives?

Satisfying answers to these questions are difficult to come

opposite: Glazed bridge leading from the penthouse to the squash court, SC Johnson Company Administration Building, Racine Wisconsin, 1939. Architect: Frank Lloyd Wright. Wright said of glass: "This dawning sense of the Within as reality when it is clearly seen as Nature will by way of glass make the garden be the building as much as the building will be the garden: the sky as treasured a feature of daily indoor life as the ground itself."[3]

by. Certainly, when architecture fails it's glaringly obvious; it draws attention to itself like a sore. When it succeeds, it is in ways that are subtle, almost invisible. Consequently, we take good architecture for granted.

It might be, as with art, that the very questions themselves are more important than any supposed answers. Sometimes questioning our questions tells us something: when we say success, for instance, do we mean material success? Emotional well-being? Spiritual realization?

Looking at architecture helps; experiencing it first hand is even better. Remarkably, we think that architecture can be appreciated vicariously, through mere description, without experiencing its volumes and voids, its forms and spaces in time. All too frequently we study structures as if they were mute objects that could be understood through diagrams, drawings, or with the aid of the camera. Many volumes have been written through second- or, third-hand experience.

Perhaps we need to look at what architects call the "program" and then have each building reveal its successes (or failures) to us. If building buildings is the result of solving problems, then what kinds of problems are we talking about?

An architectural program is a set of parameters that are established at the outset of any project. They may change as a project moves along, but these parameters comprise the bases of the myriad number of problems to be solved. It is here that problems are created as much as they are found. Architects put a different spin on what constitutes a problem; rarely a negative obstacle, a problem is more frequently a positive challenge—it is the resistance that design needs in order to be any good.

A buiding's program, simply put, always relates to people, places, and things. People are the many individuals it takes to make architecture; building is, after all, a collaborative effort. People are also the users of architecture. Places are the sites that architecture occupies, and all that that includes from geography, to history, to weather and other natural phenomena. Things are the materials, the practices, the technologies, and even the ideas that go into making a building.

Henry-Russell Hitchcock didn't accept Drexler's notion. In the very same catalogue he said, "If there be a 'school,' it would be that of Gropius, whose leading position as an educator and whose discussion of theory in lectures and books provides a more coherent body of architectural doctrine than do Wright or the rather inarticulate Mies van der Rohe."6
left: Frank Lloyd Wright in front of the skyscraper proposed for the *San Francisco Call*, 1914.

1 People

Good old Crow Island,
The best school ever made.
Yes, good old Crow Island,
From kindergarten to fifth grade.
The building's not too low or tall,
It's just right you might say.
And, because it is the best of all,
We enjoy it every day.

— Crow Island School song.

Crow Island School (page 92) is neither iconic, nor well-known (except perhaps with architecture buffs). It presents us with a deceptive sensation of familiarity; to see it for the first time is to think, "I went to school here!" (if you are an American under the age of 65 and attended a school built after 1939). The low, single-level horizontality, the diminutive scale, the ordinary materials, and simple construction techniques have become part of the vocabulary of the public elementary school building-type.

So, why is Crow Island often referred to as one of the best schools in America (and, because of its architecture)? Larry Perkins, one of the school's architects, was characteristically modest:

"You have to understand what you are starting with. First, you have kids from families whose parents follow up on every aspect of their development. Winnetka provides a superb base of citizenship. Or take the teachers. For the last 50 years you haven't been able to teach at Crow Island unless you have pretty showy credentials. So you have had good kids and good teachers."[7]

Nevertheless, the teachers do feel that the building has served them well. "The feeling of being alive was reflected there," says one teacher. "It was light and cheery, and there was always a lot of materials." Another teacher, who taught at Crow Island for nine years, thinks the quality of the staff made more of a difference than anything. Still, he says, "the

And Mies said . . .
"God is in the details." Or, did he?*
  In 1936 Mies, unwilling to compete with Gropius as a candidate for the chair at Harvard, was invited to head the department of Architecture at the Armor Institute in Chicago. He was at first reluctant, but visiting Chicago and finding an openness to his ideas, he eventually agreed. Ironically a visit to Taliesin may have contributed to his decision. Wright, who had refused to see either Le Corbusier or Gropius, welcomed Mies. He admired his work, particularly the Barcelona Pavilion and the Tugendhat House. Mies in turn was moved by what he saw at Taliesin. Indeed the two architects, placed by Henry-Russell Hitchcock in virtually incompatible stylistic compartments, met as equals and as two leaders of the same broad architectural movement. Mies took up the position permanently in 1939 and immediately took part in the creation of the new Illinois Institute of Technology with which the Armor Institute was merged.
  It has long been a popular belief that Mies was single-handedly responsible for the profoundly mundane design that transformed the American and, indeed, the entire world's landscape in the 1950s and 1960s. This wide-spread misperception is to a great extent due to the way in which the "Miesian" became the order of the day in architecture programs across the country and, in the hands of lesser teachers, contributed to a formulaic mediocrity.
  One just has to look with care at one of Mies's buildings to see the difference.

*Mies was known to use this expression, but it may have originated with Gustave Flaubert who said, "Le bon Dieu est dans le détail."

above: Mies with a model of Crown Hall, IIT, from TIME magazine, June 14, 1954. In his critical biography of Mies, Franz Schulze points out that "at the height of his American popularity it became conventional wisdom to acknowledge that Mies's architecture, because it was reasonable and systematic, was the most teachable of architectures. Indeed, it was not at all, and may have been among the least teachable."[8]

Plain and Fancy

Louis Sullivan (1826-1924) set down his life story, in the third person, in THE AUTOBIOGRAPHY OF AN IDEA (1924). In it he says the following concerning form and function: "For his view, his conviction was this: That the architectural art to be of contemporary immediate value must be plastic; all senseless conventional rigidity must be taken out of it; it must intelligently serve—it must not suppress. In this wise the forms under his hand would grow naturally out of the needs and express them frankly, and freshly. This meant in his courageous mind that he would put to the test a formula he had evolved, through long contemplation of living things, namely that form follows function, which would mean, in practice, that architecture might again become a living art, if this formula were but adhered to."[9]

Upon completion of his studies in Dresden, Adolf Loos (1870-1933) spent three years (1895-98) in the United States, where he worked as a mason, a floor-layer, and even as a dishwasher, and where he visited the World's Fair and became familiar with the Chicago School. He familiarized himself with the writings of another architect-writer, Louis Sullivan, who suggested as early as 1885 in his essay ORNAMENT IN ARCHITECTURE that "it would be greatly for our esthetic good if we should refrain entirely from the use of ornament for a period of years, in order that our thought might concentrate acutely upon the production of buildings well formed and comely in the nude."[10]

On his return to Vienna, Loos developed this proposition further by decrying ornament all together as socially and economically wasteful. The theoretical result of his stringent thinking was published in 1908 as ORNAMENT AND CRIME.

The architectural result was the shop he designed the following year for Goldman & Salatsch on the Michaelerplatz in Vienna, 1909-11 (above).

building cut down on intrusions. You didn't have to worry about filling up a bulletin board—you just tacked things on the walls. You could be more dynamic."[11]

Perkins did admit that:

"The building structure counts for something, . . . Yes, it's a factor. But then I have to say that to justify my right to breathe. It's like asking whether in an opera the stage set enhances what's occurring. The set helps some. I believe that. But nobody can prove it. How many saints has your church produced? Donald Rumsfeld would have gotten a good job somewhere, with or without Crow Island."[12]

U.S. Defense Secretary Rumsfeld attended Crow Island for three years in the early 1940s. "I loved going there. I went early and stayed late," he says, but, "I never found that architecture made a lot of difference. . . . One of the best schools my own children ever attended, in Brussels, Belgium, was in an old house with 40 code violations."[13] He feels that Crow Island's architecture had no effect on him, while the quality of the teachers and students mattered a great deal.

Other alumni, however, recall the building and its setting lovingly. "I remember the sense of space in that building," says Marianne Goldberg, a writer-choreographer in New York City. "Everything was your size, so when you reached up, you actually got to something. You had the classroom area and the work area. I don't remember the curriculum at all, to be honest." Victor Bernstein, a Chicago psychologist, remembers the story hours. "We sat by the windows, where there were these incredible views to the woods outside. Those woods were a gas."[14]

Among all the constituents of the Crow Island School project, the architects paid particular attention to the children; something that never happened before and, sadly, may not have happened since. Schools built since owe a great deal to the Crow Island model, yet few of them

above: The Goldman and Salatsch building by Adolf Loos. Since the building's façade lacked the customary decoration, it was nicknamed "the house without eyebrows." Loos's prohibition of ornament was a response to a bourgeois malaise he felt had fallen on Vienna like a pall. left: Merchants National Bank, Grinell, Iowa, Louis H. Sullivan, 1914.

got it right. Even in Crow Island's addition, built just a few years later, hanging fluorescent fixtures were substituted for the original recessed incandescent lights; everyone there feels the difference.

The care given by the architects to the needs of *all* users made the difference in the end. Those who sense the rightness of the spaces and enjoy Crow Island School's textures and proportions, contribute themselves to the palpable aura of the place. A building's success is contagious, affecting everyone, even those who don't pay particular attention.

2 Places

I placed a jar in Tennessee,
And round it was, upon a hill.
It made the slovenly wilderness
Surround that hill.

The wilderness rose up to it,
And sprawled around, no longer wild.
The jar was round upon the ground
And tall and of a port in air.

It took dominion everywhere.
The jar was gray and bare.
It did not give of bird or bush,
Like nothing else in Tennessee.

        — Wallace Stevens *Anecdote of the Jar.*

There is no one element of a program that is more significant than another, but the relationship between architecture and its site is certainly of paramount importance. In recent decades the concern for "a sense of place" has been rekindled as if it were something we had forgotten. This sense is a combination of bodily experience and memory.

One of the most eloquent spokespersons for place as an essential ingredient in architectural practice was Charles W. Moore (1925-1993). An inspired teacher and writer as well as an architect, Moore had a long-standing, abiding interest in how the "spaces we feel, the shapes we see, and the way we move in buildings . . . assist the human memory in reconstructing connections through space and time."[15]

West Meets East
Two important instances of exposure to Japanese architecture in the U.S. before the turn of the last century were the Japanese Pavilion at the Philadelphia Centennial Exposition in 1876, and the pavilion at the World's Columbian Exposition in Chicago in 1893 (above).

Japanese design immediately inspired all manner of artists, designers, and architects, including Bruce Price (1845-1903) who designed the William Kent House (Tuxedo Park, New York, 1885) after a visit to the Philadelphia pavilion, and the Greene brothers who designed the Gamble House, in Pasadena, California in 1908 (page 196).

Few American architects were as enamored of the Japanese as Frank Lloyd Wright. His interests made their way into print when he visited the publisher Ernst Wasmuth, in Berlin, who published the AUSGEFUEHRTE BAUTEN UND ENTWUERFE, in 1910. The WASMUTH PORTFOLIO as it has come to be known, was an oversized monograph with 100 plates showing both architectural plans and details of Wright's ornament.

No creative architect of the time missed seeing the folio. It solidified the new modern direction and became a reference point for decades of European architecture.

above: The Ho-o-Den, a half-scale reproduction of a Japanese pavilion, World's Columbian Exhibition, Chicago, 1893. This was the first time many Americans saw Japanese design.
right: Susan Lawrence Dana House, Springfield, Illinois, Frank Lloyd Wright, 1900. The Dana House was not a new structure by Wright, but a skillful renovation, with turned-up copper eaves like a Japanese temple, and a main door in the manner of H.H. Richardson.

The original state of a site may be retained in part, or reintroduced after construction. Or, nature may be added for the first time, particularly in urban settings. Or, architecture itself may act as what Moore describes as nature's "surrogate." He wrote:

> "Buildings must be inhabitable, by the bodies and minds and memories of humankind. The urge to dwell, to inhabit and enhance and protect a piece of the world, to fashion an inside and distinguish it from the outside is one of the basic human drives, but it has by now been so often thwarted that the act now often requires help, and surrogates which can stand upright (like chimneys or columns) or grow and flourish (like plants) or move and dance (like light) can act as important allies of inhabitation."[16]

Moore often referred to his mentor, Louis I. Kahn with admiration and affection. Kahn's is an architecture of pure geometry that reflects a reverence for materials and light. The integration of these, with the special qualities of a singular place, has rarely been achieved so harmoniously as in the Research Institute that Kahn designed for Dr. Jonas Salk, overlooking the ocean in La Jolla, California (page 44). Moore was particularly struck by Kahn's treatment of the garden at the Salk Institute when he wrote:

> "It's funny how the Salk Institute lurks in the memory, whether or not one intends it to. It comes to mind again when we speak of gardens—albeit somewhat ruefully. When I first visited Salk it was just being completed, and I wrote about it then, enthusiastically, summing up with a description of the stacked office clusters bracketing the central open space 'waiting for the garden to grow.' The garden in question was one that I was then told was planned for

above: Winning entry, Chicago Tribune Competition, Howells & Hood, 1922. Other entry drawings affected the prevailing style, contributing to an American form of Art Deco, Streamline (page 35), or Moderne. far left: Second place drawing by Eliel Saarinen, 1922. left: A rendering by Birch Burdette Long of the American Radiator Building, New York City, Hood & Fouilhoux, 1924.

the space between the two buildings. I don't remember that I had seen a plan for the garden, but somehow I had imagined it would be a fragrant oasis, akin probably to the sacred playgrounds of Krishna found in Indian paintings. That space, of course, became instead the famous paved court opening baldly, some say cosmically, to a stunning view of the ocean to the west.[17]

"The court, as it finally came to be, is a bare, bright, hard surface of travertine paving blocks, screened at one end by a thicket of Monterey pine, open at the other to the ocean's horizon. It is split down the middle by a narrow channel of water and animated only by the stalking shadows of the columnar office towers and by the occasional passing of white-coated workers, their deliberate pace syncopated to skip across the shallow chasm. The space, as it is, is a far cry from what I had imagined, but it is arguably a garden still: a controlled space open to the air, bounded so that experience is set to measure and sequestered sufficiently to nurture reflection and enjoyment.[18]

"Gardens come in all shapes and sizes, from the most intimate and personal to the most public and sublime, and with every conceivable level of sophistication in design, execution, and maintenance. They merit attention especially because they are so thoroughly invested with care, and more linked to the elements and cycles of nature than most buildings are. Gardens remain gardens only with effort; bereft of attention they decay (as indeed do buildings, though generally at a slower pace).[19]

"Most interesting, though, is the capacity gardens have to civilize, a capacity to mediate between nature and humankind. The fascinat-

STRUCTURAL STEEL is the bone and sinew of every great modern building and bridge. It lends courage to design, inspiration to imagination. Founded on steel's known safety . . . confident of steel's adaptability . . . rise the cities of the future.

Equally important is the service steel must perform in the development of small structures—homes, small apartment and mercantile houses, schools and small bridges. Here also steel brings sooner occupancy, greater security, longer life. Structural steel eliminates shrinkage; facilitates alterations or additions. In small as well as large bridges, steel long since proved its economic and esthetic excellence.

Before building anything find out what steel can do for you. The Institute serves as a clearing house for technical and economic information on structural steel, and offers full and free co-operation in the use of such data to architects, engineers and all others interested.

The co-operative non-profit service organization of the structural steel industry of North America. Through its extensive test and research program, the Institute aims to establish the full facts regarding steel in relation to every type of construction. The Institute's many publications, covering every phase of steel construction, are available on request. Please address all inquiries to this Madison Avenue, New York City. District offices in New York, Warrenton, Philadelphia, Birmingham, Cleveland, Chicago, Milwaukee, St. Louis, Topeka, Dallas and San Francisco.

A FREE ENLARGEMENT OF THIS HUGH FERRISS RENDERING, ON SPECIAL STOCK FOR FRAMING, WILL BE MAILED TO ARCHITECTS ON REQUEST.

AMERICAN INSTITUTE OF STEEL CONSTRUCTION
STEEL INSURES STRENGTH AND SECURITY

The Architectural Record, April, 1936

Power of the Press
Journals and magazines were the quintessential 20th Century mode of communicating architectural ideas. Professional magazines in the U.S. such as ARCHITECTURAL RECORD, ARCHITECTURAL FORUM, and ARTS & ARCHITECTURE played extremely critical roles, occasionally sponsoring competitions (page 158) or publishing popular books (page 153).

American architects became far less provincial in their views by reading foreign publications such as L'ARCHITECTURE D'AUJOURD'HUI or DOMUS.

As for the popular press, everything from THE NEW YORKER to HOUSE BEAUTIFUL to LIFE magazine, became a vehicle to reach the growing interest in architecture and to affect public taste. Other popular forms—film, radio, television, and all forms of advertising—round out the picture.

This enthusiastic picture of life in the future is from a 1939 issue of AMAZING STORIES magazine:

"The city of tomorrow . . . will tend first to vastness; gigantic buildings connected by wide, suspended roadways on which traffic will speed at unheard of rates. . . . Helicopter planes, capable of manuevering about between buildings and rooftop airports, will take the place of the ground taxi. Each building will be virtually a city in itself, completely self-sustaining, receiving its supplies from great merchandise ways far below the ground. . . . Many persons will live in the healthy atmosphere of the building tops, while others will commute to far distant residential towns, or country homes."

above: A series of visionary ads for steel delineated by Hugh Ferriss.
right: Cover of POPULAR MECHANICS derived, without credit, from Ferriss.
In his early drawings, Hugh Ferriss wielded his charcoal with a particular ferocity that resulted in an inner glow, a burning, demonic mood that was distinctly romantic and highly influential.

activities. This feeling in regard to machinery is one of respect, gratitude and esteem.

Machinery includes economy as an essential factor leading to minute selection. There is a moral sentiment in the feeling for mechanics.

The man who is intelligent, cold and calm has grown wings to himself.

Men—intelligent, cold and calm—are needed to build the house and to lay out the town.

Towards a New Architecture

Originally published in 1923, VERS UNE ARCHITEC-TURE (TOWARDS A NEW ARCHITECTURE) *by Swiss-born architect and city planner Le Corbusier (Charles-Edouard Jeanneret, 1887-1965), became the most influential architectural book of the 20th Century. Expanded from articles written for his journal* L'ESPRIT NOUVEAU, *which spawned at least three other books, this work is part manifesto and part interpretation of architectural history.*

Its publication brought Le Corbusier to the atten-tion of those who sought a new style of architec-ture applicable to modern, urban needs. The book's radical format mixed photographs of bridges, factories, ships, airplanes, and machines with classical structures. The many plans, draw-ings, and sketches included his designs for the Palace of the League of Nations, in Geneva. His entry was disqualified on a technicality prompting much furor among progressive architects and led to the formation of the CONGRES INTERNATIONAUX D'ARCHITECTURE MODERNE *in 1928.*

CIAM, as it was called, "convened with the aim of establishing a program of action to drag archi-tecture from from the academic impasse and to place it in its proper social and economic milieu." It met regularly over the next three decades.

Although its membership constantly changed and its influenced waxed and waned, in two vital peri-ods—1930-34 and 1950-55—CIAM was the instrument through which many important ideas of modern architecture and town planning were made known to the world.

ing thing is that gardens create a middle ground that can work both ways: gardens in the wilderness are evidence of human control; a garden in the midst of buildings reasserts nature's presence. At Salk it does so by turning attention starkly to the sea, the sky, and the sun."[20]

3 Things

They all laughed at Rockefeller Center—
Now they're fighting to get in;
They all laughed at Whitney and his cotton gin.

. . . For ho, ho, ho—
Who's got the last laugh—
He, he, he—
Let's at the past laugh—
Ha, ha, ha—
Who's got the last laugh now?

— Ira Gershwin *They All Laughed*

Ideas can be more powerful than conrete, steel, or technology. The dense ideological thickets of the past century were born of a collective faith in progress. An example of a progressive idea is that certain archi-tectonic forms will inevitably emerge and express themselves as if they were forces of nature. Largely deterministic, this kind of thinking has resulted in generations of critics and writers who have crafted a single point of view, a vision which has irrevocably changed the way we look at and describe architec-ture. Whether one subscribes to the tenets of mod-ernism or not, these ideas are now received wisdom.

Louis Sullivan's oft-quoted dictum reads in its entirety: "So remember, and bear ever in mind in your thinking and your doings, that form ever follows function, *that this is the law—a universal truth.*" A truism such as this brings inevitable moral obligation with it; we are told in so many words that to not fol-low the law is to be dishonest. Critics such as John

The First CIAM Congress, 1928. Group photo in front of the chapel of Castle La Sarraz. From left, standing: Mart Stern, Pierre Chareau, Victor Bourgeois, Max Haefeli, Pierre Jeanneret, Gerrit Rietveld, Rudof Steiger, Ernst May, Alberto Sartoris, Gabriel Guevrékian, Hans Schmidt, Hugo Haring, Zavala, Florentin, Le Corbusier, Paul Artaric, Héléne de Mandrot, Friedrich Gubler, Rochat, Andre Lurçat, Robert van der Mühll, Maggioni, Huib Haste, Sigfried Giedion, Werner Moser, Josef Frank. From left, seated: Garcia Mercodal, Molly Weber, Tardevossian.

Ruskin and architects such as Frank Lloyd Wright were great moralizers.

Deterministic thinking can also be pseudo-scientific. Walter Gropius and Sigfried Giedion saw architecture as a kind of biological imperative, an ecology of sorts. The forward march of progress may be slowed down, even temporarily thwarted, but eventually things will right themselves and advancements will be made.

All this is nowhere demonstrated as blatantly, and with such convoluted logic, as in the arguments over the relative merits of Rockefeller Center. According to Giedion for instance, the avant-garde overthrows the old order, in this case, through the use of the *slab*—an inevitable form just waiting to emerge. He writes:

"After the passage of the New York zoning law of 1916, the chaotic state of building development was reduced somewhat by the use of the setback and the application of other zoning regulations, but fundamentally no real order was achieved until an entirely new architectonic form was explored, a form for the high structure which was adapted to the requirements of its unusual height and to its internal necessities. This change did not come about until nearly four decades after the skyscraper problem had presented itself. How this new form developed step by step, here and there in various cities, cannot be outlined here. We can only note the final image of the skyscraper as it eventually, came into being in the R.C.A. Building of 1931-32."[21]

He footnotes this passage with the following:

"Steps on the way to this overthrow of the tyranny of the tower, with its medieval echoes,

above: Installation view of the exhibition *MODERN ARCHITECTURE: INTERNATIONAL EXHIBITION*, The Museum of Modern Art, New York. February 10, 1932 through March 23, 1932. Though the catalogue title, *THE INTERNATIONAL STYLE*, has since been recognized as a misnomer by everyone including the curators, the compelling power of its label is difficult to remove. It is hard to imagine structures from so many countries sharing the same style, yet the term continues to be applied to buildings of the period that are monochromatic (usually white), have flat roofs, no decoration, ribbon windows, and skeletal structures.

The International Style

Since its first architecture exhibition in 1932 New York's Museum of Modern Art has played a pivotal role in defining and promoting modern architecture in America. The INTERNATIONAL MODERN ARCHITECTURE *exhibition toured the U.S. for two years. Curated by Henry-Russell Hitchcock and Philip Johnson, the exhibition and its catalogue was central to the transformation of American architecture in the decades that followed.*

Not everyone reacted the show with the same degree of high praise. J.J.P. Oud, on receiving a copy of the catalogue from Johnson, commended the authors on their choice of illustrations and on the text, but objected to what he called "the schoolmastering under the illustrations." Hitchcock's most serious exclusion was Frank Lloyd Wright.

The Museum followed this exhibition's success with an unbroken chain of important exhibitions, far too numerous to list here, except for a few that relate to the material in this book.

In 1938-41 an exhibition called WHAT IS MODERN ARCHITECTURE?, *especially prepared for schools, to explain architecture here and abroad, toured 71 cities and was sold to other museums.*

A 1938 exhibition called BAUHAUS 1919-1928, *organized by Walter Gropius and designed by Herbert Bayer, contributed to the fame of the Bauhaus in America.*

There was a Frank Lloyd Wright Retrospective in 1940, and the first retrospective of Mies's work was organized by Philip Johnson in 1947.

BUILT IN THE USA: A SURVEY OF CONTEMPORARY ARCHITECTURE, *a follow-up to the* INTERNATIONAL *show, was curated by Elizabeth Mock in 1945 (page 28 and 94).*

BUILT IN THE USA: POST-WAR ARCHITECTURE, *the second follow-up to the* INTERNATIONAL *show, was co-curated by Henry-Russell Hitchcock and Arthur Drexler in 1952 (page 129).*

COMPLEXITY AND CONTRADICTION *was organized by Robert Venturi in 1966 (page 174).*

are, for example the Civic Opera House in Chicago (1928-29), by Graham, Probst and White, three slablike wings, yet without any new spatial relationships: the Daily News Building in Chicago, by Holabird and Root (1929), with its blunt, obtuse T-shaped plan in the upper stories; and also to a certain extent Hood's McGraw-Hill Building (1930), which perhaps unfortunately, had no influence on the architectural features of Rockefeller Center. The Daily News Building, with its upthrust of piers, in which there lingers a last implication of Gothic, is much more clearly reflected in Rockefeller Center."[23]

So, some found the McGraw-Hill Building flawed by its horizontal banding, while others felt that the upward thrust of Hood's New York Daily News Building was more modern in its accentuated verticality. Giedeon wished that the Associated architects had used McGraw-Hill as their inspiration and faulted the Daily News setbacks as too old fashioned.

Ironically, the horizontal *versus* vertical question was less of an esthetic consideration than a financial one. In an article in *Architectural Record,* written while the clients were deliberating, one member of the architecture team, L. Andrew Reinhard wrote:

"How was window spacing determined? Purely from a renting standpoint. The fenestration was a natural development from the plan, inasmuch as the service and elevator areas and steel framing were all definitely determined. The steel span of 27' 6" working thus became the working unit. By using four windows to a bay the most flexible subdivision of space was secured. Units of two, three or four offices can be easily provided as the tenants may desire. At the same time there is plenty of window area for large working space. What materials will be used for the exterior walls? This is still an open question. Much study has yet to be given to the external appearance of the buildings. The model, as it stands, represents the rentable cubage. . . . At all times the owners' interest —that is, the renting schedule—was paramount. A sound plan, like a machine, can always be made beautiful!"[24]

Of course, these flippant remarks belie the design decisions that were made around considerations of light and elevator service discussed on page 22. And, it is sound design, finally, that we want to see.

To be sure, there is more than enough of real value beneath the vicissitudes of academic and critical argument; value that will show itself in spite of all the moralizing or the pseudo-science.

Listen closely to Charles Moore's gentle and poetic reflections on the continuity of style:

"Yet another modern and more recent expression of the pilaster can be found on many of Mies van der Rohe's buildings—the Seagram and Lake Shore Drive Apartments, to name a couple. These may be the most distilled versions of the pilaster, being slender I-beams welded and stacked on top of each other, stretching up into the city skies. What a far cry from the more familiar pilaster, but what similar functions. The thin strips rigidly articulate the glass surface, and they wrap the boxes in a uniform cadence of bronze or steel."[25]

In 1938 Walter Gropius, the new Chair of the Harvard Graduate School of Design, invited the Swiss critic Siegfried Giedion to deliver the Charles Eliot Norton seminars at Harvard University. His brilliant, albeit determinist, analysis of the growth of the modern tradition in architecture was published in book form as SPACE, TIME and ARCHITECTURE in 1941.

Another Point of View

The most influential book on architecture to appear in the last half of the 20th Century was Sigfried Giedion's SPACE, TIME and ARCHITECTURE. *Giedion concludes the first edition by claiming to have restricted himself, as if he were a research scientist, to "observations [of] architecture and its interrelations." Giedion regarded architecture as an "organism" that can be isolated and observed "scientifically" in order to gain an understanding of its "nature and growth." He goes on to say, "we have pointed out why architecture reflects the inner tendencies of the time and therefore may properly serve as a general index." In his book's concluding section called "City Planning as a Human Problem," he praised the recently completed Rockefeller Center as the perfect example of a "new tradition of Space-Time."*

"Such a great building complex presupposes not the single point of view of the Renaissance but the many-sided approach of our own age. The difference can be indicated by comparing it with such thirteenth-century structures as the leaning towers of the two noble families of Asinelli and Garisenda in Bologna. Private patrician fortresses, they rise up magnificently into the sky, but they can be embraced in a single glance, in a single view. There is no uncertainty in the observer concerning their relation to each other. On the other hand, nothing of the essential character of an organism like Rockefeller Center is revealed in a view restricted to its central axis. It possesses symmetries which are senseless in reference to the aesthetic significance of the whole. It requires comprehension in space and time more closely analogous to what has been achieved in modern scientific research as well as in modern painting."

The photomontage above appears in the book as a means of conveying the sensations of Rockefeller Center that one only comprehends in space and time. The caption reads: "Expressions of the new urban scale like Rockefeller Center are forcefully conceived in space-time and cannot be embraced in a single-view. To obtain a feeling for their interrelations the eye must function as in the high speed photographs of Edgerton."[26]

This last comment makes little sense, but it makes up in enthusiasm what it lacks in logic.

1

the

garden

in

the

city

Rockefeller Center
Baldwin Hills Village

Today, we just assume that conscientious private developers will think of the coordinated planning of all the buildings on a large site, arranging and graduating their sizes to give each the maximum open space, light, and view, and providing for adequate pedestrian as well as vehicular traffic. Zoning laws may, in fact, oblige them to offer these features of design, or to provide landscaping, or links to mass transportation, or a covered parking garage. But few of these aspects of planning were common in 1927 when John D. Rockefeller Jr.'s associates first became interested in acquiring a lease on the three blocks of midtown Manhattan where Rockefeller Center rose a few years later.

What little construction took place during the 1930s was mostly residential, usually low-cost housing. It was often in this arena, if at all, that architects concerned themselves with amenities that would positively impact the quality of life. But, there was no guarantee here either.

From its beginnings in the United States, the housing movement was centered on the East Coast and in in New York in particular. Ralph Walker, Joseph Urban, Harvey Wiley Corbett, and William K. Harrison led teams of investigative architects in a project for The New School for Social Research—an examination of slum conditions on New York's Lower East Side.

In 1932 Clarence Stein, Henry Wright, and

"If buildings do not express an integrated society (or at least a desire for such a society) they merely state the fact that society is discordant—and little more."[1]
— Catherine Bauer, Modern Housing, 1934

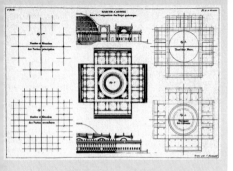

Beaux Arts Classicism

In the 19th Century the Ecole des Beaux Arts, Paris, had an unrivaled reputation among schools of architecture. The first American to attend was Richard Morris Hunt, followed by H. H. Richardson. By century's end the architectural profession in America was dominated by those who followed their example.

The typical Beaux Arts plan essentially meant that massing of buildings was symmetrical; larger buildings had a five-part composition with a climactic central mass and wings as terminal features.

Rockefeller Center is essentially Beaux Arts in its conception. Raymond Hood was a member of the Beaux-Arts Institute of Design in New York; he competed for its re-design in 1927.

Many claim the Beaux Arts approach never died. Kevin Roche, commenting on his education at IIT in 1947, said, " . . . what I didn't realize then was that I was going through another kind of Beaux Arts education. It was a formalist architectural education, one which dealt with the elements, the vocabulary, the syntax of architecture, separated from its social and cultural service. It was as if the whole process of architecture were placed on a laboratory table and dissected very slowly to study its components. Students were then trained to reassemble these components."[2]

Catherine Bauer, three of the founding members of the Regional Planning Association of America, curated a separate section on housing for the *Modern Architecture* exhibition at the Museum of Modern Art. A special catalogue for their section was introduced by Lewis Mumford, a fourth founding member of the RPAA.

That same year the Federal Government laid the foundations of its massive housing program.

Both of the projects in this section began in the Depression while these changes were taking place. Both are somewhat self-contained, urban complexes for large numbers of people—both have gardens. But, this is where the similarity ends. In every other respect one couldn't find two more dissimilar projects: one is strictly commercial, the other strictly residential; one was built for unheard of sums of private money, the other was subsidized by government loans; one is in New York City, the other is in Los Angeles. Their gardens aren't even similar.

The word garden is used here metaphorically, to connote the desire to make urban living humane. It is not used frivolously; indeed, the metaphor has substantial meaning. In this deeper sense both projects share something of the ideals of the Englishman Sir Ebenezer Howard, publicized in his book *Tomorrow, a Peaceful Path to Real Reform* (1898).

Howard's Garden City, as he called it, had two interrelated sources: on the one hand, the tradition of the Utopias of the first part of the 19th Century, particularly that of Owen, understood as a perfect and self-sufficient community, a synthesis of town and country, with the social implications traditionally connected with it; on the other hand, the concept of the single family house set amid greenery, which was in a sense an adaptation of the preceding ideal elaborated by Victorian thought in the second half of the century, with the emphasis on privacy rather than social relations: an attempt at releasing family life from the crowding and disorder of the metropolis and at making the town as much like the country as was reasonably possible.

These ideas spread rapidly to the United States, but they

above: Plate 21 from *Précis des leçons d'architecture*, by Jean-Nicolas-Louis Durand, 1802. Durand (1760-1834) wrote the most significant treatise in architecture of the first half of the 19th Century. Its many engraved plates served as patterns for planners for over 150 years. left: One of many conceptual drawings of Rockefeller Center drawn up for Raymond Hood by delineator Walter H. Kilham, Jr. In this early Beaux Arts scheme a central building is connected by bridges to four more peripheral buildings in a system of symmetrical wings.

commonly resulted in residential suburbs of individually owned homes. Under the auspices of the Regional Planning Association of America, the Garden City idea was more fully realized in the community of Radburn, New Jersey, designed by Clarence Stein and Henry Wright. Most of these satellite towns, however, failed to attain Howard's ideal, since local industries were unable to provide employment for the inhabitants, many of whom commuted to work in larger centers. Nonetheless, the open layout of garden cities had a great influence on the development of modern city planning.

A City Within a City

Ambition, flexibility, astute management, the idealism possible within enlightened self-interest—all these are important indications of the successful commercial culture exemplified by Rockefeller Center. Granted, it's rare when they don't, but these things needn't constrict the social value of a building enterprise. The size, scope, and location of this project, and the sheer amount of money spent, were unheard of even in the best of times—this after all was the depression. It was enough to disturb almost any citizen and distract them from whatever merits the architects might bring to the enterprise.

The reigning king of neo-gothic—Ralph Adams Cram—reacted in 1931 "with wonder and indeed, some measure of stupefaction" at the project. He wrote, "Here is the apotheosis of megalomania, of a defiant egotism that not only disregards the city as a consistent unity (if it still is this: the question is open to debate), hoisting its miscellaneous masses in the midst of less arrogant shops, dwellings, churches; it is even less at unity with itself, sprouting amorphous and cubicular mushrooms, each of which is some sort of a cosmic law unto itself. Individualism here reaches its perfect flowering."[3]

Vertical? Horizontal?

Louis Sullivan established the rule—verticality is what a tall building's elements should express.

Howells & Hood designed the vertical Daily News Building. Good.

Along comes the so-called International Style with an emphasis on the horizontal. In their International Style catalogue, Hitchcock and Johnson say of Hood's new McGraw-Hill Building: "The lightness, simplicity and lack of applied verticality mark this skyscraper as an advance over other New York skyscrapers and bring it within the limits of the International Style." The rule is broken, so now horizontal is a good thing.

Meanwhile L. Andrew Reinhard wrote about four published variations on an exterior for the RCA Building: "one shows a horizontal treatment (to satisfy the "horizontalists"), another a vertical treatment (to satisfy the "verticalists"), the third a wall pattern arrangement (to satisfy the decoratively inclined), and the fourth an unadorned arrangement (to satisfy the functionally minded)."[4]

The vertical treatment was chosen.

above: The Daily News Building, New York City, 1930. Designed by the same team that built the headquarters for the *News's* parent company, the *Chicago Tribune* (page 6).
right: Hood & Fouilhoux: The McGraw-Hill Building, New York City, 1931. Despite the praise of Hitchcock and Johnson, there were others who decried the building's horizontality. The fact is, on close inspection, it is horizontal *and* vertical.

A Town for Tomorrow

Clarence Stein's and Henry Wright's work on the New Jersey suburb of Radburn, New Jersey, was a fundamental departure from the American planning traditions in the 1920s. Since its partial completion in 1929, Radburn has served as the ideal model for the building of suburbs.

Radburn's genesis was with the REGIONAL PLANNING ASSOCIATION OF AMERICA, a loose organization of intellectuals who came together in New York in the 1920s to wrestle with problems of livability in the modern industrial city. Clarence Stein and Henry Wright, Radburn's chief planners, were part of the RPAA, as were urban historian Lewis Mumford, housing expert Catherine Bauer, region and neighborhood theorist Clarence Perry, and conservationist Benton MacKaye. The group's combined expertise led it to conclusions about the future of cities that remain remarkably influential on patterns of urbanization to this day.

The RPAA followed Howard's logic that liberation from the exploitation and degradation of the city could be achieved through decentralization of population and economic activity throughout the metropolitan region.

In 1929 Geddes Smith described Radburn as:

"A town built to live in—today and tomorrow. A town 'for the motor age.' A town turned outside-in without any backdoors. A town where roads and parks fit together like the fingers of your right and left hands. A town in which children need never dodge motor-trucks on their way to school. A new town—newer than the garden cities, and the first major innovation in town-planning since they were built."5

On November 1, 1939, the last rivet in Rockefeller Center was driven with considerable ceremony. The Federal Writers' Project had the final word:

> "In its way, the Center is an effort to reduce New York to order, still keeping it New York. The Center retains the gigantism, the ruthless preying of the large upon the small, the close packing, the impersonality of the whole; and yet attempts to secure sunlight and air (at least for itself), pleasant promenades, gardens (with Hollywood costumes for the attendants), art, a sense of scale and drama, and such other pleasures as the metropolis can afford . . ."6

By this time even Lewis Mumford had come to appreciate the virtues of the complex. When the Fifth Avenue Association awarded it a prize in 1939, he admitted that:

> "Purely as a visual contribution to the mid-town section, this group of buildings has turned out so well that one can afford to forget about all the stunts that have accompanied its exploitation . . . ."7

Victory Garden

The Regional Planning Association of America maintained a Ruskinian dislike of the metropolis and preached the end of all great cities, which were to be replaced by settlements scattered over a large area. It produced several formulae, such as the "self-sufficient district," concepts that have burdened town-planning for too long, as they often conceal the real nature of problems. Only the city can be said to be self-sufficient in any way.

But this misplaced Romanticism and love of the picturesque also led, on the other hand, to important changes in architectural thought; they accustomed architects to considering the townscape as an organic whole, and drew their attention towards a number of factors—paving, trees, fencing, benches, signs—that completed the architectural scene and brought about important modifications in the fabric of towns generally; in short, they laid the foundations for the

left: The Gate to Radburn, New Jersey, Clarence Stein, Henry Wright and Associates, 1929. Catherine Bauer described Radburn as "the first American attempt to build a complete pre-planned community on English Garden City principles. Here the idea of the superblock, with indented dead-end streets, as used in ordinary practice in English housing, was carried one step farther to accommodate that particular American condition, the automobile. All the houses face inward on continuous parks, traversed by footways entirely separated from the streets. Underpasses link one super-block to the other, and it is possible to go from any house to school or shops without crossing a street."8

modern theory of townscape.

Radburn, New Jersey, designed by Clarence Stein and Henry Wright, was advertised as "A Town for the Motor Age." It had carefully planned road systems where pedestrian and vehicular traffic were separated. The roadways formed superblocks of 30 to 50 acres. Within each superblock narrow *cul-de-sacs* led to houses that faced interior parks. Radburn was a success because it planned for its inhabitants by planning for their cars.

When he was invited to Los Angeles in 1938 by Johnson, Wilson, Merrill & Alexander, Clarence Stein brought the idea of the superblock with him. Together the five architects created one of the most successful communities on record.

In May 1990, when he was 83 years old, Robert E. Alexander returned to Baldwin Hills Village. He remarked on the high integrity of the physical site after a 50-year period. But, he was primarily interested in seeing the social and humanistic results of the community envisioned by him and his colleagues. He favored the community that now governed itself, who are condominium owners, and have joint ownership of the property. This is a far cry from when Alexander lived there in the late 40s, when the original residents rented property that was strictly controlled by an insurance company, and had no voice in its management. As a longtime social activist, Alexander was deeply impressed that the community now attracted residents with a wide variety of ethnic backgrounds and religious beliefs—a sharp contrast to its beginnings when the community was restricted in terms of race and religion.

Finally, Alexander commented how grateful he was that children are now an integrated part of the community as he and the founding architects had this in mind when they designed Baldwin Hills Village. In the early '50s, children were excluded. This was successfully challenged by a Village Green resident in a landmark state Supreme Court ruling in 1983.

Robert Alexander concluded: "Everything is for the better, as far as I'm concerned."[9]

above: The Trylon and Perisphere, New York World's Fair, 1939, Harrison & Abramovitz. Commissioned to design a Theme Center, the team created one of the most popular architectural symbols of our time. The largest globe ever built, the Perisphere contained a space more than twice that of Radio City. It housed an exhibit called DEMOCRACITY, a city of the future designed by Henry Dreyfuss.

The World of Tomorrow

From the first World Exhibition in London in 1851, to Philadelphia in 1876, to Paris in 1889, to Chicago in 1893, World's Fairs became influential showcases of new architecture and breakthroughs in technology.

The particular message of the Fairs of the Great Depression—Chicago, 1933 and New York, 1939—was that a better life could be achieved through advanced technology.

The New York World's Fair (above) was originally called "The Fair of the Future"—futurism manifested itself in every form imaginable, from the "Kitchen of Tomorrow," to the "House of Tomorrow," to "Cities of Tomorrow." These technocratic utopias were cleaner, safer, more efficient places, with plenty of labor saving devices. Intriguing images of industrial progress were mixed with reassuringly familiar domestic settings. The motto of the New York World's Fair was "Building the World of Tomorrow with the Tools of Today."

Leading Designers of the day—Raymond Loewy, Norman Bel Geddes, Henry Dreyfuss—were hired to create their images of our future. At the General Motors Futurama exhibit (page 184) visitors were informed that "by the Spring of 1939 [engineers and inventors] had cracked nearly every frontier of progress."

Throughout the design process, the Associated Architects worked in reasonable harmony in an office set up especially for them in the nearby Graybar Building. Although Corbett, Reinhard, Hofmeister, and Harrison all actively participated, it was Raymond Hood who at first took the lead.

It was Hood who shaped the massing of the RCA Building, whose Daily News Building provided the model for Radio City's elevations, who convinced John R. Todd to clad the buildings in limestone rather than brick, to put a fountain in the plaza and gardens on the roof.

But, as L. Andrew Reinhard pointed out, building the Center was like building a twentieth-century cathedral town: "The architect is not one man; the design is the result of many minds working on the same problem from many angles. The results will be attributable to the group, to the 'guild of master builders' if you will. All are architects in the sense that all contribute to the creation and modification of the final result."[1]

Rockefeller Center • New York City

Rockefeller Center began as a city-within-a-city to be built around a new Metropolitan Opera House, the opera having outgrown its quarters on 39th Street in Manhattan. Benjamin Wistar Morris and Harvey Wiley Corbett—both architects experienced in large-scale undertakings—drew up grandiose schemes for the developers. However, among other things, the Depression finally brought an end to the opera project.

The withdrawal of the Opera House from the larger plan threw everything into turmoil. John D. Rockefeller, Jr., by then the major investor, recalled the moment bitterly:

"Thus it came about that in the early fall of 1930, with the depression under way and values falling rapidly, I found myself committed to Columbia [University] for a long lease, wholly without the support of the enterprise by which and around which the development had been planned."[2]

With the general financial climate steadily worsening, there wasn't even the possibility of subletting a portion of the site in its unimproved state. It was clear that the choices were to either abandon the entire development, or, as Rockefeller later put it, "to go forward with it in the definite knowledge that I myself would have to build and finance it alone, without the immense impetus that the new opera house would have given, and with no escape from the fact that under the changed conditions it would be necessary to improve all the lot in order to lease it, thus involving immense capital outlays never contemplated. I chose the latter course."[3]

This was the beginning of the Rockefeller Center we see

above from left to right: Hood, Harrison, and Reinhard inspect a model, c.1931
opposite: The roof-top gardens today are not open to the general public.
Never fully realized, the grand scheme was gloriously described in the October 1931 issue
of *ARCHITECTURAL RECORD* as the "HANGING GARDENS OF RADIO CITY—The roof terraces . . .
will be landscaped with pools, fountains, tiled paths, flower mosaics, trees and shrubs."

today. L. Andrew Reinhard and Henry Hofmeister are generally credited with its basic scheme, with Raymond Hood contributing significantly to the design of the main buildings. Together with Corbett and four others, they called themselves the Associated Architects.

They worked exceedingly well together. Hood was a kind of team leader, but went to great lengths to downplay the role of any individual participant. In 1932 he noted that,

" . . . it would be impossible to estimate the number of official minds that have engaged in untangling the complexities of the problem; and certainly the number of unofficial minds that have pondered over it is an even more meaningless guess."[5]

The design process underwent constant revision as one visionary scheme after another was put to the test of economic viability.

"Architects, builders, engineers, real estate experts, financiers, lawyers," Hood wrote, "all have contributed something from their experience and even from their imagination."[6]

Raymond Hood was certainly happier to be designing a purely commercial project. One of Hood's draftsmen drew up at least eight different super-block schemes that included the entire three-block site. Most were variations of the "City under a Single Roof," a project for an idealized Manhattan that Hood had conceived earlier. The "Loft and Office Scheme," for instance, proposed second-story pedestrian walkways on each block ringing three massive loft buildings. Rising above the lofts on the middle block was a long thin slab crowned by a central tower, while smaller transverse slabs bridged the side streets. Hood also presented a more personal conception: low, square blocks at the four corners of the site were isolated by private streets. Forty-ninth and Fiftieth streets changed their courses to meet in a cross-shaped intersection at a tiny "Rockefeller Square." Four towers faced one another across the square, their masses step-

above: New York in 1980 as envisioned in the futuristic musical *JUST IMAGINE*, Fox, 1930.

Architectural references in the film include skyscraper bridges designed by Raymond Hood in 1929, the recently completed, setback Chrysler Building and Bank of Manhattan (1929), as well as the Empire State Building, which was nearing completion in 1930.

ping down in radiating diagonals toward the edge of the site. In spite of all the alterations that took place over the many months that followed, most of this early thinking found its way into the final project.

Talks had begun with General Electric, the parent company of the Radio Corporation of America (RCA) whose affiliates included the National Broadcasting Company (NBC) and the Radio-Kelth-Orpheum (RKO) theater chain. Reinhard & Hofmeister drew up a new conception of the project, a design intended to lure the prospective tenants by offering them a prominent, centrally located office structure —the present RCA Building.

The complex was to be called Radio City. The involvement of the entertainment industry, and the opportunity to do something monumental, provoked another outburst of artistic passion, as Hood and Corbett sought to inject a greater degree of unity into the isolated blocks. They came up with a proposal to stretch a vast enclosed promenade across the entire width of the site, and 49th and 50th streets would dip below grade. This forum would serve as a grand lobby for up to five separate theaters and for the RKO and RCA office buildings. The drama each night would be played out on a stage of hitherto unimagined scale. The scheme was costly and raised the danger that, if one element of the composition failed, the entire development would be jeopardized.

As a group of buildings the Center heralded a whole new concept of coordinated city development: each building working with the others and all with the street. In the end, even one of the buildings was turned to cast less of a shadow over the plaza. An underground pedestrian concourse— which boasts over two hundred shops and restaurants—ties the entire complex together.

The slab form and setbacks of the RCA Building give it its distinctive character. Setbacks were, of course, required under the Zoning Law of 1916 (page 180), but the slender structure and the open space in front of it exempted it from the law. In the case of the RCA Building, the setbacks perform a practical purpose. In tall buildings all elevators don't

top: Lee Lawrie's Atlas, unveiled in 1936, stands in front of the International Building.
above: The Channel Gardens at Christmas.
above, right: Lawrie's relief, "Wisdom: the Voice From the Clouds," embarrassed Nelson Rockefeller when he learned it was based on William Blake's drawing of "The Creator."
right: An entrance to the underground pedestrian concourse.

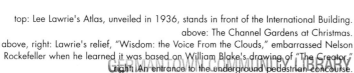

A Slab of Rugged Honesty

Raymond Hood felt that 20th Century building technology had made for "an architecture of plain surfaces, with slight ornamentation, the decorative effects being obtained almost wholly by the . . . color, texture and the contrast of materials. . . . Stone in slab form, for example, direct from the saws with solid masonry and carving reduced almost to the vanishing point, is the logical, durable and beautiful material for the exterior."[7]

To Raymond Hood, the RCA Building was a true skyscraper, but "it does not ape the aristocratic silhouettes of the past. It comes by its own form honestly and is not ashamed of it. First there is its spinal column, the vertical elevator and utility system, planned as simply and directly as we know how to plan them. Then about this spinal column is wrapped uniform office space of the proper depth with the exterior wall pierced by windows four and one half feet wide, every nine feet. With the successive stopping off of the elevator banks to the lower floors, the sides are set in to eliminate the dark useless space that would other-wise be created. So the tall, thin slab with its giant steps on the side is a true expression of the problem. It may not be orthodox beauty according to some standards but it has a rugged honesty that is akin to beauty."

serve all floors; they are built in banks that only ascend to a particular level. In this case, the setbacks actually mark the floors where the elevators change. Raymond Hood was determined that no office worker would sit more than 27 feet from a window. In the RCA Building the elevators are located in the middle of the structure, meaning that once an elevator bank terminates, that area becomes empty space in all the floors above. And because that space is in the center of the structure, a desk located where the elevators would have been would be more than 27 feet from the edge. The solution is to shrink the envelope of the building as it goes up. Not only is that a good thing for light-starved office workers, but it makes the space very valuable, allowing the management to charge premium rents. Through his setbacks, Hood found a way to simultaneously assure architectural beauty, worker satisfaction, and a good return on Rockefeller's investment.

The significance of Hood's bold massing was misunderstood and sharply criticized. Rockefeller himself disliked the expansive side views. In fact the entire project drew negative criticism—from its inception to its completion and beyond—for at least the first few years. Given the magnitude of the Center's ultimate appeal for tourists world-wide, it is hard to believe now that this could have been so.

Ralph Adams Cram, still building the gothic Cathedral of St. John the Divine uptown, likened the buildings to "quadrangutar prisms, casually disposed, towering incontinently and sliced off at a certain height, not for any considerations of design or proportion but, perhaps—there is no other reason—because the stock of modeling clay gave out."[8]

Lewis Mumford, who harshly criticized the project all along, said, "The opportunity has been wantonly wasted . . . This is the sorriest failure of imagination and intelligence in modern American architecture. If Radio City is the best our architects can do with freedom, they deserve to remain in chains."[9]

When the French architect Le Corbusier visited New York City in November of 1935 he was taken to the Rockefeller

left: Wenrich's drawing looks South with the Empire State Building to the left. "In the development of the walls and surfaces that clothe the buildings," said Hood, "our twentieth century industry has had an immense influence. Materials have been sought whose durability, quality of surface and ease of manufacture and application preeminently fitted them for the places where they were to go."[10]

Center complex. The New York Times reported that "the modern architect was not particularly impressed. He was looking for architecture not theater . . . the city that is a machine for living in—not merely frightfully expensive scenery built to knock the beholder's eyes out."[11]

The plaza was particularly slow to become the attraction it is today. Originally, it was a dreary, purposeless place that few seemed attracted to. "The public," wrote Talbot Hamlin in the New York Times,

"had been led to expect a superb piece of town beautification, carefully thought out. They received only another real estate promotion, high class, to be sure, but a monument not to city beautification or city pride, but to the hope of profits. The general plan was a real estate promoter's plan; and however beautiful the detail, it is the general plan that controls effects. The much heralded plaza at the center turned out to be an insignificant open space completely dwarfed by the 60[sic]-story cliff of building at whose feet it is placed."[12]

How did all this turn around? Tastes do change (note the taste in question belongs to critics and other architects), but it's not enough to say that we simply grow used to things. The raw material was always there; well designed structures, and particularly well designed urban spaces. The Channel Gardens invite people in, the RCA Building is a pivot, and the reconfigured streets move them along naturally, comfortably, and with pleasure. Once people began to use it, they did the rest.

The blocks that stretch from Fifth to Sixth Avenues in Manhattan are particularly long. Since little of interest breaks up the walk from one avenue to the other, the trip can often seem tedious. As Jane Jacobs aptly points out, long blocks keep people from forming "reasonably intricate pools of city cross-use." It is her contention that ". . . if city mixtures of

above: Radio City Music Hall, Associated Architects, 1932. Donald Deskey, chosen in a competition, decorated the interiors.

right: Auditorium under construction, The New School for Social Research, New York City, Joseph Urban, architect, c.1930.

Expressionist Sunrise

Ironically, designs for the ill-fated 1927 Metropolitan Opera House, by the Viennese architect Joseph Urban, resurfaced as partial inspiration for Radio City Music Hall.

The Music Hall also used a number of features Urban described in his 1929 book, Theaters. It was to be egg-shaped, with an acoustical plaster ceiling, such as Urban had recently built at the New School (below). Balconies were to be shallow and pushed to the back of the room, while the stage was to thrust out along the sides of the auditorium, a further development of Urban's vignette stages.

The Associated Architects' first models followed the Urban design more explicitly: the smoothly curving ceiling punctured by a coffer-like pattern of grilles and the semicircular proscenium was a strangely streamlined interpretation of the auditorium in his Scheme IX for the Metropolitan Opera. The final design merged the curving ceiling with the transverse bands of Urban's Music Center.

But, in the end it was the gilded vaults of the Music Hall that were most unique and impressive, turning the stage into a metaphorical sunrise.

Showman that he was, the hall's impresario, Samuel "Roxy" Rothafel, claimed it had been his inspiration: "I didn't conceive the idea. I dreamt it, I believe in creative dreams. The picture of Radio City was complete and practically perfect in my mind before artists and architects put pen to drawing paper."

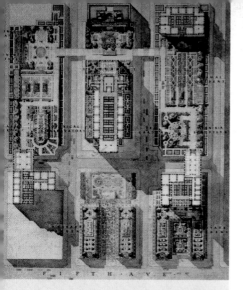

The Gardens of "New Babylon"

Looking over the city during a meeting one day, Hood said, "Look at all those roofs down there cluttered with bulkheads, ventilators, chimneys, elevator penthouses, water tanks and God knows what else. I was wondering if office space that looked out on a garden would be worth any more."

Hood was aware that the project began as a grand opera square and had upset the community by turning into Radio City. He declared, by virtue of the gardens, "John D. Rockefeller, Jr., will . . . make amends for not creating a classical setting for a Roman Holiday in the busiest part of Fifth Avenue."

At first Hood envisioned a continuous sequence of rooftop terraces (above) linked by bridges that soared high across the streets, evoking what he called the "fabled living tapestry of the Hanging Gardens of Babylon."

While the bridges were quickly eliminated from the plan, four gardens were constructed between 1933 and 1936 on the buildings facing Fifth Avenue, and more were located on the third- and eleventh-story setbacks of the RCA building. Though they were considerably diminished versions of Hood's original vision, they nonetheless provided the center with almost two acres of greenery, much of which was opened to the public during the Center's first years of operation.

use are to be more than a fiction on maps, they must result in different people, bent on different purposes, appearing at different times, but using the same streets."[18] By way of contrast to the existing condition, she notes that the Rockefeller Center project transformed "stagnation" into "fluidity of use" with the addition of an extra cross street. Jacobs felt this to be the salient feature of Rockefeller Plaza:

> "The most artful design in other respects could not tie [the Center] together, because it is fluidity of use, and the mixing of paths, not homogeneity of architecture, that ties together city neighborhoods into pools of city use, whether those neighborhoods are predominantly for work or predominantly for residence."[13]

Fluidity of use certainly makes the promenade an exemplary focal point in the urban fabric. For a city to be coherent to its inhabitants and visitors, it needs certain reference points which shape the neighborhoods and mark one's progress around the town. A single tower may suffice, but a clearly definable group of buildings, distinct from their neighbors, but not totally different from them, will provide orientation for a far larger area.

The promenade is a place to meet friends or for sitting beside some of the few ornamental plants in the area. People come to watch the ice skaters, watch performers, or listen to free concerts. They browse in shops that sell exotic and more costly products than those offered in the average New York neighborhood. Rockefeller Center offers accessible, open public space; cafés, restaurants and theaters; a skating rink and dance floors. It maintains gleaming lobbies and clean public restrooms, and provides sheltered underground streets which many people use to avoid crowds and inclement weather. Through careful planning and constant attention to its public image, it has fashioned itself into a busy center for many kinds of activity, not simply of office work and entertain-

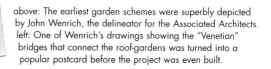

above: The earliest garden schemes were superbly depicted by John Wenrich, the delineator for the Associated Architects. left: One of Wenrich's drawings showing the "Venetian" bridges that connect the roof-gardens was turned into a popular postcard before the project was even built.

ment. As such, it draws visitors and local people and provides them with an orientation point, a stopping place within a city that was designed to fit an otherwise monotonous grid.

Rockefeller Center is a veritable mecca for tourists, especially during the holiday season. For many the Center conjures up iconic images that are synonymous with Christmas. If they can't see it in person, people world-wide will watch the tree-lighting ceremony *via* television. And, of course, there are the popular seasonal pageants at Radio City Music Hall.

Though founded on the bedrock of traditional composition, Rockefeller Center was the first building complex to use the skyscraper not merely as a commercial accommodation, no matter how artistically expressed, but as an integral element of a complex urbanism.

The Swiss architectural historian and apologist for modernism Sigfried Giedion prophetically hailed "the new scale of Rockefeller Center, which coincides with the scale of modern bridges and parkways. . . . Rockefeller Center simply is in advance of its period in the urban scale. What must change is not the Center but New York itself. The city must adopt the new scale which is identical with that of its bridges and parkways. Until then it will stand as a reminder that the structure of the city must be transformed, not in the interest of single individuals but for the sake of the community as a whole."[14]

And, in the end, though he was still critical of much about the complex, even Lewis Mumford had to agree that " . . . none of these things shows from the outside, externally the Center is a serene eyeful."[15]

The Associated Architects eminently succeeded in building their city-within-a-city and gave New York, and indeed the world, a lasting legacy.

right: A children's book from 1954. When asked to sell his tree Mr. Judson tells his little girl, "Just think, Ellen. More than a million people will see your tree at Rockefeller Center. Nearly fifty million people will see it on television."

The Most Famous Tree in the World
In its original form, the plaza was a failure. The statue of Prometheus by Paul Manship was universally criticized; the Federal Writers' Project reported that it had been nicknamed "Leaping Looie." Manship himself was disappointed by the statue, explaining that because of the tight construction schedule and an inadequate budget, he had not been allowed to erect a full-scale plaster model on the site. He felt that "the group . . . tends to sink and flatten the Plaza, instead of lifting it up, blending it in with the general architectural scheme."

The original plaza was rather bleak and unadorned. Small shop windows and sober signage were not enough to lure pedestrians. But, over the next few years the plaza was gradually transformed. In 1934 the City Garden Club was invited to mount an exhibition, and its floral displays succeeded in bringing the romance of the roof gardens down to the ground. In the following year the shops were transformed into restaurants, and the stone walls of the plaza were pulled down to make way for huge sheets of plate glass. The restaurant owners commissioned James Thurber and William Steig to draw cartoons on the walls. In summertime café tables and trees filled the plaza. There was still the problem of how to animate the space in the winter. It was not until 1936 that a brilliant solution was found in the form of an ice-skating rink. The plaza and its double ring of promenades— one at street level, one sunk to the level of the Channel Gardens—had at last found their proper role as an open-air urban theater. The photo above shows the rink's inauguration on Christmas day 1936.

THE MOST BEAUTIFUL TREE IN THE WORLD

A CHRISTMAS STORY FOR CHILDREN

Baldwin Hills Village • Los Angeles

Lewis Mumford said, "One of the handful of projects that stands out as a fundamental advance in both planning and architecture is Baldwin Hills Village in Los Angeles. Here every part of the design speaks the same robust vernacular: simple, direct, intelligible. I know no other recent community that lends itself so fully to strict scrutiny, simply because every aspect of its physical development has been thought through."[1]

Baldwin Hills Village's successful design is noticeable in the unusually high level of historic integrity. The buildings, garages, drying yards, garbage areas, driveways, and pedestrian circulation walkways have been maintained essentially intact since they were built.

Toward the end of the Great Depression a group of forward-looking Los Angeles architects devoted three years to planning a new community to be built on a great, flat empty farm bordering L.A. Much of the three years was spent securing loans and mortgage insurance from cautious government officials in the Federal Housing Agency and the Reconstruction Finance Corporation. Thanks in some measure to the red tape there was plenty of time to thoroughly refine the original conception; some fifty plot-plans were developed and the buildings were redrawn in detail ten times. All things considered, the project was surprisingly simple and straightforward when it was finally realized in 1942.

The idea for Baldwin Hills Village (now known as the Village Green) originated with Reginald Johnson. He worked in close association with Lewis Wilson, Edwin Merrill, and Robert Alexander to design and construct this community. They were inspired by a number of model communities, particularly Radburn, New Jersey, that were designed by Clarence Stein and Henry Wright. The Los Angeles architects made a critical decision that ensured the success of their project when they decided to hire Stein as consulting architect and site-planner in 1938. Stein was influential in shaping the philosophical and design parameters of the project.

Stein's own ideas owed much to Garden City planners in England such as Ebenezer Howard, Raymond Unwin, Patrick Geddes, and, in this country, Frederick Law Olmsted. He had numerous and devoted associates and allies; in addition to his partner, Henry Wright, there were Benton MacKaye, Stuart Chase, Catherine Bauer, and Lewis Mumford. They all endorsed a kind of sensitive and humane planning that was

Catherine Bauer said that "Baldwin Hills is in many ways the most attractive, liveable rental community in the country . . . "[2]
While Radburn, Baldwin Hills, and the Greenbelt towns are still with us and still demonstrate the wisdom of their original concepts, the forces that have produced suburban sprawl have taken little notice of them.

Built in the USA

Three events occurred between 1944 and 1945, just two years after construction, that helped Baldwin Hills Village gain national attention. First, New York's Museum of Modern Art selected Baldwin Hills Village as one of twelve well-designed communities to be included in a special exhibition called: LOOKING AT YOUR NEIGHBORHOOD *that was held from March 29 to June 25, 1944. The exhibition traveled from 1944 to 1949, and gave national exposure to the outstanding design of this community.*

The second event was in 1945 when the Museum of Modern Art selected Baldwin Hills Village as one of 47 outstanding examples in contemporary architecture for an exhibition called BUILT IN THE USA: 1932-44.

The third event was the publication of two articles written about Baldwin Hills Village for the September 1944 issue of PENCIL POINTS, *a national architectural journal. The authors were Lewis Mumford, noted architectural historian and critic, and Catherine Bauer, leading housing expert. Mumford and Bauer described Baldwin Hills Village as an outstanding example of well-designed, contemporary housing.*

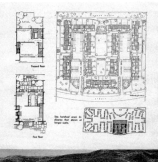

in the air in the 1920s and 30s, when the solution to many of society's ills seemed to be providing better places to live.

Stein succinctly states the objectives: "The purpose of Baldwin Hills Village was to demonstrate the practical possibilities of spacious homes and surroundings in an orderly community at low rentals, using the basic features of the Radburn Idea: superblock, homes facing central greens— twenty acres of green parks—pedestrian and auto completely separated."[3]

All of Stein's garden cities contained parks or common open spaces. But, it was only at Baldwin Hills Village that Stein was able to find a project and fellow architects that could give full rein to his progressive approach toward landscape. This type of intricate landscape design is not found in any of Stein's other sites. For one thing, the richness and variety of Baldwin Hills Village landscape is a contrast to those at the Eastern sites because of Southern California's year-round warm climate.

Baldwin Hills is not so much a landscaped community as it is a landscape. One quarter of the site is devoted to green commons consisting of inner parks and garden courts. The landscape is the driving force, the architectonic support upon which rests the program of this most unusual undertaking. Almost all the photographs of Baldwin Hills show the apartments shortly after they were built, when the trees had recently been planted and had barely grown. Now, sixty years later, the architects' vision can be seen as it was intended. A lush park, capable of rivaling the best of Olmstead's designs, covers 64 acres of midtown Los Angeles, with 629 units integrated within its varied settings. Each and every apartment has a view, each different, each something special. Through a sensitive relationship of house to site, each resident feels a personal sense of ownership for the landscape.

One reason that this is at all possible in an urban setting is that the

left: BUILT IN THE USA: 1932-44.
The catalogue remarks: "The private housing scheme is all the more remarkable when one knows the tenacity with which FHA has fought the advantages of modern architecture and modern site-planning."

car is banished to the periphery. The one superblock configuration makes it possible to relegate all automobile traffic to the edge of the site and thus provide uninterrupted open areas for safe pedestrian circulation. Garages and ample residential parking areas are grouped in 17 *cul-de-sacs* or courts on the outskirts. The close proximity of garages to residences means a short walking distance from car to house. Without the automobile there's an incredible sense of peace—an absence of noise—an uncanny sensation that you've been transported elsewhere.

To be accurate, the site is not a true superblock, but organic sub-groups or clusters of housing. In Sunnyside and in Radburn there's much less private space; people reportedly don't want all their exterior space to be public. Baldwin Hills solves this by creating courts—mini-divisions of the overall acreage—thereby making each cluster of houses appear fewer in number; small enclaves within the whole.

Baldwin Hills' site plan contains no social hierarchy, but emphasizes a community that is characterized by the Garden City concept of social and political equality. This is evident in the Village's pathway design. The meandering paths are planned to anticipate where one might walk to take full advantage of numerous and varied views. They are also designed to guide the individual efficiently from home to any other residence in the community and also to the community center. This is in contrast to the earlier garden cities where pathways are parallel to the buildings. At Radburn the pathways also hug the configurations of the buildings. Radburn residents frequently walk on the grass in the open areas to go from one location to another. This seldom happens at Baldwin Hills Village because the paths are well thought out.

In contrast to the public interaction in the common park spaces and courts, there is privacy in the patios. Stein said, "The patio is the indigenous private outdoor livingroom, dating back in California to the Spanish conquest." Hedges are used as structural—architectonic devices—while providing additional privacy.

The architecture is straightforward, unpretentious, service-

In most suburbs, it's the street system that determines the sub-division.
In Baldwin Hills Village the entire scheme is determined by a flowing central park.
The landscape was designed by Fred Barlow and Fred Edmunson.
Baldwin Hills' original name was "Thousand Gardens."

The Village Plan

Clarence Stein writes about Baldwin Hills Village seen from the air (above): "'Very pretty' says the Californian as he flies over, 'but is it practical? Where are the streets to take autos to the houses, and where do folks park and garage their machines?' There is no parking or storing of autos on public streets—in fact there are no streets within the 1100-feet by 2750-feet superblock. The highways that surround it are exclusively for movement—as they should be everywhere in all our cities.

"Not only are there no streets within the eighty acres of the Village, but even the dead-end of the Radburn type has been replaced. It has here been changed into a concentrated but adequate garage court. A new form has developed and come of age. Here is realistic modern functionalism replacing outworn traditionalism. Within the court is one garage for each home around it; also parking space for one car per family or its visitor . . . The automobile—arriving, departing, at rest, in storage—has all the room needed."

Referring to the other developments in the photo, Stein says, "The outstanding feature of [the other] subdivisions is the undue importance and comparative spaciousness of streets. There is no concentration of green open spaces. Yet there are only 3.5 to 4 houses to the acre as against 7.8 dwelling units per acre in Baldwin Hills Village, with its spacious, verdant openness."

able. The buildings' very lack of stylistic distinction has made them wear well, and the passage of time has given substance to their most positive virtue: a consistent simplicity of massing and detail.

Stein and his colleagues designed the architecture of the Garden Cities (both on the East and West coasts) to reflect the surrounding cultural and physical environments. Baldwin Hills Village has a distinctive modern vernacular architecture that was planned to accommodate outdoor space because of the Southern California mild year-round casual life style.

The Baldwin Hills Village architects derived this community's architectural style from Greenbelt's box-like government buildings. However, they incorporated four changes that made the architecture more elegant in design compared to the Greenbelt architecture.

First, bungalows or three-bedroom units were added to each end of the main buildings to give it a less institutional appearance and to create a feeling of a village.

Second, a low pitch roof was added to each building that is reminiscent of the roofs that lead designer Reginald Johnson built for his mansions.

Third, simple but elegant architectural details were incorporated. This included front steps and entryways to the individual homes; large picture windows and balconies; and a low fence or wall that wrapped artistically around the back of each patio to insure privacy and to prevent exposure of the residents' private possessions. This feature was not found in other large housing complexes. The patios were also designed as an extension of the indoor living area to take full advantage of the year-round warm climate of Southern California.

Fourth, the stucco buildings were painted in the familiar pastel colors of the Southern California region. This is a contrast to the heavy brick and wood structures (painted in conventional colors) of the eastern Garden Cities.

The basic interior architecture of Stein's Garden Cities is the same. It reflects a mass market approach in design to reduce costs and yet provide a range of options for different

above: An aerial photo of Baldwin Hills Village from the 1950s. Stein remarks that in the adjacent communities, "built about the same time as the Village, a few meaningless curves are added to the typical gridiron. The through streets do not tie into any scheme of circulation—they go from nowhere to nowhere."
Today, the City of Los Angeles completely engulfs everything in the photo.

ages and different types of families. Baldwin Hills Village is the culmination of this type of interior architecture because the spacious design incorporated both indoor and outdoor living that gave it the maximum benefit of ventilation and light.

The basic units are simple rectangles with remarkable consistency in the plans. Units may be off-set to provide variety within blocks, but the plans are clear and efficient. Plumbing is grouped, circulation is centralized, construction spans are kept modest; ample storage has been provided. Proportions are extremely chaste; Stein conceived of rooms as boxes, and was not concerned with developing space beyond bare necessity. But, since every unit has a spectacular view of the landscape, the simplicity is offset by the lush exteriors that virtually permeate the living spaces.

Though there are no longer restrictions of race, or religion, or against children, the majority of the residents are older, middle-class people looking for an alternative—a bucolic idyll in the middle of urban sprawl. Shopping and schools lie outside the boundaries of the community—something that would be a drawback for some.

People have maintained the integrity of their properties for 60 years without undo pressure. Very few of the residents are aware that Baldwin Hills is architecturally unique—they simply have a love for the place and pride in its care. This is as it should be; the place itself has inculcated a devotion to its perpetuation.

Thus, Clarence Stein and the founding architects' noble vision of a Garden City continues to persist through six decades of social change and temporary setbacks. The site's high historic integrity and its vibrant community life are a testament to the architects' original intentions.

Lewis Mumford, a champion of Baldwin Hills Village, said, "These houses are, happily if a little ironically, the crown of Reginald Johnson's career as a designer of spacious private mansions; and in the plan itself, for which Clarence Stein was consultant, his experience, with Sunnyside Gardens, Radburn and Greenbelt came to its richest fruitage."[4]

An important story about Baldwin Hills Village by Catherine Bauer appeared in the architecture magazine, *PENCIL POINTS*, in September 1944. The 17-page article, with an introduction by Lewis Mumford, cited three reasons "for its markedly greater livability and attractiveness": lower density; bigger rooms and more storage; space for private outdoor living for every family, whether in patios, enclosed gardens, or good-sized balconies.

"What do I mean by New Towns? Not merely that they are newly created. Many towns have been and are being built that are immediately obsolete and out-dated. They may have been fitted to an age long past; but they have nothing whatsoever to do with the life people now want to live, or would if they thought it were attainable.

"New Towns are contemporary. This does not necessarily mean that they should have any particular type of 'New Look,' a different architectural style or veneer. By contemporary I mean towns that are planned, built, and operated to serve present day needs and conditions."

— Clarence Stein

2

elevating

the

user

experience

**Johnson & Son Administration Building
Salk Institute for Biological Studies
Ford Foundation Headquarters
Philips Exeter Academy Library**

How does one design spaces for large groups of people with very specific needs, who perform highly specialized tasks, while creating conditions that will improve their productivity and enhance their well-being? This is a tall order, indeed. For all those there are who may wish to lift the human spirit with their architecture, there are many more who fail due to the immense difficulty. The four projects examined here vary in scope, size, and intention. They all succeed with distinction.

This chapter is about people working together—in labor, in research, in contemplation, in communication—people whose lives benefit from the conditions in which they work. Featured are corporate administrative offices, a biological research institute, a philanthropic foundation, and a library on a small school campus.

Apotheosis of Work

Frank Lloyd Wright's *tour de force* of the mid-1930s was the Johnson Wax Administration Center in Racine, Wisconsin. Wright was no stranger to the problems of organizing a workforce on a mass scale. Thirty years earlier his Larkin Building in Buffalo, New York, radically changed the way we work.

The Larkin Company found an architect in Wright who believed in the spiritual value of work and its redemptive power. He despised the values represented by most business buildings—profiteering, brashness, the uniformity of the hive. Instead he molded

"Life, forever dying to be born afresh, forever young and eager, will presently stand upon this earth as upon a footstool, and stretch out its realm amidst the stars."[1]
— H. G. Wells, The Outline of History, 1920

Ask And It Shall Be Given You

Larkin executives recognized that clerical staff needed a clean, well-lighted place to work—a feat not easily accomplished amid Buffalo's smoke-wrapped railroad yards. Frank Lloyd Wright created a beautiful light-filled interior and he is justly celebrated for the inventive way he filtered the fetid air. He also made a highly efficient machine of work, using emerging technology to handle the thousands of items of correspondence that poured in daily. From a lower-level receiving area, mail was moved to the upper levels, then processed downward. Wright installed cabinets in alcoves below high windows for a system of card filing. Company correspondents dictated responses to inquiries into gramophones, which were taken by messengers to a typing pool, then checked and mailed.

The building boasted such self-improvement opportunities for the Larkin "family" as a library, lounge, YWCA, and classroom. The solid piers of the central light court gave way, as they soared upward, to elaborate decorations, hanging plants, and the sun's rays picking out gold-leafed inspirational inscriptions such as "Ask and it shall be given you. Seek and ye shall find. Knock and it shall be opened unto you." The evangelical quality of the inscriptions is as much Wright as it is Larkin. Throughout his life, Wright studded his talks and writing with such comments on poetry, truth, beauty, and ideals.

spaces of a certain richness in which life, work, and art might enhance one another. Wright proved the perfect person to put the Larkin ideal of moral uplift into place; in the process, he created one of the most conceptually and technically rich commercial buildings of the twentieth century.

Unlike the managers of the giant, impersonal corporations beginning to dominate American life by 1930, the S. C. Johnson Company thought of their organization as a kind of extended family under a beneficent patriarchy. Wright grasped this at once and attempted to form an inward-looking community for them that would foster togetherness while mirroring the hierarchy of the firm. The result was no ordinary office headquarters: it was a collective machine in which the social relationships were institutionalized into regulated cooperation.

Wright's solution was to put all 200 clerical workers in one, great sunlit space. He and Johnson felt that, in addition to creating a greater sense of cooperation, it would be more efficient for employees to have immediate access to one another. A study showed that after moving to the new building, office operations became 15% more efficient, with some departments improving over 25%. More important than increased worker productivity is the fact that the design of the building attracted the most creative people in the field.

Uniting Art and Science

Louis Kahn, on the other hand, preferred to segregate activities while finding ways for them to intersect. In his approach, Kahn would first probe the nature of the activities to be physically accommodated as well as the concepts implied by each activity. He then created a space that was appropriate for each, a space that not only was big enough, but that also evoked its particular use. The end result is that the building's spaces are naturally harmonious and have physical and symbolic cohesion. Meanwhile, he would attend to the integration of all the necessary systems, always with a clear view of the distinction between the "served" spaces for human activity, the primary use areas, and the

---

Wright described his Larkin Administration Building as "a simple cliff of brick" with "a single large room in which the main floors are galleries open to a large court . . . lighted from above." With all the natural light there's no way to look out. "All the windows of the various stories are seven feet above the floor . . ." Wright did the same thing at Johnson & Son.

"servant" spaces—stairs, bathrooms, storage, mechanical systems, and other non-primary functions.

At their first meeting, Louis Kahn was impressed that Jonas Salk wanted his laboratories to be the kind of place where "Picasso could come to visit." This image of uniting art and architecture, and the humanizing of science, struck a responsive chord in Kahn, for whom making the "immeasurable measurable" continued to be a personal quest. Kahn later said, "there was something else that [Salk] said which became the key to the entire space environment. Namely that medical research does not belong entirely to medicine or the physical sciences. It belongs to population. He meant that anyone with a mind in the humanities, in science, or in art could contribute to the mental environment of research, leading to discoveries in science."[2]

Kahn placed studies overlooking the courtyard at the Salk Institute, each with a view of the ocean. Whereas the building is of carefully detailed reinforced concrete, the rooms are fitted with naturally finished wood. The work area is thus divided into two parts—one for active investigation and one for contemplative analysis of the work in hand, one for scientist and one for the human being. Perhaps nowhere else has Kahn's concern for the whole of the human experience been so carefully and patiently realized.

Stimulating the Senses

By the time Kevin Roche and John Dinkeloo established their own practice they were already past masters at providing enriched community environments. They continued in the monumental spirit of the work they had done in the offices of Eero Saarinen. After his death they established themselves as sensitive specialists in designing large-scale corporate environments while completing Saarinen's unfinished projects, including John Deere & Company (page 194) and Dulles International Airport (page 110). They returned to Deere & Company in 1975-79 to design the West Office Building, a seamless addition to an already near-perfect building. The success of the extension is due in large meas-

From Sublime to Ridiculous
Curvilinear forms were commonly used by architects of the so-called International Style long before streamlining made them popular here in the United States. Curves abound in the works of Scandinavians like Alvar Aalto, and in the work of Dutch architects such as J.J.P. Oud (above).

The concept of streamlining originated with airplane and ship designers who created forms that would meet with the least resistance in air or water. In the mid-1930s streamlining became a symbol of the future, as the public associated its elegantly curved, clean forms with man's increasing technological conquest of the elements. By 1937 all mass produced automobiles were streamlined.

Since streamlining conjures up images of speed and efficiency, the look began to be applied to everything from radios to tea services. Soon the idea of streamlined efficiency reached the workplace. It was only fitting that after gas stations and drive-in restaurants, that architects would apply the forms to factories, banks, and even corporate offices.

above: Workers' Houses, J.J.P. Oud, Hook of Holland, the Netherlands, 1924-27. What we refer to as streamling is at once a high and a low art. Though often perceived as a vernacular style found in banks, gas stations, and drive-ins, the practice of curving brick around corners has precedent in the buildings of German Expressionists (Poelzig and Mendelsohn) as well as architects such as Oud.
right: Academy Theater, S. Charles Lee, Los Angeles, 1939.

ure to the integration of an atrium garden into the workspace itself. This genre of structured nature has become somewhat of the hallmark of that office ever since the success of the Ford Foundation Building in New York in 1967. The working part of the building is comprised of tiers of offices in the form of an L along one side and the rear. The remainder of the building is a vast, glass enclosed space with a terraced garden. Thirty percent of the building is given over to a perpetually blooming greenhouse open to the public. The private, cloistered world of the foundation offices has equal access to the garden from above and on the opposite side.

Exaltation of Knowledge

The Philips Exeter Academy in Exeter, New Hampshire, asked Louis Kahn to consider designing a library. Kahn, who had never built one, knew exactly what he wanted to do. He systematically avoided consulting with any of the librarians and he devised the spaces as he saw fit. However, it seems that he designed a very successful space. The exterior is not without its share of surprises and delights, but the greatest surprise, and delight, awaits the visitor upon entering the main space inside.

The power and the beauty of Kahn's buildings are due in large measure to the qualities of light that invade, permeate, and define their spaces. He once said, "A man with a book goes to the light. A library begins that way." His buildings have an alchemical mutability that belies their geometry and their materials.

Future Perfect

The Johnson Wax project was begun a couple of years after the close of the "Century of Progress Exposition" in Chicago and was finished just after the opening of the New York World's Fair in 1939. This was the Great Depression, but it was also a period of great optimism about the role technology would play in our future. The Chicago show, originally scheduled to last five months, was extended by a whole year. The architecture at both these shows was designed to attract potential buyers to the exhibitors' pavilions so designers

In the final scenes of Things to Come, *the old Everytown has vanished completely, the surface of the earth has been returned to Nature, and the new Everytown is located in a gigantic underground cavern. The skyscrapers of New York, Lang's departure point, remain but a faded memory in* Things to Come, *only to be seen in educational films. "What a funny place New York was," says one little girl, "all sticking up and full of windows."*

were encouraged to give free reign to their imaginations. The promise of industrially manufactured goods and environments paved the way for architecture—public, corporate, and domestic—to change the condition of our lives.

On May 8, 1939, just two weeks after the company opened its office, LIFE magazine ran a lead story on the new Johnson Wax headquarters. Wright's exalted reference to the cathedral is there. So too, is an anonymous reference to a more popular sort of exaltation—proving that the human spirit may be touched by architecture at every level.

"'The World of Tomorrow' was officially born at 2 p.m. April 30 on a onetime dump in New York City. Grover Whalen's $155,000,000 World's Fair, sprawling its gigantic mass of freak and futuristic buildings, is undeniably a great show. But future historians may well decide that a truer glimpse of the shape of things to come was given last week by a single structure, built strictly for business, which was opened in a drab section of Racine, Wis.

"The new administration building of S. C. Johnson & Son (wax polish) was designed by the master modern architect, Frank Lloyd Wright. It is genuine American architecture, owing nothing to foreign inspiration, different from anything ever built in the world before. Spectacular as the showiest Hollywood set, it represents simply the result of creative genius applied to the problem of designing the most efficient and comfortable, as well as beautiful, place in which Johnson Wax executives and clerks could do their work.

"This building," says Architect Wright, "was designed to be as inspiring a place to work in as any cathedral ever was to worship in." Wrote the financial editor of the Milwaukee Journal on viewing it last week: "It is like a woman swimming naked in a stream. Cool, gliding, musical in movement and in manner. The inside of an office building like a woman swimming naked in a stream? Yes, that's right."[3]

Reading Room, Bibliothèque Sainte Geneviève, Paris, Henri Labrouste (1801-1875). The library was the first public building to use iron in a visible, prominent fashion. Labrouste was able to create an open, well-lit space and allow the technology that made it happen to express itself in the process. The double-vaulted roof and columns that support it are independent of the walls.

Lofty Aspirations
The first monumental public building in which iron was flaunted rather than hidden was the Bibliothèque Sainte Geneviève (1838-50) in Paris. Its architect, Henri Labrouste (1801-1875), was a rebel. Although trained at the Ecole des Beaux-Arts, he broke with the dominant Neoclassic style. Labrouste believed the century should develop an architecture for contemporary needs and made of modern materials.

The radical novelty of Labrouste's design combines a traditional masonry exterior with an interior like none before it. The library's plan is simple—a two-story rectangle, where the entire upper floor is one vast reading room.

Covering the reading room are 211 barrel vaults supported by openwork, transverse arches of wrought and cast iron. In the center, dividing the room into two naves, is a row of slender cast-iron columns. Both functional arrangement and circulation are clearly expressed in the structure, using new materials without Classical overlay.

The Renaissance-style facade contains another innovation. In place of decorative stone columns, Labrouste had the names of 810 authors carved in rows of letters like the columns of a newspaper.

Labrouste's masterpiece served as the model for McKim, Mead and White's Boston Public Library.

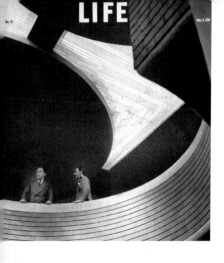

Johnson Wax President Herbert F. Johnson, Jr. and Advertising Manager William Connelly survey the new building from one of its balconies.

Torkel Korling, a Chicago botanist and nature photographer who was fascinated by the forms of the building, sold his photos (including this and the one opposite) to LIFE magazine for a May 8, 1939 feature article. The sunlight that floods the building through the glass tubes was sufficient for him to dispense with the usual floodlights or flash.

Wright, who understood well the value of publicity, wrote Johnson, "We are in line for a section of LIFE—a big spread in FORTUNE—and several pages in TIME if we are a success. Publicity equal to that costs many hundreds of thousands of thousands if it could be bought. But it couldn't be—for money. Let's not throw it away."[1]

SC Johnson & Son Administration Building • Racine

There was a high level of enthusiasm on the grounds of the new Johnson Wax Company headquarters on Friday, April 21, 1939. The work was finally finished and the employees were being shown around. The company held an open house for the entire city that weekend—a third of the population of Racine took up the invitation and were joined by visitors from all over the world—26,000 people stood in line for two hours. Once opened for business on Monday, the 24th, the building would attract immediate interest nationally and internationally. The lead article in *LIFE* magazine two weeks later featured the project; there was extensive coverage in newspapers as well as on the radio and in the cinema.

The building's architect Frank Lloyd Wright noted that there was "something universal . . . in the air . . . High time to give our hungry American public something truly 'streamlined,' so swift, so sure of itself and clean for its purpose . . . that ANYBODY could see the virtue of this thing called Modern. Many liked it because it was not 'modernistic,' but seemed to them like the original from which all the streamlining they had ever seen might have come in the first place."[2]

Wright said the building "was designed to be as inspiring a place to work in as any cathedral ever was to worship in." He was referring to more than the appearance of the building and its workspace. The space of the building itself represented Wright's view of the spiritual value of work. Though lower, lighter, and certainly less inhumanly massive than his Larkin Building of three decades earlier, this building, too, was meant to be a sealed environment—a temple—honoring labor as a redemptive force. As with his Unity temple, he

Comforting thoughts: the building is earthquake-, fire-, and sound proof.
Heat radiates through steam pipes laid in the concrete floor slabs.
Two "nostrils" (as Wright called them) suck air into the air-conditioning system.
The brick, which was baked in 200 different shapes to fit
the building's design, was lined with cork.

Testing the Limits

Wright claimed he got the idea for his column by watching a waiter carrying a tray on an upraised arm. He wanted his column to taper down to only a nine-inch diameter at the base.

According to Wisconsin state codes at the time, twenty-one-foot-high columns with a design load of six tons were required to be at least thirty inches thick. Local building commissioners argued with Wright until they agreed that he could build a column and test-load it. The State Industrial Commission said they'd be happy if it carried twelve tons without collapsing.

Workmen erected a test column on the site and hoisted sandbags to the top with a crane after only one week of curing time. At twelve tons the inspectors were satisfied. At thirty tons Wright said, "Keep on piling." Wright hit it occasionally with his cane. Soon there was soon no room at the top. It carried sixty tons without falling.

turned the true meaning inward and created a series of physical effects to get us there beginnning the moment we approach the building.

Wright carefully considered spatial event in sequence as you drive through the gate, park in the low, shadowy, enclosed carport (surrounded by diminutive versions of the mushroom columns yet to be encountered),[3] pass through the lobby doors (impressive, but squeezed under the canopied ceiling), and enter the sunlit lobby itself (dramatically rising several stories overhead). None of this compares to the next step—finally entering the bright, expansive space of the Great Workroom itself. We moved from compression to release; from darkness to light. By controlling our sensation of each successive space, Wright creates an experience very much like entering a real cathedral.

While the experience certainly inspires awe, it is neither melodramatic nor oppressive; the overall sensation is much more human in scale than that conveyed through photography. The color is warm and inviting. The materials are simple yet luxurious (brass is plentiful). Visitors, having passed through the town of Racine, bring the memory of the ubiquitous red brick with them so that, although the undulations that Wright puts the brick through are unlike anything else in the world, the material itself serves as a contextual anchor to the region.

The design of the administration building is basically similar to earlier buildings of Wright's.[4] It is a large, windowless rectangle lit from above through skylights and a series of clerestories. Balconied mezzanines are suspended inwards from its edges and look down on a two-story hall. The well-scaled, luminous space is defined by rows of tapered columns in concrete and is given over mainly to clerks and secretaries, while management is placed on upper levels off the balconies. The president and senior executives were inserted in a superstructure, visible on the exterior as two symmetrical, rounded, stepped forms. A bridge of clear glass, very striking in appearance, passes on towards the research areas of the organization. On the face of it, the design is sim-

above: Papyrus columns, Saggara, Egypt, 2600 B.C.

left: Testing the column became a spectacle that drew a crowd of onlookers including engineers, inspectors, product manufacturer representatives, press photographers, company employees, and Herbert Johnson himself (in straw hat).

plicity itself. But, it is simplicity that called for the highest level of precision in its details.

The difference between this and his earlier schemes is that here Wright designed his first streamlined building. Wright's champion at Johnson Wax was advertising director William Connelly. It may be that together they saw streamlining as good business and the wave of the future.

However, Wright's idea of streamlining was more profound than most. It's the essence of streamlining, not just its surface features, that he integrated into everything from the building's form to its lighting system, to its furniture. It gives meaning to the form.

Entering the building through a carport was a way for Wright to celebrate the automobile which he saw as a means of decentralizing society without suffering isolation. By the late 1930s the automobile had become *the* exemplary streamlined object, especially for the way it takes turns, curves through space, and cuts corners. The exteriors of the Johnson Wax Building have curved, streamlined corners. Cars sweep to turn into the covered parking area where the dynamism of the mushroom columns is first encountered.

The streamlined quality is continued in the interior in the horizontal attenuation of balconies and parapets, the undulations of the brick, and in the sleek, integrated lighting.

The columns are really the most extraordinary feature of the building. It is an indication of Wright's unusual intuitive grasp of structural principles that after quickly sketching them, without calculations, they needed no substantial changes to be built. The columns start out at the floor only nine inches in diameter. Set in a virtually hinged, steel bearing at the base, each column rises to an eighteen-and-a-half-foot in diameter disk at the top. Each disk is joined to its neighbor by small beams placed above in such a way as to allow for an 18-inch gap: they don't actually touch one another. This fact, along with the light filtering down from between them, gives the columns as well as the room itself, an eerie, otherworldly effect. Wright called them "stems and petals." The effect, as Wright describes it, is that of being

from top to bottom: Streamlined light wells in the company cafeteria, 1939.
The reception lobby viewed from the east end mezzanine, circa 1970.
The reception lobby at ground level looking west, 1969.
The lobby entrance doors with the carport in background, 1939.
The carport today.

An Upright Posture Spells Success

Furniture design was an integral part of Frank Lloyd Wright's public and corporate architecture ever since the Larkin Building commission (page 32). At Johnson Wax the furniture was especially wedded to the building's conception and its streamlined forms.

Over 40 different pieces of furniture were designed. With particularly sophisticated paper-handling systems, they are the precursors of much contemporary open office furniture design.

Nine different versions of the basic desk were designed for clerical employees to accommodate different tasks. There were also square, rectangular, and round tables for use in the mail room and other departments, as well as one-of-a-kind pieces, such as the President's desk and the conference room table (opposite).

Wright specified four fabric colors: red for the credit department (below), blue for the branch house records department, green for the billing department, and beige for the sales promotion department. Chair cushions acted as accents of color in the otherwise almost monochromatic Great Workroom.

Company employees were pleased with the desks and most found the three-legged chairs comfortable after they learned how to sit in them. The chairs were unstable if one leaned back, and a number of employees fell over in the first few days. Samuel Johnson recalls how his father told him that even Wright fell out of one, but still insisted that everyone would grow used to them.

"among the pine trees, breathing fresh air and sunlight."[5]

The columns have been compared to many things—mushrooms, toadstools, lily pads, golf tees. Meanwhile, they have become so recognizable that they are seen for what they are—the extraordinary creations of Frank Lloyd Wright. Whatever they remind one of, in person the underwater analogy is strongest due to the quality of light coming from the network of glass tubes that serves as skylights above the column rims. These tubes, sometimes lost in photos due to glare, are a ubiquitous feature of the entire building. There isn't a conference room, an office, or a hallway that doesn't have this glass tubing in some form.

Wright recognized that, having encircled the workroom with a tall, solid brick wall to shut out the surroundings, if it was not to become a dark tomb-like enclosure he would need to introduce generous quantities of natural light.

He had maintained an interest in the prismatic qualities of glass ever since he served as architectural adviser to the Luxfer Prism Company in Chicago many years before. Early design studies for Racine demonstrate a cumbersome use of traditional glass block. Wright examined a number of alternatives including cast glass panels which were investigated in collaboration with Libby-Owens-Ford, but it was a technical representative of Corning Glass who suggested that the use of glass tubing might satisfy Wright's requirements for special structural glass design and also achieve the streamlined curvilinear forms which his drawing suggested.

All light in the building is provided through double layers of horizontally stacked bands of Pyrex tubes, just like those used to make test tubes. The tubes are set in steel racks, secured by wires and sealed. The tubing admits light by day and emits the interior light to the outside at night.

This system of glazing was completely new—Pyrex had not been used in building before, the assembly systems were untested and there were many joints—and it continued to create difficulties both in its constructional detail and in the time required for assembly on site. The joints between the tubes, which required sealing, created a problem—one that

left: Wright's furniture reflects the forms of the building.
He also designed a major piece of built-in furniture—the information desk—located at the junction between the lobby and the Great Workroom. The desk runs directly beneath the mezzanine bridge. One end of the desk wraps around a mushroom column, representing the most complete integration of furniture and structure in the building.

has persisted throughout the life of the building.

Alongside his work on the new building Wright had also been designing special furniture for the project. This was a logical extension of his interest in developing an integrative approach to design and one that had been a consistent preoccupation throughout his career. Wright designed a range of furniture that touched the floor lightly, leaving its polished surface as a clearly visible advertisement for his client's products. He designed a desk with nine variations which incorporated file storage, trays for equipment, waste bins, task lighting and surfaces for office machinery at different heights. In addition he developed a range of three- and four-legged upholstered chairs with tubular frames. The system was developed with a range of variations.

Much has been made of Wright's difficulties with clients. He could certainly impose his ideas on them. He could also make major, even unreasonable demands of them. He would often come to a situation with an unbuilt project in mind and would see an opportunity for its realization; the Johnson Administration Building was no exception. He pretty much tried to do what he wanted to do.

For many architects this kind of behavior would spell disaster. But, idiosyncrasies aside, Wright had an incredible intuition about space and its uses. He built a world entirely of his own imagining—a parallel nature, a world that resembles no other. Yet, it's magical and it works.

The Great Workroom originally housed the company's entire workforce. The expanding company soon filled the space to a point where it needed additional room which Wright provided in a subsequent design.

From the beginning employees chose to linger after work, as if the place were an oasis against the chaos and economic depression in the world outside. Times have changed since then, but the polished glass and metal surfaces chosen with Johnson's wax products in mind, have been lavishly cared for and kept shiny ever since. At Johnson Wax, Frank Lloyd Wright made something of timeless beauty. It is beloved by the people who work there to this day.

above: Dome in the reception room of the advertising department (added in 1947). Bronze grilles hold individually produced tubes, each wired in place by hand and caulked. The dome is a reworking of a design originally planned for the Guggenheim Museum. right: Penthouse conference room in 1939. The table is a variation of Wright's desk. Above the display rack at right is a mural composed of the Pyrex tubing.

The Meaning of Glass

As early as 1894 Frank Lloyd Wright exhorted architects to "bring out the nature of the materials." From March 1908 until December 1928 he wrote a series of eloquent articles for ARCHITECTURAL RECORD entitled "In the Cause of Architecture," where he focused on materials—stone, wood, tile, brick, concrete, metal—and, in July 1928, he wrote of glass:

"Perhaps the greatest difference eventually between ancient and modern buildings will be due to our modern machine-made glass. . . .

"The demand for visibility makes walls and even posts an intrusion to be got rid of at any cost. . . .

"Shadows have been the brushwork of the architect when he modeled his architectural forms. Let him work, now, with light diffused, light refracted, light reflected—use light for its own sake—shadows aside. The prism has always delighted and fascinated man. The Machine gives him his opportunity in glass. The machine can do any kind of glass—thick, thin, colored, textured to order—and cheap. A new experience is awaiting him. . . .

"Glass and light—two forms of the same thing!

"Modern architecture is beckoned to a better reckoning by this most precious of the architect's new material. As yet, little has been done with it but the possibilities are large."[6]

Salk Institute • La Jolla, California

At the Salk Institute Louis Kahn created an open-air version of the classic cathedral effect he used later indoors at the Exeter Library—compression and release, expectation and revelation. Perhaps, at Salk, it's more accurate to make a comparison to ascending the Acropolis than to entering a cathedral. Or, as Kahn himself might have preferred to think of it, it's like approaching Hadrian's Villa in Rome. One mounts a short rise—just five steps—the plaza lies below out of view. We reach the top step and then—one of the most sensational experiences in all architecture—the austere, travertine-paved plaza, the watercourse, the concrete-and-wood volumes of the buildings stretch out below, all organized around the infinite vista of the sea.

The effect of the court is mesmerizing. One is instantly fixed by the space and by the thin channel of water bisecting the courtyard and aimed at the Pacific. This soundless, open space is focused on infinity. Even the travertine paving is patterned to emphasize the vanishing point, an impression abetted by the insistent perspective of the flanking, angled walls of the studies. One experiences a kind of timeless order made manifest—something man-made, but almost of the mind. "Architecture is what nature cannot make," Kahn once said. "Nature cannot make anything that man makes. Man takes nature—the means of making a thing—and isolates its laws."[2]

What's just been described is the experience of a visitor, at the moment of arrival, when they see the court for the first time. It's what has been photographed innumerable times. It's only one aspect of the Salk Institute. There are as many ways to experience the Institute as it has purposes. There's

One essential quality of Salk's and Kahn's master plan was the relationship of all the Institute's buildings, present and future, to the powerful and inspirational focal point that is the central court. Each element remains separate—resonating with its own life—but, is also unified in the mind and when viewed from the court.

Monastic Retreat

While the laboratory spaces were very flexible, in keeping with Salk's directive, they were not designed to contain all of the research activity of the building. Kahn also proposed small studies for each of the principal scientists, which were attached to the sides of their open-plan laboratories. These studies were grouped into towers that rose in the two courtyards between the paired laboratory blocks.

The researchers at first professed no desire for these refuges, they were willing to remain all day beside their apparatus. But, Kahn seduced them and Salk with the image of "an architecture, of the oak table and the rug," separated from the hard, "clean architecture" of the laboratory.

From outside, the cells appear to be teak cubicles inserted in pairs in the simple concrete study-towers.

Each tower seems animated, turning its face towards the sea to catch a glimpse of the view. In spite of the materials used the towers almost have the air of beach houses.

the experience of the casual, first time visitor. There is the experience of the Science Fellows who occupy rooms in the study towers. There are the experiences of the researchers, students, and others who use the laboratories daily. And, there are the experiences of technicians and service providers who oversee the so-called interstitial spaces.

One of the things that Louis Kahn did best was to create different spaces for different purposes and integrate them into one seamless whole. Each element of the Salk Institute remains separate and unique in its own life, but unified in mind and sight to the court—its inspirational focal point.

The east-west-oriented court is lined with study towers—the private offices for 36 Fellows—arranged in two-story banks of nine per side and angled to face the sea. These retreats are separated from the two enormous blocks of laboratories, which frame the far sides, by an elaborate, semi-enclosed circulation cloister. The offices for the Fellows bridge to the laboratories half a flight down. Three floors of laboratories are interspersed with full-height service floors that carry the trusses, freeing the labs beneath of the need for columns. In addition these floors provide total flexibility for the elaborate pipe- and duct-work which feed the experiments below. Projecting behind each laboratory block are five service towers containing toilet facilities and fire stairs. Every element is clearly defined.

The walls of the buildings have a timeless quality that is both symbolic as well as physical. Kahn's selection of building materials was always crucial to the feeling and meaning of his structures. The impression at Salk is one of emphatic boldness created by the meticulously poured-in-place concrete. This is one of the first times where the structural element—the poured concrete—was left unfaced or unfinished, or more properly put, where the concrete was left as the finish itself. The surfaces, which seem at once found and crafted, civilize an otherwise industrial material. The walls have a finish almost like marble.

Kahn researched the pigmentation of ancient Roman concrete in order to achieve the particular reddish hue. Dr. Salk

Kahn was sensitive to the color relationships of his materials as much as their textures. He left unfinished the teak surrounding the study towers and the west office windows, as well as the steel placed throughout the facility's exterior. He wanted no sealer or stain to be applied to the wood so that it would weather into a natural gray color. For the metal work he chose a steel which, also left untreated, formed a dense patina that prevented further corrosion.

was particularly interested in the color and quality of the concrete and became involved in the approval of test walls, which would eventually be used as retaining walls. He, along with Kahn, rejected several batches before the final mix was accepted.

Once the concrete was set, Kahn allowed no tampering with the finish—no grinding, no filling and, above all, no painting. It was, therefore, critical that the forms themselves be extremely well finished. The 3/4" plywood forms were filled, sanded, and coated with six layers of polyurethane resin in order to produce a smooth finish in the concrete. To avoid leakage and bleeding, the contractor used solid corners and gasketed joints between sets of gauged forms. The forms were able to be used as many as eight times before being repaired and refinished. Rather than try to hide the joints between the form panels, Kahn elected to accentuate them. The edges of the panels were chamfered to produce a raised V-shaped ridge in a grid pattern. The module of the pattern is the standard 4' X 8' and the occassional 4' X 12'.

The conical holes left by the form ties were also left unpatched, so their spacing was carefully considered. Each hole was later filled with a lead plug, hammered tightly in place to prevent corrosion of the steel ties.

Kahn also chose an unfinished look for the teak surrounding the study towers and west office windows. He directed that no sealer or stain be applied to the teak so that it would weather into a natural gray color. This may have been an unfortunate decision as the wood has weathered very unevenly over the years.

All these moves emphasize the relationship between the construction process and what constitutes the idea of finish. It should be noted that the results are anything but rough. The tolerance while building is even more critical than usual because you can see where everything comes together: you can't hide errors of judgment with shims and veneer. The process is unforgiving. In sum total, the effect of the finished product is elegant.

In spite of the decision to have the processes show, there

Each of the two buildings is six stories tall and contains three working levels (that house the laboratories), and three interstitial levels (that house the utilities). Clinging to the outsides of these two buildings are numerous structurally separate towers that provide space for utilities, elevator shafts, stairwells and private studies.

Luis Barragán

By 1965 a substantial amount of work had been completed and Louis Kahn still had not decided what form the court-yard should take—he had always visual-ized it as a lush garden with poplar trees. That year he had seen an exhibi-tion of the work of Luis Barragán at the Museum of Modern Art in New York. Barragán (1902-1988), a Mexican architect, combined his heritage with a modernist sensibility to create poetic works of archetypal power. His forms seem conditioned by the winds, rains, and sun of Mexico.

Kahn was so inspired by Barragán's work that he wrote to him with an offer to collaborate on the court. Barragán came to the Institute early in 1966, and as he later recalled, told Kahn at first sight of the muddy field between the laboratories, "'Don't put one leaf nor plant, not one flower, nor dirt. Absolutely nothing—and I told him, a plaza . . . will unite the two buildings, and at the end, you will see the line of the sea.' Lou was thinking, and stated a very important thing—that the surface is a façade that rises to the sky and unites the two as if everything had been hol-lowed out."[3]

Kahn took his advice.

are classical decisions regarding proportion and how those proportions reveal things. Kahn uses the seams in his cement work to delineate the different areas from outside even though there is no need to do that. Careful looking at the out-side reveals just about everything that's going on inside.

Blackboards are inset in the walls under the overhangs around the perimeter of the plaza so that anyone with an inspiration can make notes or work out a problem. This is something one usually finds indoors in a university. To find them placed within reach outdoors demonstrates a certain generousity of spirit. Kahn, an avid draughtsman, couldn't resist a blackboard anymore than a scientist could.

The Fellows, who occupy the 36 studies in the tower units, experience the Institute from the individual module that, in some sense, determines much about the place—the room. From inside these rooms one feels the entire complex as an extension of self. It's a very different sensation. Although not luxuriously appointed by any means, these are not monasti-cal cells, either. There is inviting warmth to the rooms, a combination of the wood and the sunlight. They feel larger inside than they appear from outside. The impression from the room is as if the whole complex was conceived as radi-ating from these centers. One feels as if the entire Institute were an expansion of one's own mind.

The cantilever solution implemented for this space protects the glass walls of the lower-lying laboratory rooms from direct sunlight. In the scientists' study cubicles situated toward the ocean, and in the library rooms, Kahn installed horizontally sliding wooden panels in a novel manner. These sun shade elements feature panels which can be adjusted as the occupant wishes. To provide ventilation, one can hori-zontally slide the entire window frames; the same is possible for the mosquito screening.

Kahn said, "Natural light is the only light that makes archi-tecture." (Nevertheless, Kahn also excelled in the design of legitimate and motion-picture theaters, lecture halls, and other auditoriums, i.e., rooms with artificial illumination, including the Kimbell Art Museum—page 226).

above: Kahn was a great admirer of the work of Luis Barragán, an architect of light, air, earth, and water.

left: A drawing by Kahn showing his early thinking about the court. The poplars would have blocked the views from the study towers.

Due to the incidence of earthquakes in the San Diego area the zoning prohibits anything higher than four stories. As a consequence Kahn put two of the six stories of the lab buildings below ground. To avoid having any level of laboratories without natural illumination he created great light courts.

He designed 40′ long by 25′ deep light wells on both the north and the south sides of each building to bring daylight into the two underground levels. The light wells lie between the tower structures, which surround the main buildings, and they are so successful that researchers on the first floors often forget they are actually underground. But Kahn did not stop at just bringing natural light into the laboratory levels. He also placed 6″ wide, full height windows in the stairwells; large screened openings (to bring in both daylight and natural ventilation) in the interstitial spaces; and large glass panes to serve as an east wall in the mechanical room. These glass walls in the mechanical room, besides bringing in daylight to maintenance workers, serve an additional important purpose: they can be easily removed to create an access for large machinery to be moved in or out of the mechanical room. This feature has been utilized extensively throughout the building's life as new equipment has been brought in to expand the energy plant's capabilities.

The design collaboration of Jonas Salk and Louis Kahn produced a facility uniquely qualified for scientific research. The laboratories themselves, with their divisible-at-will loft structural framing, stand in pointed contrast to Lou Kahn's famous Richards Medical Laboratory in Philadelphia, whose genesis was the intimate in-touch-with-neighbor approach.

At one point in their discussions Salk suggested to Kahn that the Institute might be modeled on the monastery of San Francis of Assisi. Salk had visited the monastery in 1954. As it turned out, Kahn had sketched it in 1929. Given the repeated praise for historical sources that dot Kahn's talks since the 1940s as well as his interest in monasteries, it can be assumed that he took this suggestion to heart readily. The results of the Salk Institute are truly a collaboration between the minds and the spirits of these two rare individuals.

One architectural feature that plays a key role in the Institute's spatial success is something called the Vierendeel truss. Located in the interstitial spaces, the trusses are 9 feet high and span each building's 65-foot width. These unique structural elements provide both support for the laboratory floor above and lift for the ceiling below. In turn, they allow the laboratory spaces to be completely free of load-bearing walls or space-inhibiting support columns.

Interstitial Spaces

Kahn always drew a clear distinction between the "servant" space and the "served" space. He felt that mechanical equipment, which he once called the great destroyer of space, should be confined to a servant space and kept completely separate from the laboratory.

By creating large interstitial spaces between each lab floor, he succeeded in confining all the electric lines, piping systems, and ventilation ducts to this servant space. This kept the laboratory environment completely free of mechanical equipment and was a key factor in meeting Dr. Salk's demand for an open, unobstructed laboratory interior.

But the interstitial spaces have served an even greater benefit than simply keeping laboratory space unobstructed. Because of their 9-foot ceilings, natural ventilation, adequate equipment clearance, and easily penetrated aluminum boxes cast into their concrete floors, the interstitial spaces have allowed in-house maintenance personnel to continually repair, renovate, and expand the engineering services provided to the laboratory below.

In this way, the researcher is completely free to redesign his laboratory as his scientific needs change. Since the early 1960s, the needs of science have changed dramatically, yet the Institute was able to change right alongside in a quick and economical fashion. The interstitial spaces, therefore, have been a key factor in meeting another of Dr. Salk's visions— laboratories that are adaptable to the ever-changing needs of science.

Kevin Roche assembling the Ford Foundation model, 1963. Roche comments on his vision: "I have departed very much from a rigid perception of architecture and I am obviously much more influenced by Eero Saarinen and Charles Eames and their investigative approach to the nature of architecture. And, we're bringlng to it other elements also, a strong social commitment which I have always felt. And we are exploring different ideas which are current because from one year to the next, the cultural environment changes perceptibly, subtlely but perceptibly. So one is also influenced by emerging ideas and changing values."[1]

Ford Foundation Headquarters • New York City

Entering the Ford Foundation Building is like lowering one's heart-rate: we leave the frenetic pace of one of the busiest cities in the world and enter a bucolic natural universe of semitropical plant-life and quietude. The contrast is surprising, pleasant, and in a sense, profound. It comes as a gift—which is ironic, since this is the headquarters of the largest philanthropic foundation in the world.

Kevin Roche John Dinkeloo and Associates aimed at producing an environment for the prestigious Ford Foundation in which the individual worker or visitor could identify "with the aims and intentions of the group." They created a new kind of urban space that stands between the sealed environment of a modern office building and the harsh and uncontrolled urban landscape outside. Roche has said of his structure, "It's not an office building in the normal sense. This is a home for a foundation which is really quite different from a commercial office building."[2]

The building's form, generated by a square plan is, for all intents and purposes, a cube. The cubic form contrasts as much with its contents as anything else in the structure since this rare shape among buildings holds everything as if it were a giant box. Its working area is concentrated in an L-shape that enfolds the garden on the north and west sides. Inside, a vertical conservatory shaft rises to the full height of the building with windows opening towards the planted space from all floors. Except for the offices facing 43rd Street, most open onto the enclosed court to its full ten-story height. The eleventh floor completely frames the court on four sides, but allows the space of the courtyard to burst through in the center to a great skylight that caps the building 160 feet above.

The Ford Foundation Building is a provocative gesture in an already provocative environment. Roche and Dinkeloo divided the building's monumental form by means of a great void—a surprising covered court garden. The garden is a respite between the chaos of the city and the quiet order of the offices, both of which reveal themselves through the building's transparencies.

Back to Eden

The atrium garden was designed by Dan Kiley. As he describes it, "Unlike the typical urban tower rising out of an exterior plaza, the Ford Foundation presents a well defined built edge to the street. I strove to compose a spatial statement that would fill the loftiness of the hundred-foot-high glass room.

"The original planting plan included a rich variety of species, some of which failed while others survived in this then-experimental microclimate. We installed jacaranda, evergreen pear, eucalyptus and Japanese cryptomeria-, an under-storey layer of camellia, fuchsia, andromeda, azalea varieties and star jasmine-, and baby's tears, mondo and Korean grasses, roundleaf and tassel ferns and spleenwort. Red bougainvillia, creeping fig and blood trumpet Vine reached up walls. In choosing the plant palette, we purposefully avoided species that are always found, dust-covered, in offices and hallways (such as rubber plants).

"I took a Darwinian attitude towards the installation's survival. Warren Manning, whom I worked for early in my career, delighted in letting plants fight it out—he could purposefully over-plant in some cases, then evaluate which species dominated. To my knowledge, the magnolia trees grew well for over eighteen years. I believe that our innovation at the Ford Foundation produced positive results. In the end, how-ever, I never did get to see my best inspiration materialize: a glistening, noisy thunderstorm inside the atrium each afternoon to greet workers as they left the office."[3]

The eleventh floor contains the chairman's office, a small conference room, and the executive and employees' dining rooms. From the ground floor to the tenth, the east and south sides enclosing the garden are largely of glass, through which the sun pours by day, and thus lights the offices on the court side; by dusk the court is internally spot-lit and thus delights the passersby on the street.

Before context ever became a buzzword in architecture the building was sensitively contextualized, if not in style, by its color and height. It is a dark red granite chosen to match the color of Tudor City across the street. The building is lower in height than most from the period—twelve stories—which also matches the Tudor City buildings.

In spite of the fact that the building is a cube, and sits on the regular street-grid of Manhattan, it seems shifted slightly off square by virtue of the fin-like forms of its granite piers (these contain fire stairs and air-conditioning discharge). The piers produce two interesting results. They appear to turn the building towards a more southerly light in spite of the restraints of the city and they act as giant baffles or louvers that block our sight from the west side. Since the majority of visitors are approaching the building, coming cross-town from the west, they will not really be able see the interior until they have practically arrived. All this gives life to other-wise inanimate container.

Encouraged by the generousity of the Foundation, Roche and Dinkeloo, along with landscape architect Dan Kiley, conceived the garden court, an oasis in the city that shines forth now, 35 years after it was built, as much as ever. More than just a garden in a lobby or even a full-fledged atrium greenhouse, this total environment is an integral part of the building's form and its meaning.

The garden court is conditioned to keep a year-round tem-perature of a low of 50°F/10°C in winter to a high of 85°F/29°C in summer. Heating coils along the window-walls keep the glass-conducted cold of winter in control. The gar-den is interconnected with the air conditioning system of the entire building. A mere third of an acre, the garden deploys

"As the first major interior atrium in the United States, the Ford Foundation project embodied both risk and fun. Although it may not have been what the clients expected to hear, I told them frankly that the project was an experiment." — Dan Kiley

an intriguing series of levels (it steps down 13 feet from 43rd to 42nd streets), so that its exploration produces new and unexpected vistas at almost every turn: it is not a two-dimensional layout, but a bountiful bit of landscaped witchcraft. The earth colors of the exposed, weathered steel and the granite give the greenery a sympathetic background. Among the trees are a magnolia, eucalyptus, Japanese cedar, plus a vast assortment of shrubs, vines, and flowers. There are numerous planting zones—all in New York City's temperate growing belt—each automatically watered and nourished with liquid fertilizer by underground piping.

Though the Foundation is private, the garden is open to the public. It is always crowded with visitors eating their lunches or taking casual strolls in an otherwise busy day. This patch of greenery refreshes all who see it.

In addition to providing a visual focus, the garden acts as real cohesion for the foundation—it makes a single family of all the glass-walled offices, including those of the president. All are working for a common goal—to dispense monies wisely; thus most of the staff enjoy offices that partake of a mutual and stunning collective space. The garden court ties man to fellow man and both to nature.

From the imagination of concept, to the boldness of realization, to impeccable detailing, the building is superb. The Ford Foundation has never made a more wonderful, or more lasting, bequest to the city—and indeed to all of us. "A form of this idea," explains Roche, "has now been incorporated into the zoning of New York City where, if such a space as this is provided, then bonuses of additional office space are allowed as an incentive. The Ford Foundation space was provided for no reason other than to make a public gesture . . . A developer could never be persuaded to do it unless there was some significant benefit. I don't think one could convince most clients to do it just as part of the architecture."

Laying out structures around atrium spaces or winter gardens later become popular in every building type from the skyscraper to the shopping mall, but few can compare to Roche and Dinkeloo's Ford Foundation Building.

" . . . the garden is all public, to be enjoyed by the public; they can rest, meditate, or eat their luncheon, but they are not involved with anything going on in the Ford Foundation. It is maintained for the use of the public. It isn't a lobby, it is a different kind of space."[4]
— Kevin Roche

Nature is the focus for the people in this unusual structure. Kevin Roche says, "The involvement with people in the building is very important, as is the case with the Ford Foundation which provides accommodation for the working community first, and secondly, for the relationship of this community with the public."[5]

Louis Kahn once claimed that architecture itself began "when the walls parted and the columns became . . . ."[1]

In the Exeter Library the walls literally seem to part at each corner of the building. This is an inviting gesture coming from what might otherwise appear to be a formidable, even forbidding, structure. It is also a signal of the importance of the relationship of the interior to the exterior.

Philips Exeter Academy Library • Exeter

Louis I. Kahn loved books. He once said, "A book is actually an offering and should be regarded as such. If you give honor to the man who writes it, there is something in that which further induces the expressive powers of writing." Kahn saw the library as a kind of temple—a place of worship and veneration. He was not impressed with traditional libraries. He felt they were like mausoleums.

His first plans for the Philips Exeter Academy Library embodied these sentiments and would have clearly announced them from afar. He planned corner towers and exterior arcades which, though modest in their medieval appearance, were much too grand for the purposes of the Academy. They wanted a building that would easily blend with the neo-classical New England private school campus. Rightfully so.

Long before commissioning Kahn to design its library, the Academy purchased quantities of reddish-brown brick from a local company that was going out of business. The traditional material matches that used in just about every other building in this sleepy little New England town. It was stored on campus for just such a future purpose. Kahn was asked to scale his original ideas down and, whatever else he decided to do, to use the Exeter brick on his façade. He skilfully put both stipulations to work to create one of the more surprising experiences in 20th Century architecture.

Kahn used the brick to successfully contextualize his structure. As an informed nod in the direction of history he introduced irregular or faulty bricks into the walls to further rusticate the façade—a popular device on the East Coast in the 19th Century. Though set in uniformly neo-classical sur-

"The room is the beginning of architecture. It is the place of the mind. You in the room with its dimensions, its structure, its light respond to its character, its spiritual aura, recognizing that whatever the human proposes and makes becomes a life. The structure of the room must be evident in the room itself. Structure, I believe is the giver of light."[2]
— Louis I. Kahn

Homage to a Master

When asked by Lorenzo the Magnificent to help greatly enlarge the Medici Library, Michelangelo designed an imposing stairway (above) that fills the space to a point where the beholder feels an almost physical stress. Two flanking flights of steps join the central stairway at a platform midway.

In an homage to the Renaissance master, Kahn followed suit, except his stairs (below) bear more resemblance to Michelangelo's original sketches which left circulation in front and between the outer stairways.

Michelangelo's friend and biographer Vasari wrote that his architecture "broke the bonds and chains of . . . common usage."[2] This is usually interpreted to mean that Michelangelo's architectural innovations are "expressive" rather than "functional." But, as with any architect, he too had very real problems to solve. Michelangelo solved those problems by making us the subjects as well as the observers of his work. Louis Kahn accomplishes the same end though ultimately says something quite different. Michelangelo justified the fantastic design of his stairway by explaining that the central flight was for the ruler and those on the sides for the retainers. By leaving the central stairs out of his scheme Kahn might be saying, "in this library there are no rulers."

roundings the building does respectfully coexist with its neighbors. In fact, despite its modern design and the unusual weathered teak insets under the windows, the exterior of the Exeter Library is unprepossessing in the extreme. Others might have found these demands extremely limiting and would have fought to hang on to their original concept. Instead, Kahn, who delighted always in the interplay between outside and inside, employed his limitations to toy with our expectations and create a parallel for the revelation that the contents of libraries are supposed to bring.

In the finished library, a surprisingly low arcade surrounds the building at ground level, masking the main entrance which is oddly placed on the far side away from everything on campus. The arcade itself has few distinguishing features and is even a little discomfitting. The visitor is forced to circle around to the entrance, in a tightly compressed space, completely unprepared for what lies within. Only in retrospect does one realize that this is part of a carefully calculated gambit. Kahn uses a classic game of compression and release.

Enter the building and an oversized staircase immediately awaits you. There's something a bit sly about this. It's reminiscent of the staircase that Michelangelo designed for the vestibule of the Laurentian Library in Florence. But, this isn't simply an instance of one master architect quoting another; Kahn succeeds in imparting a different set of values with his gesture. It might be argued that Michelangelo causes real discomfort and that his steps are uninviting. In Kahn's case, on the other hand, the pressure on the confined space compels the visitor to ascend—it's an invitation. And, while in both instances there is an equally dramatic compression and then a release into the open, in Kahn's it is made all the more dramatic because he prevents us from seeing our destination from below. The eventual sight of the Library's central atrium is a completely unexpected, uplifting revelation. Kahn was sensitive to the emotional consequence of his scheme as well as its geometrical sequence. One influences the other. In our experience of the transition from the exterior to the

above: Michelangelo, Vestibule Stairway, Laurentian Library, Florence 1558-59.

left: Louis Kahn's stairway is a respectful homage to Michelangelo while it expresses a different purpose.

interior, we become the subjects of the architecture as well as its observers. Expression has a function.

The relationship of scale is such that the stairway appears much larger in photographs. This is also the case with much of the rest of building. In reality the scale and qualities of the Library's spaces are very human.

Once you ascend to the main level of the library you are surrounded by a roofed-over atrium space surrounded by the four circular openings which have been photographed time and again, and through which you can see the floors of the building and the book stacks. This is *the* grand experience of the building. The visitor has an unobstructed view to the roof where the indirect light of the sun, entering through clerestory windows plays on the X-bracing and other structural elements of the building. The result is a beautifully mutable atmosphere whose drama is at the service of its primary purpose—the exaltation of knowledge and the elevation of the user experience.

Once inside, a great deal of pleasure is to be derived from wondering just how all this physically fits into this building. What one thought was a four-story structure from the outside is really a good nine stories tall (including the roof garden). Kahn essentially achieved this through a trick in scale between outside and in. What appears as a single story on the outside walls is actually double—each window embraces two floors.

The interior is of poured concrete and white oak. The wood window inserts inside echo those outside in exactly the same locations, thereby giving one the impression, as a memory of the exterior, that what you saw from outside is the corresponding wood elements inside; they appear to be plugged in to the brick framework of the building.

Kahn hoped that the building would be a showpiece and a focus for the community life of the school and this has proven so. There are numbers of events that take place in the building, including concerts: the main space has proven to be successful acoustically. The quantity of wood set in the concrete probably helps absorb a portion of the sound.

Kahn achieves an uncanny balance between stability and fragility in all his later buildings, but particularly at Exeter.

He accomplishes this through the shapes he employs such as the large circular cutouts that reveal the book stacks in the atrium.

He achieves this through his use of material, in this case the combination of wood and concrete (Kahn originally thought of using brick on the interior). And, he achieves it through the effects of light.

Structure, material, and light are the hallmarks of Louis Kahn.

above: *The play of light on the X-bracing at the summit of the atrium. Circular openings reveal the stacks from every side of the space while they bring light into the interior.*

right: *The tight space of the arcade that runs around the building's perimeter.*

Windows Are For Looking Out

"Glare is bad in the library; wall space is important. Little spaces where you can adjourn with a book are tremendously important."

Always concerned with light, Kahn struggled to find a balance between natural and artificial illumination—it is far too easy to rely entirely on the latter when designing a library. He also wanted windows to be used for looking out at the world.

The lower section of each two-story window has an inset of teak. The pairs of small windows illuminate reading niches. These niches accommodate what Kahn referred to as study carrels.

The windows illuminate the carrel as well as afford the reader views to the exterior. The reader can shut the sliding panels to close off the distraction of the view into the park, in order to concentrate fully on reading. Kahn said, "The carrel belongs to the outside world. Occasional distraction is as important in reading as concentration."[3]

The central core of the building is given over to the books for practical as well as symbolic reasons. Natural light, which can be harmful to books, rings the structure. Ample daylight is available at windows if desired. Otherwise specially baffled fluorescent fixtures light the stacks and other sensitive areas. The services such as elevators, secondary stairs, toilets, photocopying, etc. are also relegated to the edges of the building. They are well designed—not forgotten or dismissed in the design scheme. In fact, every square inch of the library has been well thought out.

Every detail was attended to by Kahn: the size and shape of every room; the woodwork; the cabinetry. Some cabinets and shelf units were designed as dividers and are inserted in the archways between rooms. Spaces are very adaptive since the cabinet modules can be removed to other locations. The archways are structural in that they hold up the upper floors; they are useful for passage; they allow one space to be seen from another so that even when small no space appears as such, because your sight lines are never fully blocked. They also allow for light to enter most of the spaces no matter how deep. The bricks in the lintels of the archways are turned upwards vertically—the curve is extremely slight and, as a result, quite attractive.

The school cares for the library with great respect and makes additions or changes in keeping with the original look and concept of the building. A few have been made. It has been rare, except where lighting was an issue, in the underground areas for instance, that additional lighting had to be added. Major modifications to the space have been unnecessary.

Kahn foresaw future growth and designed forward-looking room for expansion. He left an entire floor as undesignated space and a variety of other small alcoves and offices, again undesignated, so that the librarian and her staff could decide over time how to use, arrange, or reuse that space. When the building was wired for computers which, of course, was not anticipated, there was no difficulty since plenty of room was left for wiring, extra ventilation, etc.

above: The teak insets on the building's façade.
left: The reading carrels just behind the insets.
It must be said that the use of light in some of the uppermost, individual reading rooms is not always successful. It can range from gloomy on overcast days to too focussed and bright on sunny ones.

There are the usual problems that arise from that kind of attention to detail: since Kahn attended to everything, he had certain things manufactured to his specifications. When the custom-made baffles on the fluorescent lighting fixtures were played with or broken by the young boys they were difficult to replace. But, through an extensive search for someone who could replicate the originals, the school showed it cares.

Louis Kahn was fascinated by what he believed were the transcendant properties of certain geometrical schemes. Buildings that are generated by such preoccupations often have awkward leftover spaces—usually terribly small—nooks and crannies that remain once the major spaces are designed. Not so here; geometry was employed with consummate skill. Every space in the library is useful and actively enjoyed by everyone. None are too small. You can see from one space to another at the same time that there is a level of privacy. Seeing through gives the impression that spaces are bigger than they often are and allows light to come through. Every space was carefully attended to. Kahn was very much aware of how to make space both beautiful and practical.

Returning to the first points made about the restrictions of the program: too much shouldn't be made of the limits that were put on Kahn's original intentions. He never felt hampered. Quite the contrary, his method of working was such that he welcomed resistance as an operative force in his way of solving problems. As soon as he heard about the need to use brick he was heard to say, "the brick was always talking to me, saying you're missing an opportunity. . . . The weight of the brick makes it dance like a fairy above and groan below."[4]

In the final analysis, the constraints that were placed on Kahn's first proposal were happy circumstances for everyone. He was compelled to temper his desire to announce his feelings in his façade and transfer that impulse to the interior. He made a different and a better building. He intensified and heightened the experience for us all.

above: One of several models left to the library by Kahn's office.

It has been remarked that the open corners of the Library's façade make it look like a book. Here the book is opened to reveal its valuable contents.

An Open Book

At first glance the Exeter Library has a simply structured, symmetrical form. As this picture of a model in the Library's collection demonstrates, peeling away the layers of the building reveals a much more complex series of relationships concealed behind its careful design.

A visitor to the Library needn't know that all this is happening to feel its force. In fact, it might be argued, when the geometry that generates a building's structure succeeds it is a mark of its success that it becomes sufficiently invisible.

Kahn shared a belief that the forms he employed are a lasting vocabulary drawn from a universal language and that they imbue a structure with vibrant tension and symbolic character. They bring harmony and an order that is instinctively understood.

He was very much influenced in these beliefs by Anne Griswold Tyng. Tyng, an architect and an associate in Kahn's office for 28 years, inspired his appreciation for certain three-dimensional geometries associated with patterns of growth. Her highly theoretical research involved the interrelations between physical, natural and psychic structures and their architectural application. Tyng believed that architects should conceive of forms in building based upon dynamic three-dimensional relationships rather than on two dimensions simply extended upward.

Starting with the Yale University Library (page 102), Kahn and Tyng collaborated on many projects.

3

where

nature

and

the built

world

meet

Taliesin West
Bavinger House
Haystack Mountain School
Sea Ranch Condominium I

Over sixty years ago Frank Lloyd Wright wrote of the site he chose for Taliesin West, "There was vast room so we took it and didn't have to ask anything or anybody to move out or over." Today the once isolated encampment has been overtaken by relentless urban sprawl; waves of stuccoed, tiled-roofed mission-style housing developments with exotic names are practically at its door.

What was once bucolic countryside outside Norman, Oklahoma, where the Bavinger House sits, is now that city's suburb with the usual jumble of amenities. Deer Isle, Maine is still mighty remote, but not for long if the development continues further south along the coastal highways.

Returning to The Sea Ranch seven years after they built the condominium, two of its four architects, Charles Moore and Donlyn Lyndon, wrote:

> The new "building seems to be ignoring the plan and the intentions behind it (as well as the view itself). It turns out that the condominium program was delayed and did not continue past the first building because the salesmen on the site could make their 6 percent fees much more quickly on vacant land, without more investment by [the developers] and without the trouble and complexity of showing dwellings already built. They pressed for five years to delay condominium construction, and the present work is going on only because a contractor

"Imperative requirement of each bough to stop within certain limits, expressive of its kindly fellowship and fraternity with the boughs in its neighbourhood; and to work with them according to its power, magnitude, and state of health, to bring out the general perfectness of the great curve, and circumferent stateliness of the whole tree."1 — John Ruskin, The Elements of Drawing, 1857

The Struggle For Nature

In the early 1940s Frank Lloyd Wright began to develop a new type of plan—an extension of his Usonian house—only curvilinear and partially buried in a built up earth embankment. The house, which was glazed along its south side to receive sunlight, was an attempt to develop a "low-energy" architecture, deriving a lyrical form from the need to obtain maximum solar heat and protection from northern winds. Wright called it the "solar-hemicycle."

The version he built for Mr. And Mrs. Herbert Jacobs (below) was included in the BUILT IN THE USA exhibition of 1952. They describe it best:

> "The Jacobs house on a windswept plain, is a two story hemi-cycle protected on the north by an earth bank. All rooms open to a sunken garden on the south. Bedrooms overlooking the garden, are on a mezzanine floor set back from the glass doors, so that from within the volume of the house registers as on large room with minor subdivisions. A tunnel through the earth bank leads directly into the garden—the site itself being used as an architectural material."

Wright continued to build other solar-hemicycles demonstrating his growing interest in a flowing architecture, free from the right angle. This development continued through the reflex curves of his 1953 design for his son, Robert Llewelyn, in Bethesda, Maryland, and the 1950 ramped spiral house for his other son, David, in Phoenix, Arizona, on to the Guggenheim Museum.

bought some land and brought his architect from the ski country to fashion this chalet. The residents are angry. They are also powerless."[2]

Familiar stories? Yes, unfortunately. Is this outcome inevitable? Or is it, as we hope, bad planning and insensitive building? Why are the four projects in this section so special? What makes each of these succeed while others fail? Why are they *still* successful?

There are no easy answers to these questions. For one thing each of these projects is entirely different from the others—from their geographical locations, to the times in which they were built, to the world-views of their architects. But they do succeed. A careful look at each may be the best and only way to begin to understand them and to learn the lessons they may still teach.

A Grace to the Landscape

Frank Lloyd Wright was always concerned with what he called the "kinship" of architecture with its setting, admonishing students, for instance, not to build on top of a hill but beside it in partnership, not dominance. He said, "A struggle against naure never appealed to me. The struggle for and with nature thrilled me and inspired my work."

Taliesin West was designed for the relatively mild heat of the Arizona desert winter. Originally, every room in the house was open on at least one side. The canvas roofs, with their wood-framed, canvas-covered flaps at the eaves and gables for ventilation, allowed an enormous range of adaptability to the daily changes of climate typical in the desert, and created a house where almost every space was simultaneously inside and outside. The light, coming largely from above, is extraordinary.

But the real accomplishment at Taliesin West is the integration of spaces with the land.

> "Out here in the great spaces obvious symmetry claims too much, I find, wearies the eye too soon and stultifies the imagination. Obvious symmetry usually closes the episode before it begins. So for me I felt there could be

left: Second Jacobs House, Frank Lloyd Wright, Middleton, Wisconsin, 1943.

"Whether people are fully conscious of this or not, they actually derive countenance and sustenance from the 'atmoshere' of the things they live in or with. They are rooted in them just as a plant is rooted in the soil." — Frank Lloyd Wright

no obvious symmetry in any building in this great desert . . . . A desert building should be nobley simple in outline as the region itself is sculptured, should have learned from the cactus many secrets of straight line pattern for its forms, playing with the light and softening the building into its proper place among the organic desert creations—the man-made building heightening the beauty of the desert and the desert more beautiful because of the building."[3]

The Continuous Present

Bruce Goff designed a house near Norman, Oklahoma, for Gene Bavinger and his familiy, arguably one of the most unique houses ever built.

While for Wright building *with the land* was of paramount importance, for Goff nature demanded that particular attention be paid to *time* and the forms it calls forth. The temporal element in his work resulted from what he called the continuous present. The spiral was the form that perfectly embodies the ever-present moment—a time with no beginning and no end. He said:

"Because buildings are different doesn't mean there will be chaos, either. In nature you see different kinds of things together: you see rocks that are not like trees, and you see trees that are not like water, and you have water that isn't like flowers, and all sorts of things, and they all seem to get along together, don't they? We can't criticize nature. We have all of this variety and interest that is always changing, that is always part of the continuous present, and still the only way we think we can have harmony in buildings is to say that they all have to be the same height, or the same materials, or the same something else."[4]

Main Street in the Wilderness

For Edward Larrabee Barnes certain basic architectural and architectonic shapes and forms, and their place in history are a kind of nature in their own right. Especially if the forms in

above: Hopewell Baptist Church, Edmond, Oklahoma, 1948. Bruce Goff, architect. Interior view of the skylight and chandelier of pie pans and plastic ornaments. *"Looking into things is as important as looking out, or beyond. We often think of infinity as way out there, somewhere in outer space, don't we? We also know that infinity is within, or without. I don't believe we can even grasp it."[5]* — Bruce Goff

Without Beginning or End
Bruce Goff spoke of "The Continuous Present" he observed in nature and felt he brought to his architecture.

"Say there is a beautiful woods out here with streams, maybe a waterfall, and some nice trees and rocks and so on. . . . You would be able to walk around in it, and it wouldn't have any beginning, . . . it wouldn't have any development, or any climax . . . in nature, there is no beginning and no ending; you know it is a continuing thing . . . it would always be an ever new experience. You would never be traveling the same route twice.

"Now supposing . . . someone comes in and prescribes a route. He says I want you to go by this particular place to get a view from here, I want you to see this group of trees, I want you to come over to the water at this point, I want to put some restrooms here, and I want a place over here where you end up and really knock you out, for this will be the grand climax, maybe a plaque or something. . . .

"On the one hand, you have a very free kind of composition that you can enter and go through in many ways, and on the other, you have a very prescribed route, where whoever is doing the design calls the shots and builds you up, or lets you down, or lets you rest, or catch your breath, or whatever you need to do, and rings out of you every bit of emotion that he can."[6]

Material World
The typical 17th Century New England house is characterized by a natural use of materials in a straightforward manner. The simple, box-like appearance is offset by a prominent chimney and a sparse distribution of small, casement-type windows. The one-room house was often expanded by adding a room to the rear and extending the roof slope on the one side, giving it the well known shape popularly called the "salt-box." It is clad in unpainted riven, or hand-split, wooden shingles. Edward Larabbee Barnes has used this silhouette a number of times before and after Haystack Mountain School of Crafts (page 74).

question were developed over time in coherently knit social groups. On a visit to the islands off Greece, Barnes was deeply impressed by the strong unity between villages and their natural environment. Society, rather than the individual, was the determining factor, and each building was conditioned by its context and by what had preceded it.

By no means a new idea, this is one of the elements of what we call classic architecture; it is also one of the tenets of modernism.

Barnes can be described as a modernist, but the limitations of that description don't fully do him justice. He has immense respect for the nature of a site whether urban or rural—a number of his projects being in pastoral settings. He also has a love of common materials and the vernacular vocabularies that suit them.

"For me," says Barnes, "continuity means the use of fewer materials, the elimination of expressed articulation, as little tampering with the land as possible, and emphasis on what is alike rather than different. It means designing with respect for nearby buildings—their scale and color, and mood. It means considering the space between the buildings, bearing in mind that it can be more important than the buildings themselves."[7]

The Haystack Mountain School of Crafts is classically set into its site and draws upon a whole variety of historical relationships including what we call a vernacular or commonly shared indigenous vocabulary.

Inside and Outside in Partnership
In the 1960s a few architects began to move towards a more complex and more inclusive architecture, one that viewed neighboring buildings, and context in general, with more sympathy then the repetitive, bare-bones, universalist aesthetic that had become the only game in town. Among this more pluralistic group was Charles W. Moore. Moore felt deeply that the architect should be one who acts to particularize and reinforce a sense of place, thereby letting people

above: The Jethro Coffin House on Nantucket Island, Massachusetts, is the oldest extant house in the United States.

left: Edward Larrabee Barnes during construction of Hidden Valley Camp, Fishkill, New York, c. 1960.

know, he wrote, "where they are—in space, in time, and in the order of things." Moore often spoke about a partnership between structures and the land—a kind of agreement where one could live with the other even if there were marked differences. He enjoyed differences—he delighted in contrast and idiosyncrasy. He felt that different things augmented one another, strengthening the character of a place.

MLTW designed the Sea Ranch condominium using carefully gathered quantities of ecological data *and* a deep-seated respect for the land. The shed-roofed houses, sheathed in rough siding left to weather, clustered and enclosed like a cross between a mining community and a medieval hill town, are of a piece with their surroundings. They rise above the bluff as if they were a natural outcropping of the craggy, windswept rock forms.

The concern MLTW showed later is less an admission of failure than it is an indicator of their true sensitivity and a clue to their ultimate success:

"But we guessed wrong, too, we who planned together to make this place special. We sought a partnership of buildings with this vast landscape which required more size and presence than most houses have, and more care in the arrangements than most people working somewhere else chose to give. . . .

"At the Sea Ranch, houses merge into the forest with great success; in the meadows, however, houses need to set up partnerships with the land forms and with each other which turned out to be very difficult to achieve. Most of the houses on the meadow or the grassy slope are reduced to laying claim to their patch of turf. These houses are the least successful, and having said that, we have in all honesty to admit that it is in this way that most people build houses everywhere—one by one, without any relationship to each other. What, then, are the chances for a person who wants a good house, and what, in the late twentieth century, is the place of houses?"[8]

MLTW
Four architects, each of whom had recently moved to the San Francisco Bay Area, and each of whom had commitments to other firms, came together in 1962 and formed a freelance partnership. Charles W. Moore, Donlyn Lyndon, William Turnbull, Jr., and Richard Whitaker called themselves MLTW. They worked from their tiny individual offices and met for design sessions at a local diner. Moore's indefatigable energy and leadership helped to establish their work.

"The American landscape is littered with the shards of successive environmental dreams. Our own dream, as architects, is of a built environment so richly configured that it can easily be claimed by the imagination, with recognizable places that can serve as benchmarks and identification points. Our dream is of places to live in, endowed with a structure that can be used to make sense of, but not to restrict, the circumstances of daily life—not so much to mold the circumstances as to trace them."[9]

above: Turnbull, Lyndon, Whitaker, and Moore working on the Winnetka House at Turnbull's office, August 1979.
right: Together, MLTW designed a condominium for the rustic landscape overlooking the sea in Northern California. Sea Ranch as it was called was a group of houses that would have both unity and privacy.

Wright said after his first trip to the desert in the 1920s, "there could be nothing more inspiring to an architect on this earth than that spot of pure Arizona desert."[1]

Beginning in 1937, and continuing over the next several years, Wright and his apprentices constructed Taliesin West on a spectacular desert site in Paradise Valley.

Wright frequently abstracted the forms and textures he found in the Sonoran Desert and used them as design elements—mountains, cacti, lizards, and Native American motifs such as the ones he incorporated into the stalactites on the ceilings of the drafting room (above).

Wright sits at the drafting room table. Apprentice Edgar Tafel is at the far left.

Taliesin West • Paradise Valley, Arizona

Frank Lloyd Wright spent many months on a number of projects in the late 1920s in the arid, primeval landscapes of California's chaparral and Arizona's deserts. While working on one particular large-scale proposal, he built a seasonal camp he called *Ocatilla*, partly for economic reasons, but also to experience firsthand what living in the desert might be like.

Though they were never built, these desert projects lured Wright to a landscape that he fell in love with and remained attached to his entire life. It was at *Ocatilla* that he first dreamed of an "Arizona type," an inspiration that would inaugurate a new and vital phase in his career. It was a kind of rebirth, a new beginning so significant that he made Arizona his second home.

In his earlier work Wright typically applied a single, regular grid to the landscape as in the gardens at Taliesin in Wisconsin. That all changed after he began working in the desert. He now began to adopt strategies more appropriate to the sloping, irregular terrain, adjusting to the shifts and craggy breaks, and aligning elements in response to the views. He began angling and combining more than one grid and using geometry he derived from the land. At Taliesin West he pushed this approach further still, to include the building's three-dimensional concept. The elevations of the structures cross and collide with each other, and with the landscape, echoing nearby outcroppings and the mountains in the distance.

Taliesin West is truly integrated into the land. The complex of buildings, courtyards, and gardens is oriented, angled, woven, and wedged into its surroundings. Walls, roofs, per-

"Arizona character seems to cry out for a space-loving architecture of its own. The straight line and flat plane must come here—of all places—but they should become the dotted line, the broad, low extended plane textured, because in all this astounding desert there is not one hard undotted line to be seen. The great nature-masonry we see rising from the great mesa floors is ... not architecture at all, but it is inspiration."[2] — Frank Lloyd Wright

Working the Land

Edgar Tafel (1910-), who worked as an apprentice with Wright on Johnson Wax and other major projects, went on to distinguish himself in his own career as an architect. Tafel talked about the first days at Taliesin West:

"Mr. Wright actually designed the camp on the site where it was being built. The apprentices were the surveyors, laying out the lines for the buildings. Drafting tables were set out in the sun, in the blazing light—imagine drafting on white paper in the Arizona sun!

"Mr. Wright soon devised a master plan for the camp, decided on a grammar of building, and was off to a new design concept indigenous to Arizona. Desert stone was placed in forms with a lean mortar mix. Redwood—rough-sawn, undried, and stained dark brown—was inexpensive and handsome against the white canvas roofs and the sky.

"For sculpture at the terminals of the walls, Mr. Wright had us bring down large rocks (decorated with petroglyphs) from the mountainside and set them in a natural-looking orientation. 'When the Indians come back 2000 years from now to claim their land, they will note we had respect for their orientation.' Taliesin West would make one of the most interesting ruins of all time."[3]

golas, and paths catch the brilliant sunlight and cast crisp shadows. Stones from the area are integrated into the walls. Sight lines point to distant land forms. Invisible trajectories of the angled roof-peaks connect to distant hills and mountains.

Taliesin West lies high above the Salt-Gila River Valley with a magnificent view of the entire region. It is closed in and protected to the north by the McDowell Mountains. The hillside was used by the prehistoric Hohokam for hunting and ceremonial purposes, and the traces they left behind—the petroglyphs and artifacts—add to the aura of the site.

Wright laid out the buildings along a lateral spine paralleling the mountain range, using diagonal shifts to establish connections with the surrounding landmarks and to give the projecting main terrace prow a forceful connection with the desert. The individual buildings were constructed in stone, wood, and canvas. Angled stone walls, parapets, and substructures were created by a process of agglomeration in which the variously colored volcanic boulders found at the site were placed in forms that were filled with a concrete mix and then removed after the stones had been consolidated. Heavy redwood frames were clamped over the tops of the low walls to carry panels of translucent canvas that could slide back and forth, or flip in or out, to provide ventilation.

The building is first seen, coming through the desert, silhouetted against the low mountains immediately behind, its broken, serrated profile merging with the surroundings.

A large boulder, found on the site and bearing ancient Indian markings, stands guard at the entrance. From this point, we can overlook the desert below. The pergola leads along the south side of the courtyard. At the far end, through the drafting room, the view through the loggia reintroduces the desert and invites us to move out onto the terraced gardens that occupy the geometric center of the house.

It's not just the enclosed spaces that define the architecture and experience of Taliesin West. The spaces between and around the buildings are of equal, if not more, significance—the walkways, bridges, platforms, and terraces that

previous page: Gallery terrace looking towards pool cove.
left: Entry with light tower and fountain.

Wright wrote of Taliesin, it "is a grand garden the like of which in sheer beauty of space and pattern does not exist, I think, in the world."[4]

connect building to building, visually link the entire complex to the mountains and valley surrounding it. Paths that align with mountain peaks and other topographical features direct the movement of the eye as well as the body. Often, as at the triangular prow opposite Wright's office, or on the pyramidal base above the pool in front of the drafting room, one of the Hohokam petroglyph boulders has been positioned to mark a point of orientation, thereby connecting to the landscape with a meaningful temporal resonance.

Philip Johnson considered Taliesin West to be one of the three greatest buildings of the 20th Century. He describes how Wright masterfully controls his spaces:

". . . you start down the steps, up the steps, to the left, to the right, down the long, very long pergola and you turn to the right to get out under that famous prow. And you take those few steps down onto the magnificent view that's been concealed from you for two or three hundred feet of walking. Then you see Arizona stretched out as he meant it . . .

"And then you turn and go into the little tent room where—the man, of course, understands light better than anybody in the world—and he has this tent light that trickles, filters down through into this private room. Before he opens any flaps you are just bathed in this canvas light. Then when he opens the flap into the little secret garden, you say . . . there can't be any more unfolding of spaces, but there are. And you get into this private courtyard with the green grass and the falling water . . . .

"Then you finally get into the cove and just when you're used to Frank Lloyd Wright's six-foot ceiling, it has a four-teen-foot ceiling and the fireplace runs the full length of the building. There are no windows, all of a sudden, and no canvas. You're entirely enclosed in the middle of this experience. And by the time you get there you realize that you've been handled, and petted, and twisted much as a symphony will caress you, or an opera, until you get to the crisis. That, perhaps, is not even architecture in the same sense that [Le Corbusier's Marseilles apartment complex] is, but they both have something to tell later architects."[5]

The original construction of Taliesin West was intended to be both permanent and cyclical, or seasonal, as part of the Fellowship's annual migration from Wisconsin to Taliesin. In considering any latter-day changes, it should be remembered that Taliesin West was built by Wright—and used as long as he lived—as a winter residence, with Taliesin 'North' (in Wisconsin) being the Fellowship's summer home.

above: View of the bridge with Madonna stone and pool.

middle: The sun cottage with open canvas screen.

right: The garden room with harp.

Bruce Goff and Herb Greene examining Greene's rendering (page 74) of the Gene and Nancy Bavinger House, c. 1950.

"The Bavingers have their house which is neither old or new so far as architectural fashion is concerned, but which is timeless. . . . The house, unlike other houses, will probably never be complete because it is intended to keep growing, in a state of flux, with its occupants and I hope it will continue to be inspiring and beautiful to them. The Architect did not start with a preconceived notion of the shape or form of the house. It resulted thus as a discipline of all organic elements found and growing in freedom. The Architect was the medium; he wishes to express his appreciation to the clients and all others who have helped to make, what could have been only a dream, a reality."[1]

— Bruce Goff

Bavinger House • Norman, Oklahoma

Whenever he was asked what he thought about contemporary architecture, Bruce Goff would say that "commonism" in architecture was the big danger. The generally accepted notion that architects could achieve harmony through conformity seemed ridiculous to him. He said that he hated to see anything that he liked becoming the rule.

There is certainly nothing common about the house Bruce Goff built for Eugene Bavinger and his family near Norman, Oklahoma. Designed by Goff in 1950, it was largely built by its owner over a period of four years.

Goff enjoyed collaborating with his clients. He found the Bavingers' requirements both challenging and inspiring. Eugene Bavinger was an artist who wanted a house grounded in his art. Nancy Bavinger was a ceramist. Together they wanted a large open space, liked the idea of living on different levels, and preferred natural textures and materials. They also liked the idea of living in a garden that could be cleaned by hosing it down. They had a limited budget and wanted to build the house themselves with the help of family, friends, neighbors, and students.

The Bavingers were particularly unhappy, in their former house, with the closed feeling of separate rooms and the lack of connection between the house and its surroundings. They asked Goff for more open, continuous space that would not only provide for themselves and their two sons, but which would also accommodate their serious horticultural interests. To design a house that would perfectly suit their character, Goff decided to combine the spaces into one coherent whole and integrate the structure and its site.

The chosen site was a small parcel of un-farmable land

"The Bavinger house, earth-bound as it is, is a primitive example of the continuity of space-for-living . . . it is not a back-to-nature concept of living space. It is a living *with* nature today and every day [in] space, again as part of our continuous present."[2]

— Bruce Goff

The Curves of Life

Number is a universal language; it is also an indispensable part of the architect's craft. There is another side to mathematics, however, that has fascinated many architects for centuries—the geometry associated with nature's patterns of growth. An interest in these mechanisms and their relation to architectural form was shared by individuals who often had little else in common—a group as diverse as Frank Lloyd Wright, Mies van der Rohe, Bruce Goff, and Louis Kahn.

For Goff and Wright, preoccupation with growth and pattern, particularly spirals, is central to what each believed to be organic architecture—it is inseparable from their design philosophies.

A number of seminal books were published on this subject in the 1940s. Three in particular gained a wide circulation and created and made a big impact—THE CURVES OF LIFE by Theodore Cook, GROWTH AND FORM by D'Arcy Thompson, and THE GEOMETRY OF ART AND LIFE by Matila Ghyka.

Each of these books discusses the spiral. A spiral is a curve whose radius of curvature continually increases. This gets interesting if the spiral is logarithmic; when, as is the case of the chambered nautilus (opposite), each cell or unit is in the same proportion to the one that follows it as it is to the unit that preceded it. This pattern of growth naturally appears in such diverse forms in nature as the shell, a fern frond, a ram's horn, or the bones of the human body. As Thompson says, "It follows from all this that there . . . may be a mathematical law of growth" common to all life. Bruce Goff designed nearly 500 build-

about five miles outside Norman. Goff selected a clearing beside a shallow ravine as a spot for the house. He planned the excavation of the adjoining hill to maintain a close proximity between the lower levels of the house and the stream below. The dense trees were "busily textured and looked rather hectic." The rock shelf had a natural curved space, "like part of a helix," that became the first level of the house, with the native sandstone exposed in places in the interior. Since the clearing was small, and the Bavingers wanted different levels, Goff thought it would be interesting to design a space that would grow upward, out of the rock, and wind around to continue the helix. "I never design a house starting with a form idea," says Goff "but rather arrive at it, as I did here."

Large stones that were unearthed in the excavation were combined with others from adjacent areas to form portions of the floor and enclosing wall. This wall is a continuous logarithmic spiral 96 feet long ascending from a height of six feet at its outer point to a height of over 50 feet at the center. Rising from the middle of the spiral is a steel mast, made of two deep-well drilling pipes, that supports an array of cables that hold the spiraling roof of copper-covered two-by-fours in suspension. Everything that is not masonry is suspended and seems to float effortlessly within the free flow of space.

Inside, the floor at the lower level is treated as an interior garden with large areas given over to plants and irregularly shaped pools. Except for a dining area and a kitchen tucked in the center of the spiral, rooms are not on this level, but are suspended above it, within the continuous enclosure. Each room is cylindrical in shape and hangs from thin steel rods welded to the central mast.

There are five principal areas suspended in an upward progression: a living space; the parents' sleeping area; the dining area with a stairway leading up to a child's play space from which a suspension bridge crosses the stream to a flower garden opposite; the child's sleeping area; and a painting studio at the very top.

The space within the house is dynamic and ever changing

left: Plan of the lower level of the Bavinger House delineated by Herb Greene. Greene, an architect in his own right, was a student of Goff's at the University of Oklahoma.

When a spiral moves upwards while it is circling inwards, as is the case of the Bavinger House, it creates a three-dimensional form known as a helix.

as the walls, ceiling and floors are never parallel. Rooms are suspended containers arranged at intervals inside the outer stone spiral; in elevation they step up like a circular stair. The resulting play between the two spirals creates an interior volume of unparalleled richness and complexity—one further enhanced by an equally complex system of suspended storage cylinders, by a continuous skylight that separates the suspended roof from the outer stone wall, and by the suspension bridge that links the house to the garden.

Much of the richness in the interior space results from the quantity and quality of natural light that bathes the interior, and the surprising circumstance of finding rock-rimmed pools and gardens inside a house. The skylight above illuminates the planted areas around the perimeter of the stone wall. Another skylight follows the stairway around the inner wall.

There are great contrasts in the Bavinger house between materials and elements that are grounded (stone and water) and those that are floated (suspended roof, spiral stair, room-pods, and closet elements). Goff attempted to play these competing structural elements against one another to suggest the elements in nature.

Evidence of the owner's ingenuity is everywhere in the construction. He bought six old sewing machines whose frames he used to build scaffolding. When finished, he sold them for scrap iron saving only the drawers, which he built into the cabinetry of the house. The sixty stainless steel suspension cables are biplane braces that were purchased for five cents each. Neighboring farmers were delighted to get rid of rocks from their land; the Bavingers never had to disturb their own natural rocky ravine. When a walnut tree blew down in Oklahoma City, Gene helped clear it away and was allowed to have the remains for his help—so, the buffet and stair treads of the house are solid walnut.

"Here, more completely than in any other house of this time," said Goff, "is an architectural expression of the way of life of the client; a sense of three-dimensional living space, the furniture integral with the house, and harmony with

ings—no two looked exactly alike. Many were startling in their originality, with extraordinary spatial effects, amplified by unexpected uses of materials and structure. All reflected a fundamental belief in the right to individual expression.

Bavinger house showed how Goff made a stand against an overwhelmingly orthogonal, rectilinear architecture and incorporated circles, spirals, and asymmetrical fan-shapes into its form. "We are not satisfied anymore with a box, no matter how the box looks."

"Geometry, I think, doesn't mean necessarily to stick to the rigid forms that we usually associate with geometry. I think that we can conceive of space and of forms as one: I hear Mr. Wright quoting from Lao-tze, 'The reality of the building is the space within it,' but I don't think that is entirely true. I think that is certainly an integral part of it, but there is more to it than just the space within: there is the space without it, and there is the design itself—the material and the structure of the design itself. I believe that geometry is naturally involved in all of these thinking processes. The void and the volume, the negative and the positive, all the parts that go to make up the complete design should be in this."[3]

above: Bruno Taut, Glass Pavilion at the Werkbund Exhibition, Cologne, 1914. In Taut's building, the three-dimensional spiral resembles the form of a pine cone, or the head of a coneflower or sunflower. There is a spiral staircase inside (page 150).

right: The nautilus, nature's original architect, builds a new chamber as it outgrows the old.

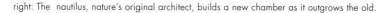

Goff on Spirals

nature, indoors and out—a do-it-yourself architecture using available materials and a limited budget."[5]

Aspects of Goff's free-flowing vocabulary appeared in earlier designs, but they were aspects only and lacked the cohesion he finally gave them in the Bavinger House. The Gillis House of 1945 (unbuilt) was the first of his spirals, overlooking an interior garden. In his Leidig House of 1946 (unbuilt) he floated the functional elements; the house includes a water garden. The Ledbetter House of 1948, published in *LIFE* magazine, has a ramp curving up over a pool. His Blakeley House of 1949 has a glass exterior with a ramp that seems to float within.

In the Bavinger house Goff combined it all—the spiral, the water garden, and suspended elements—into an organic whole. In this single project he brought together almost all of the innovations he developed in his lifetime, including open planning, the separation and suspending of functional elements, geometric innovation, and the combining of rustic masonry with crystalline elements.

Although published frequently in both the popular press and professional journals, the Bavinger House may be the least understood of Goff's houses due to the difficulty of documenting it. The interior defies being captured photographically and the complete integration of the exterior with the heavily wooded site means that it is always partly hidden. A wiry tangle of oaks now completely envelops the house.

When describing the completed house, Goff stressed that from no single vantage point could its interior be seen completely, nor could its spatial system be immediately comprehended. He said, ". . . the entire interior is a continuous flow of space wherein neither walls nor floor and ceiling are parallel."

Goff believed that a sense of surprise and mystery was essential to what he called the continuous present. He succeeded in creating a sense of surprise and mystery in the Bavinger house—that the building provides an ever increasing satisfaction for the occupants. Goff said: "It is natural that a work of art surprises us, partly because it is rare. . . .

above: Interior of the Bavinger House showing one of the pools. Some pools have been removed due to excessive moisture.

left: A delineation of the house made by Herb Greene when he was Goff's student.

RESIDENCE OF O. S. FOWLER, FISHKILL, N. Y.

Surprise engages our attention, whether it pleases or repulses us; but this is not enough. Something is needed to sustain our interest, if the work is to be meaningful to us. We call this quality 'mystery' which enables the work of art to hold our interest. If it has this and is necessarily the creation of genius, it is personal and impersonal, timely and timeless."

Even before the house was completed news spread far and wide of its unusual character. People came to look, as they have ever since, to see a house like no other. This anecdote about people's interest is best left in Bruce Goff's words:

"The Bavinger House was built out in the country on a dirt road without any fanfare and without any money. They couldn't get a loan on it, of course, and to make matters worse the man was an art professor, and you know they never have any money. He was very good at hard work; he was more like a truck driver in his build, and he liked to get out and dig and move large rocks and that sort of thing. His hobby was growing plants indoors and he was a very sensitive painter. After he got the house started with the help of some students, who had volunteered their labor in exchange for paintings, he tired of people coming around to see it. One day he decided to stop this by charging them a dollar apiece. This really encouraged it, because many people who would hesitate to come and ask to see the place felt perfectly at ease if they could pay a buck. After they saw it, they couldn't believe it; they would go back and try to describe it to their friends, and their friends couldn't believe it, and they would come and spend another dollar. So this process started making money. Then tax problems came up, of course, and they had to get a smart lawyer to show them how to get out of paying what legally is called an amusement tax. This went on until they had taken in over fifty thousand dollars, and it was getting so they couldn't eat, or sleep, or take a bath, without people coming to see the house. They finally decided it was time to stop all of this foolishness and live in it. So they stopped it."[6]

Orson Squire Fowler wrote *A Home for All* (1848) after planning his own house (pictured above). He favored an early form of concrete, promoted gravel-wall construction and recent inventions such as the gravity water system, central heating and ventilating systems, speaking tubes, dumbwaiters, and indoor bathrooms. His book also covered energy conservation, room placement to save steps, and landscaping.

What's in a Shape?

Orson Squire Fowler (1809-87) was not an architect; he was the nation's leading phrenologist. His popular book, A Home for All, established the octagon as a new, particularly American house plan. He popularized an early form of concrete and sought to combine social and architectural goals to provide substantial, economical housing for all Americans.

Fowler based his architectural model on the circle, which he felt was nature's building form and which enclosed the greatest interior space with the least exterior wall. Whereas a circular structure was difficult to build, he reasoned, most builders could construct an octagon.

In a chapter from his book entitled "Superiority of the Octagon Form," Fowler says, "But is the square form the best of all? Is the right-angle the best angle? Cannot some radical improvement be made, both in the outside form and the internal arrangement of our houses? Nature's forms are Mostly SPHERICAL. She makes ten thousand curvilineal to one square figure. Then why not apply her forms to houses? Fruits, eggs, tubers, nuts, grains, seeds, trees, etc., are made spherical, in order to inclose the most material in the least compass. Since, as already shown, a circle incloses more space for its surface, than any other form, of course the nearer spherical our houses, the more inside room for the outside wall, besides being more comfortable. . . . Why not employ some other mathernatical figures as well as the square? These reasonings developed the architectural principle claimed as a real improvement, and to expound which this work was written."[7]

The Haystack Mountain School of Crafts is a summer community of 80 students and faculty who work and live on a lichen-covered granite slope overlooking the water.

"One of the happiest jobs of my career was Haystack . . ." says its architect Edward Larrabee Barnes. "I remember first walking onto the site and looking down the rocky wooded slope to the sea. I wondered whether we should build at the top or down near the shore. Then it came to me: we could build on the slope, with a long flight of steps perpendicular to the horizon."[1]

Haystack Mountain School of Crafts • Deer Isle, Maine

Haystack Mountain School of Crafts is a cluster of small cottages, shingled in pine, nestled in a steep, forested hillside overlooking the sea. The weathered silver-gray structures are connected by a network of stairs and walkways that descend to the water's edge. The spectacular view of Penobscot Bay from the top of the stairs seems almost formally orchestrated in spite of the rustic informality of the surroundings. The impression of the whole, not unlike that of a Mediterranean hillside village, is a mixture of happenstance and planning that gives the structures a defining purpose, a reason to be at that particular, very special place.

Edward Larrabee Barnes has always been faithful to the modernist vision while able to adapt those ideals to the American tradition. Long before postmodernism was in the air Barnes was sensitive to the need to accommodate the general design ethos of modernism to the specific demands of site and client needs. Inasmuch as he is tirelessly committed to good design, his work doesn't necessarily have a recognizable signature. Nonetheless, due to his selfless resolve to express the conditions and demands of every challenge, all his projects, Haystack in particular, resonate with a sense of correctness in their circumstances. The success of the Haystack Mountain School design is that it remains fresh while firmly tied to the tradition of New England vernacular architecture. It feels absolutely right.

The Haystack concept is simple, yet never simplistic. Its drama derives from Barnes's clear organizational idea that takes full advantage of the beautiful, precipitous slope overlooking the bay. The axis of the stairs is the element upon which all else depends. It not only organizes the built envi-

"It became apparent that we were designing a village with a main "street" leading to the sea, dining hall and offices at the top, studios and decks branching out on side streets, and clusters of living units nestled in the woods. The design provides separation for work and living."[2]
— Edward Larrabee Barnes

ronment around it, it appears to have command over the entire countryside as well. Barnes achieves a quiet miracle—a made-made world that enhances its natural setting.

Although Barnes creates a romantic mood, he never breaks the regular angularity of volumes, never allows the walkways to meander—a sharp, sober geometry is evident throughout. The walks and platforms conform to the site's contours but leave it undisturbed. The wide central spine of wooden stairs leads directly down the slope to a lookout platform at the water's edge. Along the way, secondary wooden walkways branch out in either direction at right angles to the stairway, providing access to the small dormitory buildings, the workshops, and the studios.

When Barnes first saw the site, there was a fairly clear swath through the trees running off at an angle to the right from the top of the hill clear down to the water. Barnes began his initial designs based on this as the path of least resistance since it meant clearing almost no trees and would minimally disturb the landscape. However, this swath went off at an angle and would not afford a view of the water until one arrived at its shore. (If you imagine a straight line drawn from the upper center of the photo on page 77, diagonally down to the very lower left hand corner, you will have a general idea where the original flight of steps would have gone.) Very soon Barnes realized that he wanted the stairs to descend straight down in front of the visitor so that one could see right to the waterline and the result would be "at right angles to the horizon."4

"The site is absolutely beautiful—tall spruce trees against the sea, granite slopes, moss, and lichen." The integration of architecture and nature on the hillside was no easy matter. The precipitous slope to the sea had very few buildable shelves. Far from growing out of their environment, the little cabins, studios, and dormitories had to be imposed wherever footing could be found, and it required a great deal of care to avoid damaging the setting.

Barnes found the solution in the time-honored method of raising the structures up off the ground. "All structures are on

above: The walls of the cabins, as well as the steep tilted roofs, are shingled. The wood has turned silver like those in a typical New England fishing village.

left: White-washed churches on the Island of Mykonos, Greece.

stilts so that the natural ground cover, the moss and the lichen is untrampled."[5]

Twenty-three peaked roofs create a lively, sharp silhouette, sometimes paralleling the steep tree-covered slope, sometimes opposing it. One of the pleasures of Haystack is to watch the rhythms of its shifting roof-lines. The play of their forms suits a practical purpose as well. Since the pitch of each roof is determined by the structure's use which, in turn, determines the placement of its windows, the twisting and turning of each of the boxes performs the function of catching the best light. Studios receive different light from dormitory cabins.

"There are two basic building types," says Barnes, "sleeping units with ribbon windows facing the sea and peaked windows on the sides; and studios with tall windows for north light and, again, ribbon windows facing the sea. (These forms were adapted from an idea I had had for a studio a few years before—a simple volumetric form combining triangular and square geometry.)"[6]

The village concept is centered around the stairway as a main street, as Barnes refers to it. Its communal nexus is focussed on the uppermost platform, a kind of plaza where people meet, eat, and generally congregate.

Building in the vernacular kept costs down since local contractors could easily manufacture everything. The specific shapes and forms used are atypical but not difficult to accomplish. Costs of materials were kept to a minimum. Interiors could be left unfinished since the school only operates during the warmer summer months.

Contrary to the usual notion that architects leave a project at the end and divorce themselves from future obligations, Barnes continues to have a commitment to Haystack Mountain. As an honorary trustee of the school he is consulted about any and every change—adding a bay to an existing structure, building a new building, creating storage. Once he had an entire flight of steps removed that he felt was an ill fit in the landscape and worked against the simplicity of the plan.

The cabins at Haystack are the traditional salt box shape (page 64). Since the best light for studios is indirect, their windows point up to the trees. All cabins are rough, balloon frame construction; the sleeping cabins have ribbon windows that look out to the sea. They provide simple, almost spartan accommodation in warm weather.

Sea Ranch Condominium I • Sea Ranch, California

Sea Ranch Condominium I is a series of housing units, overlooking the Pacific, clustered around a courtyard as if it were a small village.

The complex preserves, even intensifies, the desolate, brooding ocean site. Untended grasses and bedrock run right up to the walls of the building; vertical redwood siding is left to weather like driftwood.

With minimal trim, and no overhangs to speak of, the mass of each structure is read as a sculptural form. Together they powerfully convey the feeling that they are a natural outcropping of the bluff itself.

The architects have said, "At once castle, compound, and promontory, it is a concentration of dwellings bunched together in the teeth of the wind."[1]

The Sea Ranch is situated on 5,200 acres of rugged exposed coast along a 10-mile stretch of cliff about 100 miles north of San Francisco. The owners, Oceanic Properties, had enough funds to plan a community that could be developed slowly and properly without the usual concern for instant profits.

They hired the firm of Lawrence Halprin and Associates to make exhaustive studies of the local ecology—wind, weather, and site. Joseph Esherick was retained to design clustered houses and a store based on these studies. The firm of Moore, Lyndon, Turnbull, Whitaker, or MLTW as they came to call themselves, were asked to plan an even tighter cluster of houses, along the shore, called Condominium I.

Because their work had been primarily residential, the Sea Ranch was a welcome opportunity for the architects to develop ideas that, until then, they had only been putting to use in individual houses.

"These ideas began with the premise that the architect particularizes. He discerns special patterns of human activity, and organizes movement. He develops a clarifying pattern, a design to which the whole process of building is subjected. Within this pattern there must be a controlling image that gives people the chance to know where they are—in space, in time, and in the order of things. People must have something to be in.

"Thus the fundamental principle of architecture is territorial. The architect assembles physical materials from which the observer creates not just an image of a building but of 'place.'"[2]

The Sea Ranch sits on a wild exposed coast—grand and very simple.
Between their collective intuitions, and the sound environmental data that was accumulated,
MTLW developed a sensible and elegant vocabulary of forms.
" . . . houses need to set up a partnership with the land forms and with each other."[3]
— Charles W. Moore

Insuring the Future

The summit of the bluffs along the shore form a coastal plain only a few hundred yards wide; beyond that is a ridge of low hills. The entire Sea Ranch site was originally covered with redwood and Bishop Pine, but was logged in the 1890s on the seaward slope. The upper areas were covered with 70-year-old second growth, but the treeless land from below the crest to the edge of the bluff had been all but grazed bare by sheep.

One of the most striking features of the landscape are the belts of Monterey Cypress planted 75 or 80 years ago at irregular intervals for wind protection. The cool wind from the northeast is almost constant, though the spot is relatively free from the fog that so often shrouds California's northern coast.

There is an air of splendid desolation to the site, typical of the whole north coast, in large part due to the absence of places to get out of the wind and into the sun. The cypress and hedgerows offer little protection.

Halprin and Associates wanted to maintain the brooding qualities of the site even though they knew that the lonely sweep of coast must eventually be carved into parcels that could be bought and sold.

The forested areas were not so much of a problem as the meadows. Land close to the water was so valuable it had to be sold, but it was clear that measures had to be taken to preserve the sense of openness of the meadows between the hedgerows.

In order to exercise some control, the developer saw to it that more than half the meadowland remained in common ownership. Much of the other half, when sold, was placed in a private restricted zone which could not be built upon. This left about one-fourth of the meadowland available for building. In the first meadows every effort has been made to have building sites relate to the hedgerows.

The place chosen for the condominium was a grassy, windswept field bordering a rocky shore where the waves break high against the cliffs. It is barren, rugged, and grand. Development was a daunting prospect given the isolation and the haunting beauty of the land. MLTW felt on one hand, that if houses were merged into the land they would provide little sense of security on the wild coast. On the other hand, they felt that if houses stood out too strongly they would emasculate the very ruggedness that made the land special. "What we and Esherick thought was needed was a limited partnership—not a marriage—between the buildings and the land. Then we developed ways of building that we thought would be responsive to the particulars of the site and climate."[4]

Because the condominium is big—ten times the size of a normal house— it holds its own against the site. The large building consists of ten smaller buildings, with tower, courts, bays, and solaria, ranged around two common courtyards— this is the first layer of "inside" as the architects like to call it. As with the coves it overlooks on either side, this inner courtyard is surrounded by forms that slope to the sea.

The buildings are all wood—heavy timber-frame structures sheathed in wide, vertical redwood siding. The roofs are angled to deflect the bracing winds. Generously proportioned windows, with almost no interfering trim, provide uninterrupted views of the landscape and the ocean beyond. Windows are high enough to let in ample sunlight, but never so high that the salt-spray can't be easily washed off. There are quantities of overhead skylights. Overhangs were dispensed with to eliminate wind flutter.

The little houses inside are made of smooth wood, and painted gray, so that they seem miniature— something between toy houses and giant cabinets. Around the periphery, bay windows reach out to special views or provide extra places for sitting or sleeping. They are conceptually outside the envelope of the house, close to the windy outdoors.

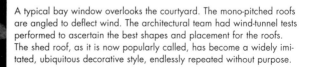

A typical bay window overlooks the courtyard. The mono-pitched roofs are angled to deflect wind. The architectural team had wind-tunnel tests performed to ascertain the best shapes and placement for the roofs. The shed roof, as it is now popularly called, has become a widely imitated, ubiquitous decorative style, endlessly repeated without purpose.

On entering the units one feels another layer of shelter and a sense of being yet farther inside, though never out of sight of the crashing surf. Every dwelling is composed of a single great room, and almost every one of these contains two little houses, one of them a simple four-posted shelter covering a hearth and supporting a bedchamber. The other is almost a miniature house that contains a kitchen below, a bath and dressing room above, and sometimes a sleeping loft above that.

The outer structure of the encompassing room is built of large rough pieces of wood used, as in a barn, to stiffen the structure against the elements. Structure is everywhere left exposed—the metal connectors and bolts that tie the joists together are visible.

The entire place is a large but measurable foil to the limitless Pacific horizon outside. At floor level one can see both. One is always near the tactile elements of the room's structure, or protected just beyond its boundaries, conscious at once of the overwhelming outdoors and the sheltering room within.

The Sea Ranch condominium was not meant to look like anything else stylistically. People recognize obvious similarities between the condominium and old buildings on nearby mining and timbering sites. The architects were not displeased by the comparison, though the resemblance was unintentional. It is interesting to think that Sea Ranch and the buildings they resemble naturally grew out of the particular conditions of similar sites.

MLTW came close to solving the insoluble—building on a site that is perfect to begin with. They were pleased on a visit seven years later. They were also disappointed with further development. " . . . since the Sea Ranch is mainly a second-home community," they noted, "people and their architects met elsewhere to develop together their fantasies, quite independent of the spirit of the place. Those same media-driven winds which blew the 'Sea Ranch idiom' abroad and made it famous also blew uncaring versions of Swiss chalets and split-levels to this splendid brooding coast."[5]

top: The sleeping loft is a room within a room suspended in space.

middle: The duplex houses are extremely economic spatially and well organized.

bottom: One can see almost eveywhere—from space to space and from inside to the outside.

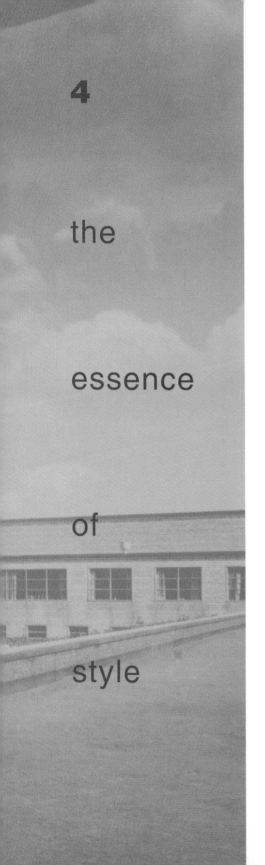

4

the

essence

of

style

**Crow Island School
Christ Church Lutheran
Yale University Art Gallery
Price Tower
Dulles International Airport**

Together we learn, play, worship, and work in spaces and types of architecture that announce their pupose, their difference, and their importance to us. We associate many of the ceremonies of our lives with structures; each has a look, a feel, a function that we expect will give us what we need. We express ourselves through their forms. We strive to improve our lives and our activities through them.

What makes one type of building better suited for its purposes than another? What makes a school good, a church inspiring, a gallery edifying, or an airport uplifting (not to mention efficient)? The answers, whatever they may be, will point us towards an understanding of style. Style and meaning are inseparable. The outward look of things is not style—a building with a steeple is not necessarily a church—not anymore.

The meanings of the forms used in particular types of buildings are derived from a combination of use and a collective, usually unconscious, agreement about what seems right. If architecture is a language, building types are a kind of grammar. And, as with grammar, there are rules. New forms change the rules. Then, before you know it, everything is as it always was—it even seems inevitable. A new word may be startling in its novelty, but after a while we wonder how we ever did without it. We come to take it for granted: so, too, with architectural forms. Then we change the rules, once again.

"Man's efforts do not create style. Style created itself through man. In the last analysis, therefore, the essense of style must be found within man."[1]

— *Eliel Saarinen, Search For Form, 1948*

Father and Son

If anyone could bring a fresh look to an existing building type it was the father and son team of Eliel and Eero Saarinen. Before he even set foot on its shores from his native Finland, Eliel began influencing architecture and design in America, beginning in 1923 with his second-prize-winning drawing for the Chicago Tribune Building (page 6).

Eliel Saarinen's (1873-1950) early work owed a great deal to the Vienna Secession movement. His monumental designs also expressed a Nordic refinement of Art Nouveau, and owed much to the combined influence of Finnish farm settlements and the Arts & Crafts movement. He abstracted classical style and Finnish vernacular to suit the Finnish sensibility. Saarinen's work was an integration of cultural symbolism with material and form. He synthesized the forms and materials of past and present, regional and international.

In 1923 he emigrated to the U.S., moved to the Midwest, and began teaching at the University of Michigan at Ann Arbor. He was invited by George C. Booth to come to Cranbrook in 1925, where he designed and later became Director of the Graduate Department of Architecture and Urban Planning at the Cranbrook Academy of Art (1948).

Eero Saarinen (1910-1961), first taking after his mother, thought he wanted to be a sculptor. He went to Le Grand Chaumier in Paris only to return to Cranbrook several years later to teach. He entered his father's firm in 1937 where, among other projects they completed two in this section—Crow Island School and Christ Church Lutheran.

Among the faculty who taught at Cranbrook over the years were Charles Eames, Harry Bertoia, Ralph Rapson, Harry Weese, and Francis Knoll. All would work together on one project or other in the next few decades.

Charles Eames worked with Eero on the now famous plywood furniture that won them first prize in the Museum of Modern Art's "Organic Design in Home Furnishings" competition (page 88).

"Because of the seemingly analogous situation between the spoken language and the language of art," wrote Eliel Saarinen, "many of those ensnared in historic styles have been eager to defend their position by referring to the 'elements' of style as a parallel to the 'vocabulary' of the spoken language. In their eagerness to defend their position they have gone thousands of years back in time in order to import the 'elements' of architecture—believing them to have become petrified into static features as soon as they were released into the market by the Greeks. But they were not petrified into static features. They were subject to change just as is the 'vocabulary' of the spoken language—which latter fact the inveterate champion of styles apparently has overlooked.

"Indeed, the vocabulary of the spoken language must be subject to changes, as time passes."[2]

If style is to be found in the delicate interrelationships of architectural form, purpose, and meaning, then we must discover it together. And, even if style is said to draw upon timeless sources, we must change it from time to time and it, in turn, will change us.

There is no single vision in all this. Each of the projects in this section evolved over time—each points up the various viewpoints of the participants.

Teaching An Old Type New Tricks

The team of architects who designed Crow Island School strove to serve the needs of one of the largest universal groups there is—children. They even included them in the design process.

When schools looked like prisons, as they almost always did (and sometimes still do, alas), it was a clear indication of how we felt about teaching our young people. Attitudes towards young children and their education certainly began to change by the turn of the last century, but progress was exceedingly slow. Children were still treated as second class

above: Eliel and Eero Saarinen in front of Hvitträsk, the family home in Finland, 1919.

In 1904 Eliel married Loja Gesellius, his partner's sister, who was a gifted sculptor, weaver, photographer, and a maker of architectural models. Eero's sister, Eva-Lisa, called Pipsan, was born in 1905. Eero, born in 1910, was a prodigy who sketched with either hand.

citizens and in few places could it be said that an educational philosophy was embodied in progressive architecture. In Chicago, Prairie School architect Dwight H. Perkins (1867-1941) designed over forty educational institutions between 1905 and 1910. He literally re-created the idea of school by adding grass and trees, sunlight and fresh air, fire safety, and good sanitation. His schools were beautiful to behold, though they still looked like large fortresses.

It took a progressive school superintendent from Winnetka, a suburb of Chicago, to go a step further, to scale things down and treat children like people. He asked Lawrence Bradford Perkins (1907-1997), the son of the Prairie School architect and a partner in the firm of Perkins, Wheeler, and Will, along with Eliel and Eero Saarinen to design his "dream school" in the Crow Island Woods.

Together the team humanized the entire concept of school. They spent time with students, faculty, and staff. Perkins listened, looked, and drew pictures of ideas, showing them to the children and teachers and noting their responses. The architectural team brought modest but profound changes to their final designs, changes that surprise us even today because we can't imagine how things were any different than they are now that they changed them.

At Crow Island School two windowed walls in every classroom invite the outdoors inside. Each classroom has an exterior door leading to it's own courtyard, so students may observe their plantings or rest for a moment. There are toilets for each classroom, so children needn't stand on line in the halls. There's running water for their art projects. And, the light switches are placed at kid level! All these things empowered the children and made for what has been hailed as the best school in America.

Expressions of Faith

A house of worship must be especially meaningful for its parishioners and its minister in order for it to work well. Its

Psychic Health

Carl Shurz High School (pictured left) is an ideal model for urban development and for its expression in architectural form. Commissioned by a reform-minded school board headed by Jane Addams, the project was one highlight of a broad program for rescuing the immigrant poor from the ignorance and isolation engendered by the industrial city.

One revolutionary aspect of this program was the linking of the development of the schools with the development of neighborhood parks. In 1904 Perkins, in partnership with landscape designer Jens Jensen, had written Chicago's first citywide park plan, promoting a network of "breathing holes" that would bring the social and health benefits of natural landscapes to the common citizen. Perkins was the ideal choice to bring these qualities to the expanding school system as architect of the Board of Education.

Chicago's typical school before 1905 was a poorly lighted and ventilated box, set into the city grid with no significant playgrounds. Toilet facilities were archaic and located in the basement. The forty-odd schools that Perkins designed between 1905 and 1910 changed all that, creating a building type with grass and trees, sunlight and fresh air, safety from fire, and good sanitation.

Carl Shurz High School asserted that the urban public school belongs much higher on the architectural hierarchy than had been allowed. Beyond its task of providing a safe, healthy, and beautiful place to learn, it towers over the trees, sheltering the entire community, an immense Prairie House for the new citizens of its immigrant, working-class neighborhood.

Carl Shurz High School (1909) Chicago. Architect: Dwight H. Perkins. Perkins introduced a domestic vocabulary into an institutional language, thereby imroving it. Although not homey by today's standards, the school sits astride its site much like an oversized Prairie House—certainly more inviting than its predecessors. Its lobby is flooded with light; the auditorium was the first in a school to open its doors for public functions.

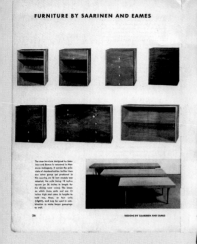

FURNITURE BY SAARINEN AND EAMES

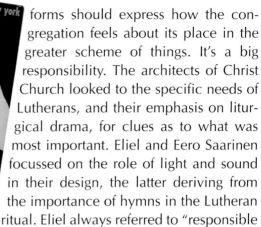

museum of modern art new york

ORGANIC DESIGN

Organic Furniture Design

In 1940, the Museum of Modern Art in New York City organized a competition called ORGANIC DESIGN IN HOME FURNISHINGS. The illustrious jury included Alvar Aalto and Marcel Breuer. A condition of the competition was that the winners would allow their design to be manufactured and offered for sale at Bloomingdale's Department Store, the competition's sponsors. Charles Eames and Eero Saarinen entered together; they had collaborated earlier on an exhibition of faculty work at Cranbrook.

The Eames-Saarinen entries, which included various kinds of living-room seating and several tables, caused a sensation due to their incorporation of two new techniques of assembly. Their designs, based on molding plywood into compound curves, and welding rubber to wood, processes being tested by one of America's leading automobile manufacturers, were so innovative, and came so close to the intent of the competition brief, that they won without difficulty. The production of the series was thwarted by the war effort, yet the techniques involved formed the basis of Charles and Ray Eames' furniture design throughout the following decade (page 160).

The furniture, which would receive international recognition, would have to wait until the war's end before it could be shown in a MoMA exhibition curated by Eliot Noyes.

forms should express how the congregation feels about its place in the greater scheme of things. It's a big responsibility. The architects of Christ Church looked to the specific needs of Lutherans, and their emphasis on liturgical drama, for clues as to what was most important. Eliel and Eero Saarinen focussed on the role of light and sound in their design, the latter deriving from the importance of hymns in the Lutheran ritual. Eliel always referred to "responsible architecture" as architecture that takes full cognizance of the complex needs of site, structure, and program, and resolves them—logically but passionately—in a single, unified "expression."[3]

Exhibiting Structure

Louis Kahn had unerring faith in the veracity of a fundamental, elemental language of geometry. He regarded its immutable laws as a universal language, a "way of life" behind the changing forms of everyday existence. He had the uncanny ability to deploy geometry in his structures without being obvious. He transformed the services of his buildings into wondrous visual displays, baldly exhibiting their functions while changing their meaning.

Clarity and power distinguish Kahn's design for Yale University's Art Gallery. The façade highlights the transition between old and new. Inside and out, the play between solid walls and glass strikes a balance between what's revealed and what's concealed. But, the real focal point of the gallery is the structure of the floor slabs which are revealed in the gallery ceilings. The patterned concrete ceilings contain continuous hollow spaces which accommodate ventilation ducts and spotlights. The resulting three-dimensionally modulated ceiling structure represents a contrast to the sim-

above and left: The MoMA ORGANIC DESIGN IN HOME FURNISHINGS catalogue with essay by designer Eliot Noyes, 1941.
In 1940, when Eero Saarinen and Charles Eames together won two first prizes in the Museum of Modern Art furniture competition, the young designers—each about thirty years old—received international recognition for the first time.

ple wall and window sections and provides a marvelous foil for the exhibited artworks. At Yale the "servant" spaces, as Kahn called them, shine forth—take center stage in fact—without overwhelming us.

Kahn once said, "An individual style must be subservient to something which is true to a way of life. The style itself can be your way of expressing something. But if it is completely out of context, with a way of life, then I believe that it doesn't have enough. No one else can take it and expand from it.

"In other words, if I produce an instrument which I only can use, it will not be of very great importance. But if I produce an ax, you see, then immediately the forests need it. Now the style, my own individual style, is the way I shape the handle. My tendency is to look at the laws of nature in such a way that I make a good rule which makes my ax somehow better than the other fellow's. My style may be adopted as being good style, but the general way of life which it is part of must be part of the making of it."[4]

Manifest Destiny

For Frank Lloyd Wright, his own vision of things was paramount. Whereas Eliel Saarinen felt that form is the natural outgrowth of an inner impulse which "springs from the physical and spiritual characteristics of the time and people,"[5] Frank Lloyd Wright saw the source of the spring in himself.

He used the word "organic" all his life, not to describe appearances, but applied it to the natural order of form and its rightness in the built environment.

In a telecast interview with Wright, commentator Hugh Downs says, "You use the word organic. Is that any different from my use of the word modern architecture, in your opinion?"[6]

Wright responds, "Very different, because modern architecture is merely something—anything—which may be built today, but organic architecture is an architecture from within outward, in which entity is the ideal. We don't use the word organic as referring to something hanging in a butcher

Containing the Void
The visitor to Frank Lloyd Wright's Unity Temple is embraced by the building's parapet before ever crossing the threshold. The inscription above each entry, "For the Worship of God and the Service of Man," reflects the Universalist belief that a house of worship must serve both sacred and secular needs.

Wright's adventurous use of concrete permitted a certain integrity in the enclosed volume that reflects the monolithic nature of its structure, which in turn grows from the functions of the different elements from which the Temple was built. For instance, the concrete roof—a coffered structure with intersecting beams—allowed for skylights between intersections that, combined with the side windows, bring light into the church from every direction.

Even before it gained worldwide renown, Unity Temple was widely praised both by its congregation and by local newspapers. Despite the unorthodox form and materials, they recognized that Wright had given substance to a deeply rooted spirituality. It is a transcendent work, bound to the earth and open to the heavens.

above: Unity Temple, Oak Park, Illinois, 1908. Frank Lloyd Wright.

right: St. Saviour's Chapel, IIT Campus, Chicago, 1952. Ludwig Mies van der Rohe. Known on campus as the "God box," this is the only church that Mies ever designed; a non-denominational, meditational chapel—all glass on one façade and brick on the others.

IN THE BOWERIE, NEW YORK "?" FRANK LLOYD WRIGHT ARCHITECT

The Vertical Street

In his "Notes on the Building of the H. C. Price Company," Frank Lloyd Wright had this to say about the Skyscraper:

"This type of sheltered-glass tower-building I first designed in 1921 for St. Mark's in-the-Bouwerie, New York City. The idea has been imitated more or less all over the world. Meantime this particular design has waited some thirty years for realization—finally finding it not where expected but in a better place under better conditions.

"Has the country meantime grown up to skyscraper status or has the skyscraper adventured on its own afield. I believe this type of structure, weighing about one tenth of say the Rockefeller Center structure, will become a desirable institution everywhere there are men and companies like the one this building tells us about. Tells us about in [ways] the buildings should tell about the people who own them.

"I wonder now where the next quadruple sky garden pent house duplex residence and office building will rise in our nation. Look for them, presently, all over these United States. It was for this the vertical street was born. To the concrete and steel construction of our modern times this type is natural."6

shop, you know.

"Organic means intrinsic—in the philosophic sense, entity—wherever the whole is to the part as the part is to the whole and where the nature of the materials, the nature of the purpose, the nature of the entire performance becomes clear as a necessity. Out of that nature comes what character in any particular situation you can give to the building as a creative artist."7

Ever since he conceived the St. Mark's in-the-Bouwerie project (pictured at left), it was Wright's dream to build a tall building of naturally dynamic form. The towers he imagined were slender and small-scale, standing free in a park-like setting. He envisioned his ideal skyscraper as a tall tree, a splendid event on the landscape, and developed what he called the "tap-root" principle. Encased in copper and glass, the tower would attend in every way to the changing light of day. The project for St. Mark's was the prototype Wright never let die. This same tall building idea remained central to his Broadacre City Plan in all the intervening years. He saw the Price Tower commission as his opportunity to realize the dream—for himself and the rest of us. To this day it remains the only tall building in Bartlesville.

Flights of Fancy

Everything about Dulles International Airport inspires awe; from the building's forms to its engineering. In the ordered rectilinear world we occupy most of the time, at least in postwar America, Eero Saarinen's architectural language so often appears utterly fantastic.

As he saw it, modern architecture, especially in the United States, lacked drama. His goal was to create a building with a memorable image, one that preferably capitalized upon daring structural techniques.

He felt that buildings with specific and different functions should look and feel different. He said, " . . . it's obvious that a hockey rink is different from an office building. It's obvi-

One of Wright's first built works (1896) was a windmill he designed for his aunts' Wisconsin property (which he eventually inherited and made famous as the site of his own house [*Taliesin*], and school). Floors within the wood-shingled polygon strengthened the tower, like the membranes of bamboo—an idea he would use all his life.

ous that in that kind of case the structure is such a strong, dominant thing that you recognize it in the form. You don't just build a box. Also certain locations and certain relations to other buildings are so dominant and so strong that you have to give it a special solution. But, perhaps, also I've been terribly worried that architecture was just going to get itself into a box and there was a very strong need for spreading out, for finding the new solutions."[8]

Eero Saarinen believed, unabashedly, in his ability to express monumentality, especially where new technologies were to be had. With Dulles he turned his attention away from a literal expression of flight in the form of a bird (TWA), to a more abstract, and in some ways more daring, expression of flight in its purest form. To do so he wrestled with one of the most intractable materials—concrete—pushing it to do new things, transforming it through grand acts of wizardry.

A search for such an architecture is in the profoundest sense an individual's quest for truth; Eero Saarinen saw it as his birthright. After all, he was the son of Eliel Saarinen, who considered "spiritual function" inseparable from "practical function," and who described civilized existence itself as a "search for form."[9]

This kind of expression transcends personal style—it belongs, as the finest architecture of the past inevitably did, to a whole epoch. Self-consciousness is a danger to it. We turn once more to Eliel Saarinen for thoughts about the impossibility of willing style into being. "Conscious conduct is of no avail in style process. As much as the fundamental form develops in a certain direction without the efforts of human decision, just so much does style move—on the basis of the fundamental form—in a direction that nobody is able rationally to control but that everyone is compelled instinctively to follow. Man's efforts do not create style. Style created itself through man. In the last analysis, therefore, the essence of style must be found within man."[10]

A Sense of Unity
Everything about Dulles inspires awe from the approach to the forms of the building to its enginering. The gyrations of the building's forms are a striking contrast to the flat, infinite stability of the plane of earth upon which one stands. As much as the building moves, the ground has never been more stable.

"Let's design the best building in concrete that we can for its purpose," said Eero Saarinen, "but a building that in every part smells concrete. Let's also design a building in steel that in every part and every joint smells steel. Very strongly I feel now that a building has to be all one thing—a sense of unity, a sense of unity in philosophy, a sense of unity in form, a sense of unity with its purpose. A building should just be one thing. A building can't have many ideas in it. It can only have one idea. You look at Wright's Guggenheim, which really looks as if it's going to be a great building. That's an all-concrete building. Sure, it has windows, but you don't see them. Now, maybe we shouldn't carry it that far. But there is an example where actually it's a concrete building and there's nothing else than concrete."[11]

the essence of style **91**

above: Notre-Dame-du-Haut, Ronchamp, France, Le Corbusier, 1954. The unusual, thick concrete form that Le Corbusier chose to use for this pilgrimage chapel filters light into its interior through the many small stained glass windows that pierce its sculpted walls. The chapel is one of the more influential buildings of the last century. right: The sculpture forms of Eero Saarinen's Dulles International Airport.

Crow Island Elementary School has been called the most architecturally influential school of modern times. One of its architects, Larry Perkins, identified 80 different people who contributed in some way during the project. One of these, a teacher who wrote a letter expressing her feelings on the purpose of materials, said, "Above all the school must be child-like—not what adults think of children. At the same time it should be dignified and playful, but not playing down to children. It must be a place for living, a place for use, good hard use, for it is to be successfully the home, the abiding place for a procession of thousands of children through the years. It must be warm, personal, and intimate, that it shall be to each of these thousands 'my school.'"

Crow Island School • Winnetka, Illinois

Carleton Washburne was superintendent of the Winnetka Schools when Crow Island School was conceived, designed, and built. "This is to be our dream school," he would say. "We want it to be the most functional and beautiful school in the world. We want it to crystalize in architecture the best educational practices we can evolve."[1]

Washburne's plan, now know as the Winnetka Plan, emphasized flexibility and the consideration of each child as an individual. Washburne didn't want a typical square or rectangular building, with two stories, high ceilings, rigid seating, and cloakrooms. He wanted a building where the classroom would be a separate, vital, self-contained unit.

In 1937, Washburne interviewed representatives from 35 different architectural firms. He was hesitant in his meeting with Larry Perkins, in spite of Perkins's father's reputation (page 87), since the firm of young, progressive architects from Chicago—Perkins, Wheeler, and Will—had done so little in three years; this was still the Depression. "We can't trust this to a group of youngsters who have only built one small house and one small church!"

But, Perkins convinced Washburne that since they were a young firm they would put more time and thought into the project. They would study the Winnetka schools and read everything Washburne ever wrote. Washburne consented, as long as the firm would consult with Eliel Saarinen.

Edward Todd Wheeler remembers going with his partners to see Saarinen at Cranbrook, in Detroit, to discuss how they would collaborate on the school. "Larry [Perkins], Philip [Will] and I went over to [Eliel Saarinen] to talk to him. He said he would associate with us, and did so. But, bless his

The outward appearance of the school was the province of the Saarinens. Perkins, Wheeler, and Will addressed the relationships between architecture and education. The two sides split the commission fifty-fifty, though Eliel Saarinen called Perkins "the hound dog who worked on this the hardest." "But the person without whom there would be no Crow Island was Washburne," said Larry Perkins.

A Sympathetic Environment

When Crow Island opened its doors in 1940 accolades were almost immediate. In addition to appearing in prominent magazines and professional journals, the school was featured in the Museum of Modern Art's 1945 exhibition BUILT IN THE USA: A SURVEY OF CONTEMPORARY ARCHITECTURE *(page 26).*

Other efforts were being made both here and abroad to further the aims of progressive education through good architecture and design. In fact, an experimental school in Los Angeles from 1935 by Richard Neutra was featured in Built in the USA as well. Though Neutra's school had many of the same features as Crow Island, the classroom units were rectangular, had high ceilings, and didn't have access to their own individual courtyards.

The catalogue to the MoMA show had this to say about Crow Island:

"Modern education is directly concerned with the psychological well-being of children, yet few educators realize the relevance of a sympathetic architectural environment. The Winnetka Board of Education, however, wanted a school which would actually contribute to the results of their famous educational system, not only through efficiency, but through encouragement of the child's sense of freedom and security. They realized that such a program called for modern architecture."

heart, he left the planning almost entirely to us." The younger architects would bring Eliel their drawings and he would pore over them, redrawing and correcting as he went. "He had a strong influence in the character of it, because he was what we came to call ourselves later as folk architects. He was very conscious of the human quality needed in buildings to reflect human scale and human emotions. . . . he was a romantic in that sense. Those qualities were his principal contribution to the Crow Island School . . . because he realized that's what we wanted him for."[2]

Washburne describes the planning process:

"Lawrence Perkins spent many weeks in our schools, watching teachers and children at work, and generally soaking up our educational thought and practice. Then he made a model of a classroom unit he thought would meet our needs. This was studied and criticized by the faculty, School Board, janitor and superintendent. When approved it formed the basic unit for the new school, which was then jointly designed by the two firms.

"Cooperation did not stop with planning. At every step of construction, members of the staff and Board worked with the architects. For the landscaping and playground, a park superintendent, Robert Everly, and a playground director, John McFadzean, of the neighboring community of Glencoe, were called in. They had specialized in what they called "park-schools" and, in consultation with the Winnetka group and the architects, laid out an ideal plan of planting, lawns and playgrounds.

"The outcome is a school which in practice works out as it was intended to do—a beautiful, homey, practical architectural embodiment of an educational philosophy."[3]

When Crow Island opened it was

left: The catalogue from MoMA's exhibition BUILT IN THE USA so successfully promoted Crow Island's progressive design, it soon became imitated nationally. The L-shaped module would be called the "finger plan" due to the way that it protrudes into the landscape.

very contemporary in style; the chimney in the front with its off-center clock was the talk of the community. The building was as abrupt an architectural move away from the traditional school building as it was from the educational philosophy of the time.

The architects were eminently successful in appreciating the needs and desires of small children; in all they designed, the pupils were their first consideration. Everything at Crow Island affords young people a comforting atmosphere while, at the same time, they are given an expansive sense of freedom.

The design is simple, practical, thoughtful. The school is all on one level. The front steps are heated at the suggestion of a custodian. A common rose-colored brick is used inside and out; a mundane material magically transformed by sensitive patterning in the way it is laid. Horizontal courses of brick are interspersed with concrete block in the auditorium adding a well proportioned decorative touch. There is an honest beauty in everything.

The classroom unit at Crow Island is the most important space within the building. Each of the L-shaped, "one-room school" modules allows for windows to wrap around three sides. Windows on two sides reach from the low window-seat storage units to the ceiling and afford views of the park space that surrounds the school. Windows on the third side are high to provide privacy. Each classroom has access to its own small courtyard. Flagstone walks and shrubs contribute to a pleasant sense of spaciousness.

Exterior wood is redwood. Ponderosa pine, treated with wax, is used in the interiors. The expanse of pine makes all classroom and workroom walls instant display areas. There is ample built-in storage. The workroom off each classroom provides a separate area where group projects can be easily overseen by the classroom teacher. The well thought-out lighting and window walls make the out-of-doors part of the interior. The original "Crow Island" still exists as Crow Island Woods. The school often uses the woods and park for nature-study and art classes. The relationship of school, park, and

From top to bottom: The school's auditorium.
A typical classroom, c. 1940.
Artrooms have their own running water at the request of the children.
The door of each classroom is painted a different, bright, primary color, so no one gets lost.
Skylights bring daylight into the hallways.

woods is unique since schools prior to Crow Island often contained children all day long.

Referring to Crow Island School in an article that accompanied the Museum of Modern Art's circulating exhibition *Modern Architecture for the Modern School* (1943), Elizabeth Mock said, "If we grant the importance of encouraging the child's awareness of nature along with his sense of freedom, we can then understand the present tendency towards ground-level classrooms, each with its own door to the outside and its adjacent outdoor class area. We can also understand why each classroom should be so designed that its enclosed space will seem part of the limitless space outside."[4]

In every way possible—through lighting and ventilation as well as texture and color—the architects provided for the welfare of the children who spend their hours of work and play in the classrooms. The plan of the building is designed to bring an abundance of light and air into all the spaces. The wide hallways have skylights mixed with the artificial light. Classroom doors are painted different, bright, primary colors so nobody gets lost.

Each classroom has a glass-paneled transom door opening onto a courtyard, linking outdoors and indoors. The one windowless interior wall in each classroom has served as the tackboard that teachers have used and loved for 50 years. Ceilings were lowered from the standard 12 to 9 feet. The low ceilings are finished in acoustical plaster. The recessed incandescent lighting contributes a calming atmosphere to the arrangement. Following the philosophy that the school should fit the child, everything is scaled to children's needs, from the height of door handles and blackboards, to the size of benches under the windows; there are no overly elaborate or forbidding refinements.

It was common at schools before Crow Island for furniture to be heavy and bolted to the floor. The furniture at Crow Island, including movable desks and tables, designed by Larry Perkins and Eero Saarinen, was made by the Illinois Crafts Project of the WPA, with the assistance of the Welfare

above: Interior of a nursery, Polhemsgaten, Stockholm, Ingeborg Waern Bugge, 1933.
left: Desk by Larry Perkins, chair by Eero Saarinen. Eero Saarinen met Charles Eames at Cranbrook Art Academy in 1938 where they organized a group exhibition the following year. Charles and Eero also collaborated on furniture for a competition that year (page 88), so Eames may have worked with Eero and Larry Perkins on the Crow Island furniture.

Engineering Company. The few extant pieces still bear the WPA stamp on the bottom. The chairs of bonded plywood (pictured) were especially designed by Eero Saarinen. The auditorium's plywood benches, also designed by Eero, vary in size with seating for the smallest children at the front and for adults at the back.

From the beginning the school was widely publicized and imitated. In an extensive article for *Architectural Forum*, Joseph Hudnut said:

"The Crow Island School is not the first in which the expanding energies of the new education, bursting that stubborn box, have found their way without the lead of tradition into outward expression. It is rather only one of the many affirmations of that liberating spirit which is making the art of teaching (the greatest of all arts) articulate in the art of architecture; but it is an affirmation clear resolute and persuasive. An inward activity has shaped this arresting building. The architects, I think, proceeded not towards, but from, the busy pattern of the society it was to shelter. The design was shaped in their minds by the pressures and recessions of this society—of which it was to be both a consequence and a cause. They saw, before they took up T-square and triangle, the making and doing and expressing in ceaseless variety which was to be sheltered here, the seeing, hearing and speaking, the experiencing and growing, and around these they fitted their fabric so closely that it seems to share them all in a way not unlike that in which the human body shares the energies of the soul; and by the same process they have written into their constructed forms, both within and without, that unity with the scheme of a wider life briefly channeled here—that awareness of a social usefulness and destiny—which are the heart of progressive teaching."[5]

above: Lily Swann Saarinen, a gifted ceramic sculptor, created colorful, playful plaques that were incorporated into the brick walls of the school. This one's in the garden.

right: Members of the Studio Loja Saarinen at the Cranbrook Academy, c.1930, with a rug they created for the Kingswood School Auditorium Lobby.

Cranbrook Women

At Cranbrook, furniture and interior design were always part of any architectural concept. Eliel Saarinen believed in the unity of all elements, large and small.

Loja Gesellius (1879-1968) studied sculpture in Paris before she married Eliel. At Cranbrook she established the Loja Saarinen Textile Studio where carpets, tapestries, draperies, and table linens were produced for many of the Saarinen projects.

Another native of Finland, Maija Grotell (1899-1973), head of Cranbrook's Ceramics Department, was known for her stoneware and her research in glazes based on Chinese techniques.

What role they may have played, if any, at Crow Island or on any other project, for that matter, is difficult to determine since the men of the family overshadowed them.

Eero's first wife, Lily Swann Saarinen, was commissioned to create ceramic sculptures that were incorporated into the walls of the school. These animal sculptures appeal to the children and lend an intimate and charming aspect to the simple, broad areas of brick construction. The 23 glazed ceramic plaques that appear both inside and outside the school were fired in Maija Grotell's Cranbrook studio. Marjorie Cast Danforth, a student of Grotell's in 1938, assisted Lily by researching glazes. In the Crow Island lobby are plaques depicting Noah, three pair of animals, and the dove.

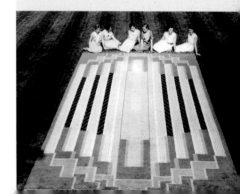

Eliel Saarinen always referred to "responsible architecture" as architecture that recognizes the complex needs of site, structure, and program, and resolves them—logically but passionately—in a single, unified "expression."[1]

The Pastor of Christ Church Lutheran spoke eloquently about the structure Saarinen had designed for his congregation: "Through its basic floor plan our church ties in firmly with the churches of all time, because ours and all others must meet certain liturgical requirements. . . . Church design must always have very firm roots in the past; otherwise it is merely an aberration."[2]

Christ Church Lutheran • Minneapolis, Minnesota

"This church is a symbol of our faith; all of us feel that this is so and we thank the day when we were given the inspiration thus to express the best in us."[3] So said William A. Buege, when Christ Church Lutheran was completed. As a young, newly appointed pastor, it was Buege who went to Eliel Saarinen's studio to ask him to design a new church for his congregation. The church would be the elder Saarinen's last completed work.

Eliel Saarinen, in consultation with his son Eero, conceived of Christ Church Lutheran as a setting for a liturgical drama of sight and sound. Because he felt that nothing should compete with the visible rite for the attention of the worshipper, he reduced the interior of the church to a background of unadorned simplicity, brought into brilliant focus by his use of light. As acoustics in a church are also important for the appreciation of the Word of God and the ritual of music, the control of sound was another equally important factor through which many of the decisions were made.

The result is a building of simple, even rare beauty without a hint of the practical and infinitely painstaking calculation that went into its design. Christ Church Lutheran is proof that new forms can be as compelling as the forms they supersede.

The basic structural system of the church is extremely simple: a steel frame enclosed by stone and brick walls, the latter exposed on the interior as well as the exterior. But, the organization of these elements to achieve the acoustical and visual goal is a more complicated matter.

The nave, which seats six hundred, provides a high central volume with low expansion areas on either side. Thus with less than a full congregation the church does not seem

The Pastor of Christ Church Lutheran was unhappy with the gothic forms of a design that had been drawn up just prior to his arrival. He and his congregation came to believe "that only a contemporary approach would have relevance in an effort to interpret our message to the present age. Our Gospel is as honest as it is simple, and we felt that the building should express these qualities."

Expressions of His Time

Before he came to the United States Eliel Saarinen was a long established and much appreciated master of the Finnish Art Nouveau movement.

Finland's Premier Urko Kekkonen gave the eulogy at Saarinen's memorial service when his ashes were returned to his native land. Kekkonen spoke eloquently of his country's affection and esteem for the renowned architect:

"We pay tribute to the memory of Eliel Saarinen. His name in the field of architecture has become a concept.

"Style is the way of expression of a certain time. What is the style of Eliel Saarinen, that noble style of architecture that is known by all the world? It is an expression of the modern age in architecture. It is also the Finnish way of expression in architecture. But Eliel Saarinen's style is far greater; it cannot be tied by the fetters of passing time any more than it can be geographically restricted. Eliel Saarinen's style embraces parts of the best of all times. It has harmony that dates from the expression of bygone time; it has values that will be preserved by the generations to come. Eliel Saarinen's architectural art has grown far outside the national boundaries of Finland; it is owned by all the world. In the true sense of the word, it is the style of Eliel Saarinen."[4]

sparsely occupied. A 36-seat chapel at the rear, behind the open narthex and placed at right angles to the nave, provides for overflow services and accommodates its own functions. The choir and organ are placed in a balcony directly over the narthex. The baptistry is at the forward end of the nave. A low curved wood screen at the right ties the nave to the sacristy, enabling direct passage to the chancel for the pastor and also forming a backdrop for the pulpit.

The shapes of the church itself are the means of controlling the sound. Since sound reverberates between parallel surfaces, such surfaces have been avoided. The flat ceiling, hung from a roof of steel decking, is canted slightly downward from side to side, thus presenting a surface that is not parallel to the floor. The north wall of the church is slanted from front to rear, angling away from the straight south wall at the opposite end. Toward the front of the church, this north wall merges with the chancel wall in a gentle, continuous curve, thereby eliminating the right-angle meeting of wall surfaces that is ordinarily a focal point for echoes.

In addition to the shape of the church and the tilt and angle of surface details, the materials used in the interior have been chosen for their acoustical properties. They take advantage of the fact that to provide clear tones without reverberation, a sound-reflective surface should be opposed by a sound-absorbent one. The hard floor and hard wooden surfaces of the pews are opposed by a suspended ceiling of perforated acoustic tile, backed at strategic areas by two inches of insulation. The solid brick south wall of the nave is opposed by the north wall, patterned with open brickwork which undulates in and out from the line of the wall. The open space thus created behind the brickwork is backed by sound-absorbent material.

The slightly angled panels of open brickwork high along the right-hand side play both an acoustic and a visual role. The ceiling is angled for similar considerations.

Because Saarinen's concern for sound control started with the basic shape of the building and extended to small details, the acoustics of Christ Church are probably the finest of any

The Cranbrook Academy, Detroit, 1938 (above), and the Tabernacle Church of Christ (now the First Christian Church) in Columbus, Indiana, 1940 (left) are some of Saarinen's most notable works in America. They demonstrate his consistent use of contrasting horizontal and vertical forms, the result of a Finnish vocabulary tempered by modernism. The freestanding campanile and nave of the Tabernacle Church served as a model for Christ Church Lutheran.

religious building in the United States. The tone and clarity of music within is incomparable, Although not small, every syllable spoken by the minister is as audible in the last row as it is in the front of the church. In effect, the congregation is in the service, at its acoustical center, rather than merely at a crossover point in a path of reverberating sound.

The illumination of the church has been given equal consideration. The only two sources of daylight are the glass walls of the side aisles and a narrow, vertical window strip lighting the chancel. The main area of the nave has no windows at all. As the interior surfaces are lightly colored, the limited amount of daylight is reflected and provides a soft yet ample Illumination throughout the church. This serves to intensify the radiant whiteness at the chancel.

Daylight pours in from tall narrow windows lining the low side aisles. The glass is set at the outer face of the brick piers whose depth minimizes glare. The sanctuary receives a dramatic shaft of midmorning sun from a floor-to-ceiling chancel window concealed behind a projecting louvered wood grille. The chancel wall is angled and curved at the right side to reflect this light and is given emphasis by having its brick painted white and then sanded. Artificial illumination is provided by indirect fixtures and ceiling downlights.

The church is as edifying an experience for the congregation as the rites that take place within. Reverend Buege made these remarks about Eliel Saarinen's ability to teach through his architecture:

"He was a teacher of us all and I can see why he used to say, 'An architect must first of all be an educator.' To further our education, we called in a competent theologian to present the history and development of church architecture so that the congregation could know that the presently accepted forms were not designs of God nor the only forms in which the church had worshipped. When Saarinen's prospectuses were ready, we used an entire week in presenting them to the congregation. I believe that these studies were important in opening the minds of the congregation to acceptance of an entirely new church design."[5]

These renderings by Jay Henderson Barr were used during the course of thinking out variations in the church's design. Barr remained a vital member of the Saarinen team long after Eliel's death. He remained with Eero up to the beginning stages of the Dulles International Airport project.

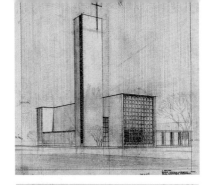

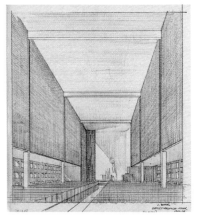

Immigrants from Germany and Scandinavia brought the Lutheran faith to North America, many of them settling in Pennsylvania and the upper Midwest. The forms of Lutheran churches are pure and simple.

Since Martin Luther emphasized the importance of the Word, the sermon is at the heart of the Lutheran service.

An equally important role is played by hymns, which not only convey evangelical teaching but allow for popular participation in the church services.

Lutheran music is world famous. Among the composers of importance are Johann Sebastian Bach, Michael Praetorius, Heinrich Schütz, and Dietrich Buxtehude.

Louis Kahn was less concerned with revealing a building's frame than he was with emphasizing its walls, floors, and ceilings as sculptural masses, planes that define the spaces within.

The entrance to the Yale Art Gallery is a break and a shift in an otherwise simple plane of brick.

Kahn also used these planes as a way to structure mechanical needs into his buildings. He said, "The feeling that our present-day architecture needs embellishment stems in part from a tendency to fair joints out of sight, to conceal how parts are put together. Structures should be devised which can harbor the mechanical needs of rooms and spaces."[1]

Yale University Art Gallery • New Haven, Connecticut

Older architectural styles represented the power of knowledge when employed, as they almost always once were, in the buildings of educational institutions, especially at a time when they saw themselves as temples or cathedrals of learning. Greek, Roman, Neo-Classical, and Gothic Revival styles dominate campuses everywhere.

Yale University in New Haven was no exception to this tradition. But, they began during the 1950s to throw off the mantle of these outworn forms under the leadership of A. Whitney Griswold. The vitality he encouraged as university president brought many of the finest architectural talents in the country to the campus, with some two dozen resulting buildings, that made Yale a mecca for architects from all over the world.

The structure that inaugurated Yale's new approach was the four-story Art Gallery—actually an addition to Egerton Swartwout's 1927 building—by Louis Kahn. This was Kahn's first major commission.

The new building was required to accommodate, for some years, almost two floors of architects and a basement full of graphic designers, as well as gallery exhibition space and offices. The whole building finally became the intended gallery when Paul Rudolph's Art and Architecture Building was completed across the street. This interim requirement of mixed use certainly made it harder to design with only the gallery in mind. All any architect could do was to make spaces which were as large and uncluttered as possible in order to allow for optimum flexibility.

Kahn fit his building into its site with admirable sensitivity, complementing the older buildings and terminating their

The horizontal concrete elements, or stringcourses, set in the brick façade, follow the lines of the moldings on the 1927 building to the right of the gallery (out of view). These in turn determine the placement of the windows and reveal where each floor is inside.

Solid Geometry

Kahn's freedom from any particular style and his concern with elemental geometric forms allowed him to monumentalize every building. Significantly influenced by Richard Buckminster Fuller (1895-1983), Kahn and Anne Griswold Tyng (page 57) designed a number of structures based on the tetrahedron and Fuller's tensegrity principles.

These explorations, together with Kahn's Traffic Studies (1953), where he suggested huge parking towers both as containers and as urban markers, intrigued the Smithsons and other groups in England. He joined Team X, whose preoccupations with society, context, and "technological man" were of interest to him.

Buckminster Fuller, Kahn's old acquaintance from Shelter, came to lecture at Yale in 1952 for some weeks. Kahn sometimes admitted, sometimes denied, that all this affected him; but the fact remains that the final, post-Fuller scheme for the gallery's floor slabs was afterwards conceived by him as a concrete space-frame of tetrahedronal elements.

line-up with authority. He enhanced, where he might easily have destroyed, the several levels of Weir Court to the north. The Chapel Street façade and entrance to the Gallery are quietly stated; the excitement begins once you're inside.

A central service core (Kahn's "servant space") cuts the building into two equal parts, galleries falling to either side. The plan of the galleries is quite simple: they are left wide open for maximum adaptablity. The core has a stair-tower at one end, an elevator and other services in the center, and service stairs (for fire) at the other end.

One of the building's most striking features is the poured-concrete, cylindrical stair-tower which accesses each of the gallery floors. The stairs inside the well move from landing to landing at 120-degree turns each time forming an equilateral triangle inscribed within the circle of the stairwell itself. Glass bricks ring the uppermost end of the cylinder allowing natural light to enter from above. The concrete plates of a triangular slab at the summit serve as "light blades" which deflect the light downward. The underside of the triangle lies in shadow while the walls of the stairwell are washed with light. The cylinder and the triangular form sharply contrast.

Kahn made drawings for a series of concrete vaults, carried on beams, which were to span the major spaces of the gallery, but things just weren't right. And, he was trying to avoid columns, anyway. Anne Griswold Tyng (page 57) was working closely with Kahn on this their first building together and may have helped with the floor solution. Tyng formed an effective bridge between Kahn and Buckminster Fuller. She and Kahn had met Fuller in 1949, and Fuller came to respect her ideas, praising her "superbly crafted and original scientific work," and calling her "Louis Kahn's geometrical strategist." One geometry they all experimented with derives from close-packing polygonal solids—in much the same way as they are arranged in molecules and organic forms.

The final scheme for the floor's span was conceived as a concrete space-frame, made up of tetrahedronal elements and poured in place. The design was modified by the consulting engineer, Henry A. Pfisterer, due to problems of shear

above: U.S. Pavilion (Geodesic Dome), R. Buckminster Fuller, Montreal World's Fair, Canada, 1967. For many the geodesic dome represented the way of the future.

left: Kahn and Tyng, *City Tower Project*, unbuilt plan for Philadelphia City Hall, Philadelphia, 1952-1957.

at the points where the tetrahedrons joined. It became a braced beam system, but the visual effect remained more or less tetrahedronal. Since the slab for each floor was poured across the tops of these shapes a continuous horizontal void resulted, through which Kahn ran channels and ducts for flexible lighting and ventilation from the central service core. The mechanical equipment was now an integral part of the building's hollow fabric. This is a lesson he later applied to the interstitial floors of the Salk Institute (page 49).

The concrete was left rough with the marks of its forms on it. The results are marvelously textured canopies that hover over exhibition and work floors. There tends to be disagreement as to whether the ceilings set off the art displayed in the galleries or compete with it: the ceilings are undoubtedly impressive in any case.

The open structure enables all spot- and down-lights to be recessed instead of dangling; to be installed, moved, and projected at will. The ceilings also allow the air-conditioning ducts to be laced through with appropriate acoustic insulation above. Equally important, almost complete flexibility in installing movable partitions is assured, as opposed to many new museums where a right angle is mandated.

From the stair-tower to the ceiling coffers, the shape of the equilateral triangle is a module that reverberates throughout the galleries. Kahn took what he used to engineer the floor slabs and left it exposed as a geometric pattern that winds up being the salient visual feature of the building. The ceilings can be seen day or night from the street or the courtyard and form an impressive backdrop for the exhibited works.

The Yale University Art Gallery was an important transition for Kahn. It can easily be labeled a hybrid with its mixture of solid exterior wall and glassed-in box-like forms. This works to the building's advantage, however, inasmuch as it all smooths out the passage from the old to the new.

In any case, between the drama of the stair-tower, the space-frame ceilings, the play of light in all the spaces, and the clarity he achieves in the marriage of geometry and form, Kahn does come into his own here.

The space-frame floor slabs contain all the gallery's mechanical systems. They are also beautifully patterned elements that define the galleries while they shine forth as architectonically conceived sculptural planes.

Harold Price and Frank Lloyd Wright look over the plans for Price's headquarters (above).

At a large gathering assembled for the opening of the Price Tower, Wright asked if there were any questions. One woman rose and asked: "Mr. Wright, what is your first consideration when designing a building for a client?" "Why, my dear lady, the first prerequisite is, of course, to give the client what he wants." There was a chuckle from Hal Price who stood up and said, "Well, now, I don't know about that. You see, I came to Frank Lloyd Wright wanting a two-story office building with parking space for about ten cars and trucks, and look what he gave me—this Tower!" Wright looked at his client with a glint in his eye, placed his hand affectionately on Price's shoulder, and said: "But in your case, Hal, you didn't know what you wanted!"

Price Tower • Bartlesville, Oklahoma

Harold C. Price, who owned and operated an international pipeline company, needed little office space for his headquarters in Bartlesville, and had no desire to build a corporate symbol of any advertising value. Price in fact preferred buildings low to the ground, and particularly admired the work of Clifford May, pioneer of the California ranch house. Early in 1952 he was thinking about new headquarters:

"We wanted a building of our own. We agreed to build a three-story building with another company taking the entire first floor. My two sons, Harold and Joe, recently graduated from the University of Oklahoma, suggested we get Frank Lloyd Wright to design the building . . . . However, I did not believe that Mr. Wright would be interested in such a small building."[1]

Wright indeed was not. Price's two sons had suggested Wright at the recommendation of Bruce Goff, then chairman of the school of architecture at the University of Oklahoma, in Norman.

Price and his family flew to Wisconsin in June to meet with Wright. "I told him I wanted a three-story building with about 25,000 square feet of floor space," Price recalled. "He said immediately that three floors was most inefficient and suggested ten floors of 2,500 square feet each." What Wright offered was a smaller version of a project he designed for St. Mark's in-the-Bouwerie in New York thirty years ealier. Price wrote later that he had revised his program to "a building of no less than ten stories." He also told Wright there was a demand in Bartlesville for "what might be called deluxe apartments" with two bedrooms and two baths.

" . . . on the rolling plains of Oklahoma comes a fresh realization of the modern advantages of architecture yet unknown to the big city. As trees in the forest have no chance to develop their own individuality to full expression of their own character as would be seen if they were isolated, so the quadruple skyscraper now has a chance to be itself, free standing in the countryside." — Frank Lloyd Wright

Excepting that Wright really wanted a building of 22 stories, everything else went his way. Three stories of the new tower would be occupied by Price's company, the first floor and one or two more would be rented to the Public Service Company of Oklahoma. In one quadrant of the tower he could at last realize the duplex apartment plan he had conceived for St. Mark's.

He began the design of the Price Tower that August. The building was finished early in 1956. Price expected to spend $500,000 for his building. When it was finally finished the tower had cost about $2.1 million.

Wright described his building as a "light-fabric," a work dedicated to "the value of sunlit space." It represented the release of the tall building, he said, from "congested areas of monstrous cities" to a typical "country town." And it showed how the tall building might become a much finer thing than a mere engine of profit. Wright set out to transform the skyscraper in a substantive way, not just ascribing to it a symbolic content. When he talked about a tree that escaped the crowded forest, the metaphor rang true because it is literally at the core of his tall, solitary tower.

Price Tower's most important feature, the concept that Wright had been trying to use these thirty years, is something he called a "tap-root" structure. This consists of a central mast-like core, containing circulation and services, with reinforced-concrete floors cantilevered out from it like the branches of a tree. Wright realized something along these lines in 1944 with his Johnson Wax Research Tower. In neither the Research Tower, nor in the Price Tower, however, was Wright able to employ a true curtain wall—a freestanding skin (page 119)—as he intended to do in the St. Mark's buildings. The edges of each of the floor slabs, in both of the built projects, support separate knee-walls and separate window sections. The continuous vertical fins of copper on the apartment side of the Price Tower give the illusion of a single sheer face.

In plan the building is comprised of two squares superimposed one upon the other with the second square rotated 30°

Wright clearly indicates the functions behind each façade by his use of the copper fins or sunshades he attached to the windows. In the three quadrants of offices, the fins shade the glass and wrap around the corners horizontally (previous page).
left: On the apartment side, fins run vertically up the building's height. The verdigris of the copper, which also appears in the fascia panels, contributes to the character of the tower.

from its center. The resulting pinwheel provides balconies at every other level. There are two floors of offices for every apartment floor, each apartment being a duplex (there are eight apartments and 14 floors of offices). Mr. Price's office was at the very top along with a roof garden.

The tower offered oddly undersized office spaces, and the deluxe apartments Price had asked for—although literally "of the light"—were hardly suited to family life. The intricacies of the building, and its surprising intimacies of scale, can be sensed almost immediately from the outside. From a plan only 46 feet wide the building is divided into quadrants and then into a unit or module shaped like a rhombus composed of two equilateral triangles. Since the unit is derived from the dynamic rotation of the plan, its dimensions of less than three feet on a side makes for a most eccentric module of construction.

By insisting that the tower was to be tall and slender, the unit system used made many situations in the plan somewhat tight and cramped. Because unit-lines determined the partitions and the placement of various items of furniture, the interior space gained fresh but sometimes awkward configurations. Wright designed all the built-ins, furniture, fixtures, fabrics—everything. It all reverberates with the prismatic, other-worldly shapes of the building. It's all of a piece—one man's insistent vision made manifest.

Because he had virtually eliminated the original purpose of a tall office building, Wright courted a certain irony when he spoke of "this release of the skyscraper from slavery (of commercial bondage) to a human freedom."[4]

In the end Wright's fastidious attention to detail, coupled with his tenacious need to impart intimacy to every aspect of his structure, worked against his ambition to build a truly tall building. He nevertheless drove to the heart of the problem, as always, and opened the walls to the light of day. The size of the Price Tower, hovering as it does between a skyscraper and a house is an appropriate resolution of Wright's aspirations. The result, like a tree, freestanding in the heartland, is resonant with a strange beauty.

From top to bottom: A typical office interior, an apartment living room, an apartment dining area, a bedroom and balcony.

Saarinen redefined the airport with Dulles and it has been imitated the world over ever since.

An obituary in TIME maga- zine from September 8, 1961, describes Saarinen's work as characteristically "controversal . . . there was always in Saarinen's designs—from his famous 'womb' chair to the soaring, winged, 6,000-ton concrete roof of his TWA termi- nal at Idlewild to his new Dulles International Airport at Chantilly, Va., with its moving waiting room—a daring, a willingness to experiment with form that few of his contempo- raries had. 'An architect must have a combination of sensitiv- ity and crust,' he said, and he had both."[1]

On his last visit to Washington before he died, Eero Saarinen remarked: "I think this terminal building is the best thing I have done. Maybe it will even explain what I believe about architec- ture."[2]

J ust as Eero Saarinen was about to finish the Trans World Airlines Terminal in New York he was asked to build for another airport. This time it wasn't a single departures termi- nal, but the whole airport—the first in the world intended exclusively for jets—Dulles International in Washington, D.C.

Saarinen gave serious consideration to what this would mean to people: "[I see] this airport [as] unique . . . in being the national and international gateway to the nation's capi- tal. It is unique in its ownership—the Federal Government. It is unique in being a part of the whole complex of buildings that create the image of our nation's capital. We felt the ter- minal should express all that in its architectural design."[1]

What exactly should an airport express? "The tradition of Federal architecture is static," Saarinen said, "but a Jet-age airport should be essentially non-static, expressing the move- ment and the excitement of travel. We thought that if we could bring these two things together into a unified design we would have a very interesting building."[3]

The idea of expressive monumentality had become the driving force for Saarinen. At a time when monumentality was simply a veneer on the small ideas of so many large- scale projects, such as New York's Lincoln Center,[2] Eero Saarinen, with his Ingalls Hockey Rink, TWA Terminal, and Gateway Arch, was one of the few architects capable of mak- ing truly expressive and monumental structures.

The thoroughness of Saarinen's working methods was impressive to say the least; they were applied to every proj- ect but none so thoroughly as this one. It's interesting to note that his father's methods, which were just as thorough and probably influenced Eero, date back to another large-scale

In this as in all of his work Eero Saarinen never forgot that buildings are for people
nor did he forget that buildings grow from need and when that need
is responded to with reason, a respect for the nature of things, and
the human condition, good buildings will always be the result.[4]
— Kevin Roche

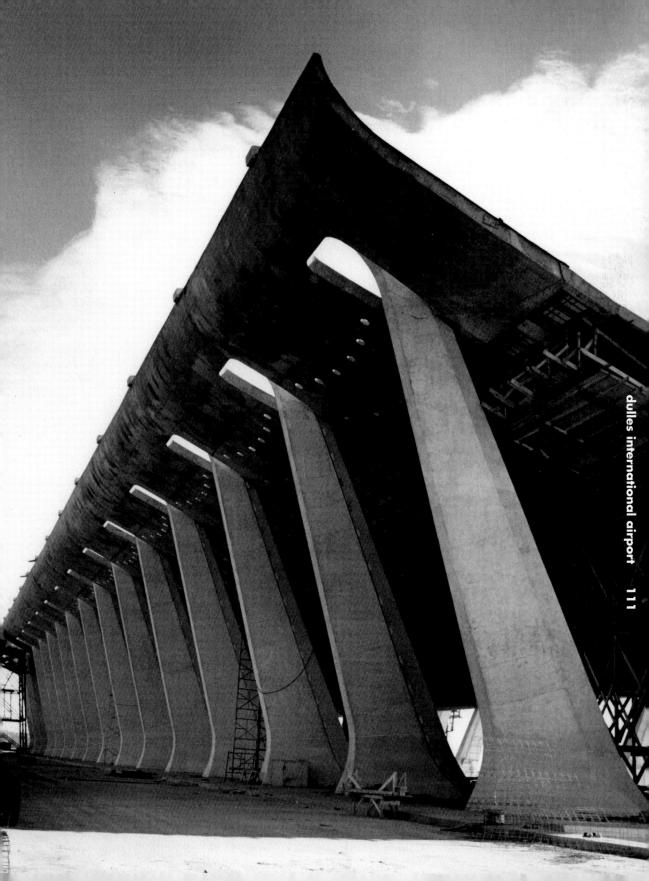

Reflections on Method

A frequent criticism leveled at Saarinen is that he was constantly changing styles; he was thought to lack a consistent approach to problem solving. However, Saarinen's work is a unique meeting place for two great, often conflicting traditions: a dominant objectivist philosophy, and a richly diversified, and therefore less easily categorized, romantic subjectivity. This meeting place characterizes his work as a whole and as such is seen either as a strength or, more frequently, as a weakness.

"I think it was Sullivan that said, 'Each problem has within it its own solution.' Where we might be criticized," said Saarinen, "is for almost trying to find a different solution for every single problem, trying to just bend over backwards to do that."

Kevin Roche got his start in Saarinen's office and in many ways approaches problems similarly. Referring to three projects of Eero's that were going on simultaneously, Roche has remarked, "They belong to the same couple of years, and it seems completely logical to me that they are different. They were built in different places, for different clients, of different materials, and most of all their functions were completely different. They had no reason to be similar. . . . This, of course, was Eero's philosophy: the Sullivan one of the solution being in the problem, and a very particular thing. What you bring to it is your art, and it brings its reason; the two come together and the answer is, specifically, that building, of that moment, for particular purpose."[5]

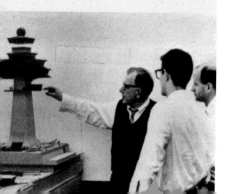

transportation project—the Helsinki Central Railway Station (1910-14). For that project Eliel scrupulously studied the mechanics of railway operation and discussed the problems of railway design with numerous experts.

Eero describes his approach to the Dulles project:

"No one asked us to grapple with the problem of a jet-age terminal beyond the question of pure architecture. But I believe the architect has to assume that kind of responsibility. Therefore, together with the team of Ammann & Whitney, engineers, Charles Landrum, airport consultant, and Burns & McDonnell, mechanical engineers, we decided to make a fundamental analysis of the whole problem of a large terminal for jet airplanes. It was a hard-boiled problem and we wanted to solve it in a hard-boiled way."

"We sent out teams with counters and stop watches to see what people really do at airports, how far they walk, their interchange problems. We analyzed special problems of jets; examined schedules, peak loads, effects of weather. We studied baggage handling, economics, operations, and so on. We reduced this vast data to a series of about 40 charts."

The careful planning paid off. The Dulles Terminal is a remarkable combination of ingenious organization and expressive architecture. It is notable for its compact plan and short walking distances, a contribution to airport amenity made possible by the concept of the mobile lounge. And it is notable for its graceful hanging roof, its colonnaded façades, and its dynamic look. The terminal manages to express the architect's desire to "place a strong form between earth and sky that seems both to rise from the plain and hover over it."

Dulles is isolated in the somewhat ordinary countryside that stretches to a spot about 20 miles west of Washington, D.C. But, the approach to the airport was skillfully landscaped and transformed by Dan Kiley. The drive is calculated to provide vistas of ever-changing perspectives which end by fully revealing the building and tower. The excitement

above: Transportation modules attached to the terminal. Saarinen said, "Gradually, we arrived at the concept of the mobile lounge; a departure lounge on stilts and wheels—a part of the terminal that detaches itself from the building and travels to the plane."

left: Eero Saarinen surveys a Dulles model with his design team. Kevin Roche is at far right.

generated at a distance is maintained to the very entrance. The terminal itself is visually dominated by its fantastic suspended roof.

Saarinen describes the evolution of the overall form:

"There was also the problem of the site—a beautiful flat plain. . . . We came to the conclusion that a strong form that seemed both to rise from the plain and to hover over it would look best. The horizontal element, or roof, would be the highest element. It should be tilted forward so the building would be seen. The terminal should also have a monumental scale in this landscape and in the vastness of this huge airfield. The mobile lounge concept allowed us to make the terminal a single compact building. We started with abstract, ideal shapes for the site and went through many forms. Gradually, we arrived at the idea of a curved roof, high in the front, lower in the middle, rising again at the back.

"But how should this strong, hovering form be placed on the site? How should it look as one approached and arrived? . . . Approaching closer and arriving, one will see the large colonnade. The control tower (whose form was arrived at after much study) was placed at the back of the terminal, to be seen in changing relationships to the terminal."

In essence the terminal is the roof—and the roof is astonishing. It is supported by heavily reinforced concrete piers, 16 per side, 65 feet high on the approach side, 40 feet at the back or field side, spaced 40 feet apart for a total length of 600 feet. From edge beams that laterally connect each of the two lines of piers are slung steel suspension bridge cables 1-inch in diameter, and from these are hung 1,792 precast concrete panels, each weighing 800 pounds. The rods which connect the piers laterally and from which the hammock roof is slung, are, contrary to appearances, not on the upper face or fascia, but at that inner point on the rear faces of the piers just behind the holes where piers and roof deck first

Fellow Countrymen

As modernism emerged as a global phenomenon extending from Europe and the United States to Latin America, Asia, the Middle East, and Africa, its interaction with regionalist modes produced complex and intriguing hybrid forms of architecture.

Compelling examples of differing national expressions in international contexts appeared at the world's fairs of the late 1930s in Paris and New York.

At these fairs, the architecture of national pavilions was of consummate importance to the identity of each sponsoring nation in the continuously shifting arena of international political, economic, and cultural relations. In the cases of nations seeking to assert their identities alongside those of the major world powers, these prominent commissions often fell to leading architects who were also considered "advanced" such as Alvar Aalto (1898-1976). He created a groundbreaking modern design for the Finnish pavilion at the 1939 New York World's Fair (below).

In the wake of the wholesale acceptance in the United States of the so-called International Style, recognition of modernist regionalism fell by the wayside.

dulles international airport 113

above: At Dulles, a complex system of mullions spanning the spaces from column to column and from floor to ceiling holds the curtain of glass in a waving web reminiscent of some of the work of Alvar Aalto, another Finn twelve years Eero's senior. Aalto's work possesses a strong feeling for materials; it often includes massive curving walls of brick and timber.
right: Alvar Aalto, Finnish Pavilion, New York World's Fair, 1939.

Sculptor at Heart

When he was a very young man in Finland, Eero Saarinen naturally gravitated to designing furniture while working on family projects. As with his mother before him (page 97) he went to Paris thinking he would be a sculptor. He soon returned to study architecture and join the family firm.

Saarinen worked like a sculptor producing rough models in clay (above) for his model-maker to realize later in more permanent form.

But, unlike architects who impose sculptural objects on us as if they were buildings, he understood the flow of architectural space as an integral part of the expression of architectural form.

Saarinen had a penchant for bio-morphic form especially when he worked in concrete. He said that a building should smell concrete. "Yes, and I think TWA will, as a concrete building, also have the sort of the total unity of the flowing, cast material of concrete. I have great hopes for that. Now I see the problem much more clearly."

The form of the Ingalls Hockey Rink has been compared to many things from a leaf to an insect. It may also be compared to an inverted Viking ship. Many cultures have overturned worn out vessels and re-used them as buildings. Saarinen's forms are decidedly Scandinavian.

meet. What hangs suspended resembles a huge, continuous hammock hanging between concrete trees. The thirty-two piers lean outward, the better to counteract the roof load.

There are two points worth noting in this description of the roof. The first concerns the connection between the roof-line and the supporting piers. This connection is purposely made to look tenuous, especially since the curved ends of the piers that are visible through the holes—the part you'd think was designed to hold it up—don't even touch the roof. It appears as if the whole thing were floating.

The other point concerns the piers leaning outward to counteract the load of the roof; they actually lean out farther than is necessary. About this decision Saarinen said, "We exaggerated this outward slope, as well as the compressive flange at the rear of the columns, in order to give the colonnade a dynamic and soaring look—in addition to its dignity."

The words "sweeping" and "soaring" are often used to describe the meaning of Dulles as well as its appearance; this is a habit that began with Eero himself. Are these qualities we really see or feel; or, are they ideas that are placed in our heads? The reality is a little more complicated.

Inside, the ceiling swoops down on us as much as it sweeps up. In spite the fact that it is rigid, reinforced concrete, the ceiling may as well be an immense expanse of fabric hanging over our heads. Even Saarinen referred to it as a "hammock." It sags with what seems like an inordinant amout of weight. Oppressive? Well, maybe at first, but it's almost comforting after a while—the equivalent in a building to Saarinen's womb chair.

Saarinen likened the columns to trees. The analogy points up a difficulty in the way we often think about buildings with expressive form. Our imaginations seek literal narratives in metaphors such as these, but we shouldn't be looking for a forest. By the way he manipulated concrete, Saarinen achieved a sense of what materials such as wood could do if wood could be obtained and manipulated at that mammoth size. As a consequence, we feel an organic rightness in the forms in spite of the fact that the material is an artificial one.

above: Eero Saarinen working with Gordon Bunshaft and Pietro Belluschi on Lincoln Center.
left: Saarinen invested sculptural power in each of a succession of buildings where he used reinforced concrete. The monumentality he achieved with its possibilities reaches a state of maturity in the Ingalls Hockey Rink, Yale University, 1958. The roof is carried on steel cables suspended in catenary curves from a parabolic concrete arch. The ceiling is wood decking.

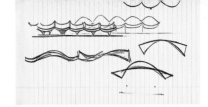

These are sensations that parallel the sensations of hammocks or trees, they are not depictions of them. As such, the forms feel new and awe-inspiring, while they feel equally right and comforting.

Everyone was convinced that a new airport needed a new method of handling passengers. Dan Kiley, who had just finished working on O'Hare Airport in Chicago, "was discouraged by the lack of insight . . . specifically the unwieldy layout of the terminals. It seemed obvious that no passenger would want to walk an entire mile between gates."[6]

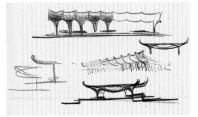

Taking cues from European airport bus systems, Saarinen's office came up with the Mobile Lounge, a modified bus that alleviated the need for airplanes to attach directly to the terminal. Instead, it carried the passenger to the plane in comfort and style. Chrysler built a prototype, and Charles Eames made a short publicity film to sell the idea—contrasting hundreds of stampeding feet with a man relaxing with a martini in the Mobile Lounge.

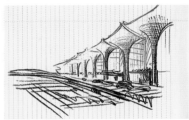

At Dulles, the endless, wearisome corridors down which thousands trudge have been eliminated. Instead, you draw up to the terminal by cab, car, or bus, walk 150 feet maximum to a check-in station on the far side, and then you're whisked by Mobile Lounge to the plane on the airstrip one mile away. Little bother for the passenger; no juggling or expensive taxiing of jet planes. The building acts as a staging point rather than a dumping ground; the bus is part of the architecture. It is a beautifully analyzed concept.

Saarinen was a prolific draughtsman who constantly sketched on yellow legal pads. Here we see how he developed a thought from the most abstract suggestion of forms of flight to more literal cantilevered structural elements. His ideas evolved from almost symbolic notations to practical architectonic forms.

Kevin Roche remarked on Saarinen's success at total architecture: "What he looked for was: what is there in this problem that is particular to it, and of its nature? He included all the factors he could: the site, structure, economics, function, the psychological needs of the people in the building, and the key question, 'Why do these people want to build this building?' The answer to that has to justify the building as a reality later on. An attitude-of-mind approach would characterize more of what Saarinen wanted to do than anything else; it was in his great ability to realize the building that he found the answers."[7]

right: Saarinen in his Womb Chair.
Saarinen's Model No. 70, with its upholstered organic form, eventually became known as the Womb Chair, since it invited the sitter to curl up into its generous proportions. He used these forms in his furniture since he and Charles Eames won the Museum of Modern Art's ORGANIC DESIGN competition in 1940.

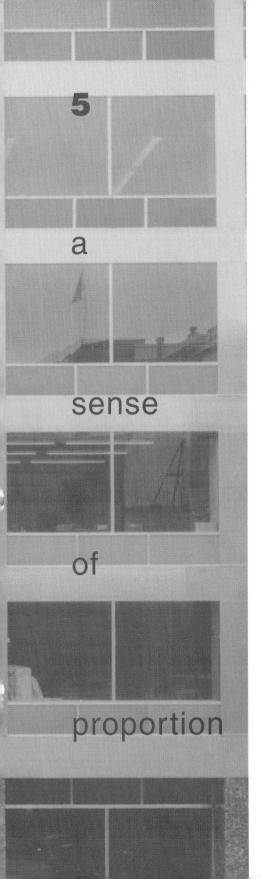

5

a

sense

of

proportion

Equitable Savings and Loan
Lake Shore Drive Apartments
Lever House
Seagram Building

The four buildings in this section, especially the two that were built in New York, have been hailed as the forerunners of what we now call the glass box. For some this means that they pointed to a better future; for others it means that they paved the way to the very destruction of our cities. It is difficult to talk about how these structures have changed our lives without addressing the legacy of woes that are (falsely) attributed to them.

The hiatus in the construction of tall buildings that began with the Great Depression ended with the close of the Second World War. The era brought with it a rejuvenated economy. Although there was no consensus as to how to remake the city, a search was soon underway for fresh architectural idioms that would represent post-war values.

In cities across America, the transplanted European modernist architecture was endorsed as the official style of a democracy that now largely championed a free market economy. In 1951, when Henry-Russell Hitchcock wrote about "The International Style Twenty Years After,"[1] he could claim that "the establishment of a fixed body of discipline in architecture," i.e. the International Style, had been "successful" in America, and that this work was "probably the major achievement of the 20th Century." Now generally associated with the accomplishments of an industrial, technological society, new building in steel and glass became, as Colin Rowe noted, " . . . a

"The history of architecture shows that down the centuries an unremitting battle has been joined on behalf of light against the obstacles imposed by the laws of gravity." — Le Corbusier

Envelopes of Glass

In his search to "wrest the impression of corporeality from unsubstantial materials," Walter Gropius (1883–1969) designed one of the first buildings associated with the look of modern architecture. He and Adolfus Meyer, a cabinetmaker turned architect, designed the brick, steel, and glass Fagus-Werk (above) in 1914.

The corners of the administration block were constructed almost entirely in glass. Gropius's first independent commission, it could hardly have had more of an impact; it established the style of modern factories worldwide.

That same year Gropius produced designs for a model factory (below) for the Werkbund Exhibition in Cologne. The twin, streamlined glass stair towers were a new device that was to influence countless architects after World War I.

By the time Gropius designed the Bauhaus buildings in Dessau in 1926 he was able to wrap entire sections in continuous glass curtain walls.

suitable veneer for the corporate activities of an 'enlightened' capitalism."[2]

As a building type, the glass box, particularly the Miesian hi-rise, conjured up images of efficiency, cleanliness, organization, and standardization. It fit the bill for developing big business. Glass boxes—perfect and economical—now characterize modern skylines all over the world.

However, from the very beginning, the concept of the glass and steel corporate structure was considered anathema to Frank Lloyd Wright. In an address delivered before the A.I.A. in 1952 (Lever House had just opened), he attacked "what he felt was a growing conception that buildings could be well planned merely as "boxes on stilts. . . . Mr. Wright called for the development of an architecture which would 'reflect the American personality,' and was sharply critical as usual of the progress thus far made in that direction."[3] One can detect Wright's usual preoccupation with the evils of un-American architecture.

Philip Johnson became one of the style's most vociferous detractors in spite of the fact that he began his architectural career with Mies working on the Seagram Building. By the 1960s Johnson was deprecating even his own efforts saying,

"Today I am ashamed for the terribly scattered work that I do, and its lack of direction . . . . It is all very well to say that we admire Mies, and that some discipline is a good thing for young minds, but what if one is bored . . . ? If you go to Germany you will see the local version of Lever House; they are worse."[4]

Lever House and, more particularly the Seagram Building (along with Mies as its creator), became the whipping boys for all that had gone wrong with the low cost, prefabricated real estate ventures that followed. Many still feel that the glass box was really a Pandora's box that opened the floodgates of bad design. Ultimately, it was standardization, and the confusion of economy with non-design, that gave this building type the bad name from which it will probably never recover.

Two of Walter Gropius's first buildings and two firsts in modernism.
above: The Fagus Works Shoe Factory at Alfeld-an-der-Leine, Germany.
left: Office Building and Exhibition Hall at the Werkbund Exhibition, Cologne, Germany.
As head of the School of Arts and Crafts in Weimar after the First World War, Gropius changed its name to *Bauhaus* (House of Building) to signify the meeting-place of all arts.

For the early modernists, "standardization" was a battle cry in a war waged against the old order. Later in the century, particularly in the United States, standardization led to a nightmare world of cheap imitation, the dreary result of purely economic considerations. A point was reached when it seemed as if architecture might make itself. Eero Saarinen remarked:

"In a way function became one of the gimmicks, one of the sales gimmicks, of modern architecture, but it was a sort of Frankenstein that was created. Architects began to believe that through the function, this Frankenstein would come up with the architecture. So they sat around and waited for him to produce, but he didn't."[5]

The building industry's interpretation of serial production led to the loss, not only of originality, but to the love of detail which was most important for Mies, and without which the standards of an architecture of "less is more" sadly declined to almost nothing indeed. No surprise that the last nail in the coffin was Robert Venturi's comment that "less is boring."

But, Lever House and Seagram benefitted by having demanding clients who were the corporate tenants of their respective buildings. What was even more unusual, in the case of Lever House, is that Lever Brothers wished to be the *only* tenants of their building and they had every desire to keep it small in scale as a result. If the entire structure were gathered together to fit the lot line of the site it would only amount to eight stories. More typical are buildings that are developed solely as real estate ventures, where the primary concern is to maximize rentable floor space—good design is not a consideration.

Too many people who should know better confused real estate speculators with tenant-clients and painted all large corporate ventures with the same bitter brush. Glass and steel become the villains. In a public talk entitled "The Death of a Street," delivered at the Museum of Modern Art in New York, Vincent Scully said that the plazas of "aggressive and

above: Hallidie Building, San Francisco, 1918, Willis Jefferson Polk (1867–1924).

Although the glass curtain wall was heralded as something new in the 1950s, Polk had pioneered the all-glass façade almost 40 years earlier with results that still command awe and admiration.

The Curtain Wall
Outer, load-bearing walls essentially became superfluous once cast-iron, then later steel, framing was perfected. Only then, when the outside walls were no longer needed for support, was it conceivable to extend the dimensions of a building's windows until they occupied the whole façade.

This method of constructing a skeleton with its "skin" conveniently independent of its "bones" allowed for non-loadbearing, or curtain walls, to be fabricated in any material, including glass. The greatest benefit of this advancement is that, since it is the skeleton and not the outer walls that holds up the floors, the building is now able to rise to just about any height (see page 202).

The first multi-story, iron-framed, fireproof, curtain-walled building in the world was the St. Ouen Docks warehouse in Paris, designed by Hippolyte Fontaine in 1864–65.

The Hallidie Building (above) was the first building in the United States with a fully glazed, non-loadbearing outer wall. The entire façade of the seven-story building is glass with the exception of four bands of superimposed cast-iron decoration and its fire escapes. The structure of the building is set back about three feet from the glass. Attached to the outer edge of the floor slabs at every third horizontal mullion is a mullion which carries the glass.

Paper Architecture

It is characteristic of much of the architecture of the last century to be disseminated, in print, in visionary—unbuilt—form and still have a profound impact worldwide.

Mies van der Rohe himself first became known to the general public through the publication of a number of visionary projects. Among them were the Glass Skyscrapers of 1919 and 1921. Mies would wait 30 yeras to realize his vision in glass and steel.

The first project was Mies's entry into the Friedrichstrasse competition and was exhibited in Berlin's City Hall in 1922. The second was exhibited at the annual Berlin Art Exhibition, also in 1922. Both were then repeatedly published in journals, both avant-garde and professional, including the Journal of the American Institute of Architects (1923), G (1924), Merz ((1924), and L'Architecture Vivante (1925). They also appeared in numerous books published in the '20s including Walter Gropius's Internationale Architektur (1925). Theo van Doesburg invited Mies to exhibit the two projects in the De Stijl exhibition in Paris in 1923. Mies also published a number of articles of his own such as "Hoch-häusser" (Skyscraper).

free-standing monuments [such as Lever House and Seagram] have shown us we cannot define a civil space with glass screens and banks of fluorescent fixtures." He said that the 58-story Pan Am Building was about to deal Park Avenue its "death blow" by blocking the view and denying "the continuity of the Avenue beyond Grand Central." It would thereby "deprecate the length of the Avenue's axis of movement and smother its scale."[6]

Richard Roth, one of the team of architects responsible for the Pan Am Building, shed some light on the problem when he said,

"Architecture mirrors the society in which we live. Why don't we admit that we are living in [a society] controlled by money and the tax structure? In our economy, the architect designs to his client's specifications. Unless the architect is among the lucky few who have corporate tenant clients—(as opposed to speculative builders)—and our firm is not—then the client's specifications are controlled by the law of supply and demand. Because our clients are in the business of renting space, they demand maximum working area and optimum working conditions. A glass and metal façade costs less, and these facts are important to our clients even though the skin of a 20-story building may account for only 1/2 of 1% of its total cost."[7]

Other glass boxes of originality and beauty have certainly been designed and constructed since these and they have been recognized as such. But one has to look beyond the category to appreciate their qualities and to learn from them. In 1954 Lewis Mumford wrote even more glowingly about Gordon Bunshaft's Manufacturers Trust Building in New York than he did of his Lever House two years earlier. He says that the bank

above: Project for Friedrichstrasse, Berlin.
Cover of the magazine G, no. 3, Berlin, June 1924.

left: Glass Skyscraper, 1920–21. Unrealized project.
Montage with photograph of model.

building "is perhaps as complete a fusion of rational thinking and humane imagination as we are capable of producing today. If you reject it, you reject many of the notable excellences of our age."[8]

What is different about the four buidings here? They all use innovative engineering and manufacturing technologies that in every case have become industry standards, yet there is nothing standard about these structures. Each is unique, well designed, well made; they are none of them pressed from a mold. They have been much imitated but never duplicated. What is singular about each of them remains singular. Their imitators have only borrowed a semblance of their style.

Equitable

In 1948 Pietro Belluschi built administrative headquarters for the Equitable Savings and Loan Association in Portland, Oregon. A reinforced-concrete frame sheathed in a skin of glass and aluminum, it was the first time these materials were used together to clad a tall building.

The Equitable Building derives much of its elegance from the interplay of its sleek industrial materials, its limpid coloration, and variations on otherwise standard modules. Though he took pride in himself as an innovator and at least verbally eschewed historical references, Belluschi certainly paid homage to the Chicago School in his structure's fine proportions. The lower story was enlarged to form a base, the uppermost horizontal element was increased in height to form a crown. The structural bays of its interior are revealed on its exterior. From the placement and proportions of its windows to the relation of the building to its site the building can be said to be truly Sullivanesque.

Lake Shore Drive

Mies van der Rohe designed the blue-black, steel and glass Lake Shore Drive Apartments in Chicago for developer Herbert S. Greenwald. "860," as the twin towers would affectionately be called, would become one of the most influential projects in the last half of the 20th Century.

Mies's American structures are collaborations between his

What in the World?
The glass curtain wall signified modernity just about everywhere. Some 17 countries from around the globe were represented in the INTERNATIONAL STYLE EXHIBITION of 1932. A number of the structures shown had curtain walls of glass.

Six structures from Czechoslovakia alone reflect the solid reputation that the country had since the 1920s for highly accomplished and progressive architecture. One of the structures exhibited was the Bata Shoe Shop by Ludvik Kysela.

A simple building of the sort that became almost routine in European cities over the next three-quarters of a century, the Shoe Shop must have been a revelation at the time. Its very clarity makes it as special today as when it was built. This clarity is achieved by facing the seven-floor concrete structure with a wall of what is as far as possible sheer glass, offset by minimal bands of white opaque glass. As evening falls, the building lights up in contrasting layers of clear and milky tungsten and fluorescent. The company had its own design and architecture department with whom Kysela worked very closely.

The Bata shop has become an icon of modern design; a benchmark for much of the architecture that followed.

a sense of proportion

121

The Bata Shoe Shop, Prague, Czechoslovakia, 1929. Ludvik Kysela (1883–1960), architect.
The caption that accompanies the image of the store in
the *International Style Exhibition* catalogue says,
"The window frames are light; the spandrels are unusually thin.
The lettering is both unarchitectural in character and inharmonius in scale."

Trouble in Paradise?

In his masterpiece PLAYTIME, the French actor-director Jacques Tati takes pot shots at what he sees as the vacuousness of our modern urban existence. "PLAYTIME is a gloriously funny movie about a Paris so modern it does not yet exist," writes Vincent Canby, "a Paris composed entirely of streets like our Avenue of the Americas, hemmed in by efficiently beautiful glass-and-steel towers in which, if we are quick about it, we may see momentary reflections of Sacre Coeur, the Arch of Triumph, or the Eiffel Tower."

Rightly called "one of the keystones of modern filmmaking," PLAYTIME developed a revolutionary approach to narrative structure and cinemagraphic space and presents a humorous but lucid comment on modern architecture. Tati accomplishes this with a cinematic space that rivals the qualities of the subject it attacks. In fact his cinematic art is so adroit as to confound his contemporaries as much as do the objects of his barbed drolleries. He was accused of coming "dangerously close to boredom," or making "serious doodles."

Continuing some of the themes of the earlier films, PLAYTIME portrays modern architecture and technology gone haywire and out of control. It sends up just about everything from the modern airport to the urban street, from fast-food stands to traffic jams, from apartment dwelling to restaurants to the workplace.

original concepts of the '20s and the developing technologies of the '50s and '60s. He wrapped the Lake Shore Drive Apartments in more steel when the code demanded that the original steel skeleton be clad in concrete fireproofing. Fundamentalists have never forgiven him for what they perceive as an artifice, but the results are what counts—the skeleton is revealed after all.

Lever House

Working for the partnership of Skidmore, Owings & Merrill, Gordon Bunshaft designed a new kind of office building for the Lever Brothers. When Lever House opened in New York City in 1952, *New York Times* critic Aline Louchheim wrote,

"Lever House is beautiful as well as functional: it uses the visual possibilities of disciplined, formal architecture for emotional appeal. Clients who recognized the public relations value of a building of distinction were intelligent enough to hire and encourage architects who could meet their challenge."[9]

Shortly thereafter, writing for *The New Yorker*, Lewis Mumford said,

"Lever House is a building of outstanding qualities, mechanical, aesthetic, human, and it breaks with traditional office buildings in two remarkable respects—it has been designed not for maximum rentability but for maximum efficiency in the dispatch of business, and it has used to the full all the means now available for making a building comfortable, gracious, and handsome."[10]

Seagram

Mies van der Rohe went to New York City and built a luxurious masterpiece for Canadian distiller Seagram Limited. The Seagram Building was markedly different from any other previous New York skyscraper. It stood back from busy Park Avenue, creating an open urban space before it.

No corners were cut when it came to the Seagram project,

From the very beginning cracks began to appear in the culture of uniformity as portrayed in literature and film. The flip-side of a corporate culture based on standardization was portrayed as an endless nightmare. Progress certainly begins to come apart in the films of Jacques Tati. above: Behind the scenes: a set with scaled-down, moveable skyscraper mock-ups.
left: M. Hulot (Jacques Tati) surveys "the open plan," searching in vain for his business partner.

particularly in the choice of materials. When initially asked what materials he liked, Samuel Bronfman answered, "Bronze and marble." Mies said, "Fine."

In March of 1957 the average American was treated to in-depth coverage of a "Master Architect" in LIFE magazine. Amongst eight pages of photographs of burnished bronze beams ready to be shipped off to New York and molten glass being poured for Seagram's windows were these words describing Mies's relationship to his materials:

> "The demands of Mies's advanced designs have pushed U.S. industry to keep pace technologically. To achieve a lighter, more waterproof 'skin' to cover the 'bones' of his buildings' steel skeletons, the aluminum industry was forced to fabricate aluminum beams long, straight and strong enough to hold and brace the expanses of glass. To cut down sky glare, a manufacturer was goaded into developing subtly tinted glass for Mies's transparent walls. To accommodate Mies's desire to use bronze for the skin of the Seagram building to New York, a metal company produced a chemically weathered alloy.
> "These innovations are accepted matter-of-factly by Mies. 'In our work,' he says, 'we don't have a grand idea, a dream, and then try to glue it together. . . . We just solve problems.'"[11]

Pietro Belluschi, Gordon Bunshaft, and Mies van der Rohe—each in his own way—rendered the forms, the materials, and the rhythms of modern urban existence into a sublime language of nuance and subtlety. Meanwhile, their imitators reduced this language to an oppressive repetition that resulted in a mundane, alienating monotony.

Merely repeating another's forms is no way to understand a language.

above: Once the largest commercial building in the world, the Pan Am Building accommodates a permanent building population of 17,000 people.
right: For some, the "XYZ Buildings," as they are disparagingly called, represent the logical outcome of standardization.

Pushing the Envelope
The Pan Am Building (now the Met Life Building) is probably the world's most detested skyscraper. Its immense bulk and height dominates and completely overshadows the former New York Central Building immediately to the north, which was designed by Warren & Westmore as part of the "Terminal City" complex of which Grand Central Terminal was the centerpiece. By shrouding a cherished building in its shadows, it was felt that the Pan Am Building had desecrated a major icon of the city. The building will never recover from this contemptible slight on such a prominent site.

From the outset the developer felt uncomfortable with the modesty of the original designs. Convinced that such an important site demanded something more, he asked Richard Roth to suggest a few possible design collaborators. Roth suggested Walter Gropius, who in turn suggested Pietro Belluschi.

When completed, the 2.4-million square-foot building became the world's largest office building in bulk. The final product was far from popular: Ada Louise Huxtable of The New York Times, for example, described it as a "colossal collection of minimums" and "gigantically second-rate."

If the building's innovative form was unappreciated, its lack of fine detailing has not gone unnoticed either. Whatever its merits, the building's form was further compromised by poor workmanship and shoddy, unattractive materials.

This image of an airplane serves as the frontispiece for ART AND THE MACHINE: AN ACCOUNT OF INDUSTRIAL DESIGN IN 20TH CENTURY AMERICA (1936). *The book's authors, Sheldon and Martha Cheney, call for the recognition of "a new art, existent in machine-made mass products: industrial design. It is not an esoteric and precious manifestation but a practical expression embodied in utilitarian forms increasingly familiar in the daily life of the average person."*

The caption under the photo reads, "Sources of idioms of machine-made art: streamline, long hard edge, sheer surface, and repetition of simple motives, as seen in an airplane." The Cheneys could very well be describing the Equitable Building.

Equitable Savings and Loan • Portland, Oregon

In the early 1940s architects were already speculating about postwar building. A great deal of thought was given to how wartime mass production methods and substitute building materials could be applied to future undertakings. Working through the mediums of museums, stores, and popular publications, architects offered up their predictions about the future.

Some of the most innovative designs for postwar building sought to take advantage of advances in aluminum and plastic manufacturing techniques that had resulted from building aircraft. The wartime growth of the aircraft and aluminum industries led to proposals for structures that would use the same tools, techniques, and workers that had built airplanes during the war.

For a special issue in May 1943 called "New Buildings for 194X," *Architectural Forum* asked a group of invited architects to propose a range of building types for a hypothetical city of moderate size, specifically focusing on the exploration of new uses of existing technology.

In his response, Pietro Belluschi of Portland, Oregon, designed a high-rise office slab raised up on stilts, set back on a lot to allow for a low, two-story retail building and landscaped court. It would seem to foreshadow Lever House in its site plan, though in fact it was based on a recently published proposal for a retail complex by Morris Ketcham.

Though there wasn't much new on the face of it, what was most interesting about the project was Belluschi's use of new technology. He recommended aluminum for structural members as well as exterior cladding. To minimize heat loss he employed double-paned, sealed windows. He utilized indi-

Photographed right after it opened in 1948, the Equitable Building shows its materials and fine proportions to supreme effect. Belluschi said, "I think that plastic and aluminum and other materials of that kind which lend themselves to be worked, just like the automobile . . . offer the greatest opportunity and the greatest change in the future."[1]

Pietro Belluschi *(1899-1994) came to the United States as an exchange student from Italy in 1923. He was trained as an engineer at the University of Rome and earned a degree in civil engineering at Cornell University. After working in the office of A. E. Doyle in Portland, Oregon, he became an associate; the office later reorganized in his name. Although his Equitable Savings and Loan Building was recognized as a pioneering structure, it's the more than 40 churches he designed in his Northwest style, influenced by Japanese wooden vernacular, that earned him an international reputation. He later served as Dean of MIT's School of Architecture and Planning, the nation's oldest, from 1951 to 1965. He was widely known as an educator during this period, writing and lecturing frequently. But, he continued his architectural practice, doing most of the work at a drafting board at his Back Bay home.*

Belluschi's work ranged from elegantly simple structures at the start of his career to such massive urban skyscrapers as the Pan Am Building in New York City and the Bank of America in San Francisco. He participated in the design of more than 1,000 buildings in all, among them the Juilliard School of Music and Alice Tully Hall in New York, which were done in association with a colleague from MIT, Eduardo F. Catalano.

Involved in the Lincoln Center project from the first, Belluschi was picked by Wallace K. Harrison who coordinated the team of six. Philip Johnson was politic and stated, "The six of us may have different ideas but we're united." Belluschi put it more bluntly when he said, "We hang together or we hang separately." Belluschi was respected for his seriousness of purpose. He brought a humanist view to the team.

vidual, standardized air-conditioning units set under windows. He included acoustical paneling, fluorescent lighting, and radiant heating. Realizing that the problem of cleaning the windows of flush-surfaced buildings had not been adequately solved, he proposed a window-washing apparatus that would be suspended from the roof, running on a track around the periphery.

Belluschi would incorporate many of these ideas in the Equitable Building after the war.

During the war's early years, Belluschi met J. Paul Raven, head of the Bonneville Dam Administration, the producer of the hydroelectric power on which the Kaiser Aluminum Company depended for the production of the metal used in the aircraft industry. Raven was fervently looking for peacetime uses for the large quantities of aluminum being produced for the war effort. With this in mind, Belluschi began looking into its potential architectural uses.

The Equitable Savings and Loan Association Building was the first large-scale postwar commission of the Belluschi office. Equitable had acquired the remaining portion of the half city block it occupied in the downtown business district. With progress halted by the war, it was awaiting the release of building materials to begin construction. Once the war ended, Ralph Cake, the president of Equitable, was eager to move ahead on the new building.

Ralph Cake proved to be the ideal client. He had an enterprising mind and an assertive nature. He also possessed an eagerness to explore new uses of advanced technology, and he took risks. Cake and Belluschi worked well together. They shared a keen business sense, a driving ambition, and each respected the other; the most progressive ideas for the building were the results of their brainstorming.

Cake had gone before the War Production Board in Washington to get an early easement on building restrictions; he was one of the first to gain approval of a nonmilitary use

above: The St. Philip Neri Catholic Church, Pietro Belluschi, Portland, 1946–1952, was inspired by the simple early Christian basilicas of his native Italy.
left: Seated left to right in front of a model of Lincoln Center are the full design team: Wallace K. Harrison, Philip Johnson, Pietro Belluschi, Eero Saarinen, Max Abramovitz, and Gordon Bunshaft.

of structural materials. In January 1945, well before peace was declared, he gave Belluschi the go-ahead to proceed with the preliminary drawings.

In the fall of 1945 Belluschi went before the Building Code Board of Appeals to request a variance for the use of aluminum facing. Negotiations began with two glass companies on manufacturing the oversized glass. And, their consulting mechanical engineer, Donald Kroeker, was brought in to design the innovative reverse-cycle heat and air-conditioning system. When the building permit was finally approved, construction documents were ready.

In January 1946, the original Equitable Building was demolished and construction begun. The new building was completed in January 1948. It was the first major high-rise to go up in Portland since the late 1920s and the first major corporate tower to be built in the country after the war.

The building was a major event. The technological advances alone made it exciting: Kroeker's experimental heat pump heating and cooling system; the specially manufactured over-sized, hermetically sealed, thermopane windows; the utterly flush, tinted glass; and the aluminum skin. A constant stream of out-of-town visitors who learned of the project through the press added another level of excitement. Belluschi's own exuberance was conveyed in his statement to the Appeals Board:

"The design of this new office building for Portland is fundamentally an expression of faith in a great future for our civilization—a faith born out of a conviction that from our modern techniques, materials, and understanding of present-day architectural problems, we are able to create not only more useful buildings, but also a new kind of beauty—a beauty which is not borrowed from the past but is our own—clean, strong, and straightforward."[2]

The Equitable Building's surfaces are absolutely flush—no projecting sills, mold-

The Bayard-Condict Building, New York City, 1897–1899, Louis Sullivan and Lyndon P. Smith
The skeleton is evident in the piers that reach from the ground to the roof. Entirely·clad in ivory-colored terra cotta, this is the only example of Louis Sullivan's work in New York City.

The Chicago Window

Increasing the ratio of glass to the overall surface area of a building's façade was facilitated by the introduction and perfecting of cast-iron and steel framed buildings. The first to do so were the architects of the Chicago School, thus answering the demand for as much natural light as possible for every room in those first large office blocks. With the Reliance Building of Burnham and Root and Sullivan's Carson Pirie Scott department store, 1899 (above), the façade assumes a modular texture, with continuous rows of closely spaced but ample windows.

The "Chicago window," as it was soon called, is a wide, horizontal expanse of glass featuring a large, fixed pane at the center and two operable windows at either end.

The Chicago School architects were well known in Portland. The Carson, Pirie Scott Store was included in a 1946 Portland Art Museum exhibition of Chicago School architecture. The simple, direct expression of the Equitable's structural grid was Belluschi's conscious continuation of the Chicago frame carried to its logical extreme.

CALDER
PAINTER HILL·ROAD
R. F. D. ROXBURY,
CONN., U.S.A.
TEL. & TEL. WOODBURY 122-2

Alexander Calder
(1898–1976) sculpted, painted, and illustrated children's books. His "stabiles" and "mobiles" (sculptures that are either stationary or that move accordingly) can be regarded as a marriage between engineering and sculpture. He worked on two projects for Eero Saarinen: the "dancing fountains" at the General Motors Technical Center [page 186], and a mobile for the TWA Terminal at Idlewild (1962).

Belluschi wrote Calder, whose popularity was widespread as the result of a recent MoMA exhibition in New York, who responded with the sketch of a mobile, together with a cost estimate of $10,000. Recoiling at the sight of the Calder proposal, a whimsical abstraction of yellow shapes suspended from fine thin wires, Ralph Cake categorically rejected it on the grounds that "too many people would ask questions and ridicule the idea, since to the layman there's no purpose to it." Belluschi wrote Calder to apologize. "I too am sorry things have come to naught," Calder responded (above)—"It's too bad I didn't meet Mr. Cake. I might at least have scratched his icing." In the end, Belluschi designed the mural himself, a combination of simple curvilinear forms that was executed by ordinary housepainters for about $50.

Dear Mr. Belluschi I am sorry that things have come to naught —at least for the present— but see no reason why you should apologize.

I certainly do hope to meet you sometime. If you're ever in N.Y. do call us and come out to see us (2½ hrs. drive)

Its too bad I didn't meet Mr. Cake. I might at least have scratched his icing.

Cordially yours
Calder

ings, or decoration—the window glass and the walls are one plane. In order to express the natural properties of the thin aluminum skin, which was no more than 1/4-inch thick, nothing —not a hinge, nor a bolt, nor a rivet —was allowed to project from the surface. The effect is as clean and smooth as the surface of an airplane.

Everywhere, and always, it is remarked that the building's surface is its most remarkable feature. All that MoMA's *Built in the USA* catalogue had to say was, "Glass and aluminum sheathing on this twelve story concrete frame produces a smooth, sparkling façade. No part projects more than seven-eighths of an inch."

The building is undoubtedly sleek and its skin has almost no perceptible differences. Yet, it is the classic proportions of the Equitable's design that are particularly outstanding. It has a refined elegance, a cool crystalline presence, where every deft decision is justified and of a piece with the whole.

The building's 12 stories[3] fall just short of the city's height limit. The rectangular box, 11 bays wide by three bays deep, abuts the street in front and is set back at the rear, with a lower, two-story portion filling the remainder of the lot. The display windows are recessed at the base to expose the structural piers. The reinforced concrete structure made use of a newly developed formula that enhanced its strength, thereby reducing its bulk to the absolute minimum. This gained extra space in upper-story offices and on the street floor, which was used for a bank lobby and retailing. It also meant additional daylight, as interstices of the thin structural frame were filled in with glass, except for a narrow concrete sill required by code.

To preserve the effect of the minimal structural frame, the sills were faced with dark green cast aluminum to distinguish them visually from the silvery sheets of rolled aluminum elsewhere; that way they read as part of the void rather than as solid. With structural members reduced to a bare mini-

A great admirer of Joan Miró, Belluschi wanted to integrate the fine arts at the Equitable. He failed to convince his client to spend the money on abstract art for the main lobby (left); instead Belluschi's own efforts can be seen. Calder's amusing reply aside (above), the incident served to demonstrate the seriousness of the Equitable team's aspirations. They sensed they were doing something momentous and little seemed beyond their reach.

mum and, except for those on the street floor, all clad with a thin veneer of aluminum, the building appears extraordinarily lightweight.

The slender two-story piers at the base are covered in richly grained pink marble in order to provide warmth, texture, and a sense of human scale at the pedestrian level and to give the otherwise lightweight, delicate building a solid grounding at the base.

As a result of the large expanses of glass, the interiors are remarkably light and spacious, albeit spare in their appointments. Belluschi aimed at maximizing the available rentable space while enhancing his client's return on the investment. On Cake's urging, he designed the most comfortable, desirable office spaces possible, in the hopes that they would remain in constant demand.

Anticipating what the postwar tenant would be seeking, Belluschi sought to incorporate the most advanced lighting, year-round air-conditioning, acoustical controls, and flexible as well as distinctively designed interiors possible. The office spaces lined either side of a central corridor, so that they ringed the building and each would have an exterior window—indeed, a wall glass—looking out over the city. The electrically powered reverse-cycle water pump ensured year-round temperature control. Eight-foot low-voltage fluorescent tubes, deliberately exposed for easy access as well as a straightforward, functional look, distributed the light evenly.

The Equitable Building's significance was celebrated immediately. Belluschi himself played an active role in making sure the building was well publicized. The direct expression of the structural frame, the sleek aluminum skin, the progressive mechanical services, the enormous expanse of windows, and the wholly modern proportions, all this came together to make the Equitable one of the most widely acclaimed buildings of the time. On *Architectural Forum's* September 1948 cover, the building was hailed as a new "crystal and metal tower," looking "the way all skyscrapers are really built but few admit," and recognized as a new standard in the design of the office building.

The photo shown in detail on pages 116–117 is seen here as it appeared in *Built in the USA: Post-War Architecture,* the Museum of Modern Art's "report on the best of American architecture today." The 1952 survey was the third in a series, in this case curated by Henry-Russel Hitchcock and Arthur Drexler. It included six of the buildings featured in the present book.

A Smooth Façade

Trained in engineering rather than architecture, Belluschi, like Frank Lloyd Wright, had an intuitive sense about what was structurally possible. He constantly pushed the limits of technology in his search for the perfect form.

The sheer amount of glazing in the Equitable Building was unmatched by any building of comparable size in the country at the time. To get thermopane window glass in the dimensions Belluschi wanted required special manufacturing. Libbey-Owens-Ford refused, saying it could not guarantee it in such large sizes. Pittsburgh Plate Glass finally agreed after Belluschi persisted. He eventually obtained the panes in the proportions he wanted.

Lingering doubts about the soundness of the building were put to test the following year when Portland was struck by an earthquake. As was the case with Wright's Imperial Hotel in Tokyo, the Equitable came through unscathed.

Lake Shore Drive Apartments • Chicago

The first high-rise building designed by Mies van der Rohe after emigrating in 1938 from Berlin to Chicago was the 22-story Promontory Apartments building (1949) on South Shore Drive. Initially conceived with a steel-and-glass curtain wall, it had to be built in reinforced concrete due to the persistence of the wartime steel shortage. Light colored brick panels and aluminum window frames are set into the reinforced concrete frame; the building's façade is emphasized by a series of projecting, stepped back concrete columns. The Promontory Apartments building was altogether modern in its rectilinear profile and Miesian enough in the composition of its façade—windows running above brick panels set slightly behind supporting columns—but little else about it is particularly interesting. The building embodies few if any of the ideas about tall buildings that Mies had been thinking about since the 1920s. It would be his next project, the following year, two 26-story glass and steel apartment towers at 860–880 Lake Shore Drive, that would give him his first opportunity to demonstrate those concepts.

The two apartment towers are rectangular in plan and are located right on Lake Michigan near the city center. They are spaced in such a way and turned at right angles to one another that each apartment gets the best possible view of the lake. Mies constructed each building on a steel skeleton which rose from a 3-by-5, 21-foot-square bay plan. His main objective was to reveal the structural cage as clearly and as forcefully as possible. The supporting columns and the spandrels provide the chief rhythm of the façade. The area enclosed by columns and spandrels and divided by mullions is given over to glass, yielding four aluminum-framed floor-

Each 26-story building is a rectangle in plan in the ratio of 3 to 5 (the heavier structural verticals make this number clear). One building is turned 90 degrees in relation to the other and set back behind its neighbor a distance equal to that of two bays.

The buildings appear to float two stories above the ground, particularly when lit at night.

to-ceiling windows in each bay. The windows, higher than they are wide, together with the mullions, accentuate the verticality of the buildings. The black plate steel construction stands out in relief against the continuous glass surface of the façades with their background of uniformly gray curtains and aluminum window frames. The steel I-beams welded to the surface of the towers appear to change in density, depending on the angle at which the buildings are viewed.

In traditional apartment buildings, the design of the facade, the composition of its surface elements, was the priority. In "860," as these buildings are affectionately called, the *construction* was the design priority: first structure, then mullions and windows—working from the inside to the outside—the architecture evolved in the sequence of construction.

Revealing the skeleton on the outside of a building is not necessarily an important, nor even an interesting idea. For Mies, it was a symbolic disclosure of his belief in the freedom it afforded the building's occupants. He said, "It makes rational production possible and yet permits total freedom of disposition on the interior." Mies had already made use of this conviction in his apartment block in Stuttgart, Germany, in 1927, and he saw the struggle for "new housing as an element of the larger struggle for new forms of living."[1]

Once the steel skeletons of 860 were erected, the prefabricated façade elements—each two stories in height and one structural bay in width—were lifted by cranes into position and welded on the spot. The aluminum windows were then installed from the interior. Mies' concern that the perpendicular I-beams should be reassembled in exactly the same order that they left the rolling mills, to exclude even the smallest errors of measurement, reflected both his own perfectionism and the logic of his design.

Mies refined his iconography as he went. The attached I-beam had the practical advantage of strengthening the mullions, thus stiffening each bay frame, but Mies himself said he employed it

primarily because without it the building "did not look right." Its purpose, then, like the famous IIT corner, was more aesthetic than functional, and his continued reliance on it for the remainder of his career signified that it had become a prime symbol for the transcendence of technology into architecture—prose into poetry.

In an interview Mies gave two reasons for applying the I-beams to the surface of his structure, both of which show that there is nothing decorative about this act. The first represents a poetic, but none-the-less real gesture, the need to express the building's verticality. The other reason demonstrates how there turned out to be two additional functions for the I-beams; we just have to ask what those functions are. Throughout the course of the interview, however, he continues to come back to the first reason as the real reason.

"It was very important to preserve and extend the rhythm which the mullions set up on the rest of the building," he told the interviewer. "We looked at it on the model without the steel I-beams attached to the corner columns and it did not look right. That is the real reason. Now the other reason is that the steel I-beams were needed to stiffen the plates which cover the columns so these plates could not ripple, and also we needed the I-beams for strength when the sections were hoisted into place. Now of course, that's a very good reason—but the other one is the real reason!"[2]

The mullions at 860 are made of commercially available standard 8" wide-flange steel. The standard steel sections were simply attached to the exterior frame. They are not customized for any special condition imposed by the overall design, but rather manufactured as independent elements for general use. Mies was always excited by the prospect of deriving his proportions from standardized elements.

The ground floor area of each tower is even with grade, walled with glass—clear for the lobby and opaque for the service area—and set back behind the supporting columns with the effect that an arcaded walkway surrounds the base. A steel-framed one-story-high canopy runs from the south face of 880 to the north face of 860. The form of this con-

Soaring Skeletal Frames

While the buildings at Lake Shore Drive are steel-framed, the Chicago building code required that they be fireproofed with two inches of concrete all around. To avoid an unacceptable visual condition and to "express the skeleton" Mies finished all his concrete-covered columns and beams with black steel plate, and then welded onto these, vertical I-beam rails eight inches deep, which soar up from the second floor of the building to the roof line 250 feet above.

Only one in every four of these regularly spaced mullions conceals a broader, load-bearing support. The two outer windows of each field are thus always somewhat narrower than their central neighbors.

During the construction of the façade four-window units were assembled on the roof and fastened from above from column to column. The windows themselves were inserted from the inside.

Mies said, "Only skyscrapers under construction reveal their bold constructive thoughts, and then the impression made by their soaring skeletal frames is overwhelming. . . . On the other hand, when the structure is covered with masonry this impression is destroyed and the constructive character denied. . . . We must not try to solve new problems with traditional forms: it is far better to derive new forms from the essence, the very nature of the new problems."[3]

Neue Grafik
New Graphic Design
Graphisme actuel

The Grid

The photograph above appears in the classic graphic design text TYPOGRAPHIE *by the eminent Swiss type designer and teacher Emil Ruder (1914–1970). Director of the School of Applied Arts in Basle, Ruder left a significant mark on the art of typography in mid-century. Ruder's caption reads, "This detail of the façade of an apartment house in Chicago designed by Mies van der Rohe reveals the beauty of technology and construction. The steel framed building produces its effect by the principle of its construction and makes no claim to be organic."*

Ruder's sensibility reflected the International Typographic Style, also known as the Swiss style, which developed in Switzerland after World War II. Built upon the foundations of Constructivism, De Stijl, the Bauhaus, and the New Typography of the 1930s, the Swiss Style sought to present complex information in a highly structured and uniform manner.

The publication of the Swiss journal NEW GRAPHIC DESIGN *in 1959 provided an influential platform for leading exponents of the style to disseminate their philosophy. In 1957 the Swiss Type Foundry issued* HELVETICA, *a sans serif typeface designed by Max Miedinger and Edouard Hoffman, which soon became internationally ubiquitous. The late 1970s increasingly identified the International Typographic Style with a corporate style of design, particularly in the U.S.*

The titles of each chapter in this book were set in Helvetica.

necting element is repeated in the canopies that project over the entrances to both buildings.

There are four apartments to each floor in one building, eight to a floor in the other. Elevators are placed in a central core so that all apartments have outer windows. The buildings are equipped with a hot water heating system at the perimeter and in the ceiling plenum. The plenum heating keeps the floor warm and very comfortable The perimeter heating, however, is not adequate for many apartments. Fifty years ago when technologies were yet to be developed, buildings were perceived as static objects and these shortcomings were acceptable standards.

A few alterations were imposed on Mies's first plans before the buildings were approved by Greenwald and his financial partners. Budgetary restrictions kept Mies from installing the central air-conditioning he had recommended, and his open plan in the apartments was changed to a more cubicular arrangement in consideration of the traditional preference of closing off rooms for privacy. The financing agent considered the original open plans, which recalled the Barcelona Pavilion, too daring; he felt the small rooms of the traditional apartment block would sell better. This now changed the relationship between the exterior and the interior. It also so disturbed Mies's sense of what constitutes good living that he thought long and hard for quite some time before deciding not to quit the project.

He was finally convinced that the exterior was worth it. With the completion of these two apartment towers Mies took a long step in adjusting his architecture to American conditions without compromising its philosophical basis. Several of his old dreams were fulfilled: for one, a tall building in steel, its form deriving from the structure—a derivation he had

above left: Emil Ruder's Typographie represents what was once the style of choice. In fact, there was no other choice.
above inset: The cover of the September 1958 issue of Neue Grafik magazine (New Graphic Design) by Carlo L. Vivarelli (1919–). Swiss graphic standards, once ubiquitous, are still the style in New York City subway signage.

never carried out in detail before, even on paper; for another, a work whose reduction to structural essence expressed the aspiration to universality he had associated with the modern sensibility. And, the towers were consonant with the technology which he had come to identify with.

In his own yearning to be rational—not to mention magisterial—he did little to correct the public impression that he was the purist of rationalists. Very likely because in the U.S. he was a teacher, not just a practicing architect, he talked increasingly about objectivity and reason after 1940 and less about spirit. But, a major element of "spirit" for Mies was aesthetic, and it is art, not reason, that most distinguishes 860, generations after it was built, from the depressing multitude of buildings by other architects who sought to emulate what they presumed to be its ineluctable logic. The excellence of 860 lies in the sensitive relationships of width to height in the windows, spandrel to column, and bay to facade, not to mention the powerful thrust and careful detailing of the connecting canopy and the secure placement of one building mass relative to the other.

Pushing the glass back behind the I-beams accomplished something else to Mies's liking besides revealing the building's skeleton—something very poetic. There is a constant play of light and shadow across the façades that exemplifies his fascination with the transformation of form. Another aspect of alchemical change occurs as we move around the structures; the blades of the I-beams alternatively reveal and conceal, turning each plane from transparent, to opaque and back again, depending on one's point of view. This temporality, built into the life of the buildings, gives them an animate existence.

He may later be best known for the Seagram Building, but no other buildings by Mies had as strong an impact on his contemporaries as 860, and their influence would forever impact modern architecture itself. In Richard Neutra's article on 860 in *Architectural Record* in 1956, he wrote, "The Lake Shore Drive Towers appeared like the wonderful conclusion of a lifelong aspiring formation of ideas."[4]

One of the benefits of the construction technique used in the Lake Shore Drive Apartments is that the windows go from wall-to-wall and from floor to ceiling. Given the location of the building this is one of it's most attractive assets.

The angling of the buildings places them as close to the lake as possible. The offset relation of one to the other insures optimal views from every apartment that faces the water.

The sensation upon entering one of the lake-front apartments is that of hovering in the space between water and sky, an experience that has made them some of the most desirable apartments in all of Chicago.

Mies insured a uniform look to the exterior of the buildings by insisting on identical, off-white draperies in every apartment. These hangings show to the outside. Behind them draperies of the tenants' own choosing, visible only from within, could be installed.

above: This artful photo from *LIFE* magazine demonstrates how "this glass and steel structure . . . provides an abundance of daylight, but tenants can pull drapes to shut out the sun and their neighbors' view."
right: Drawn in 1958 for *Architectural Record* by Alan Dunn, the cartoon's caption reads: "Oh, Mr. Mies! Tenant on the 34th floor brought his own window shades!"

LIFE *magazine reported that taxi drivers and pedestrians slowed as they passed Lever House. A writer from* Business Week *admired a new kind of working environment where it was "hard to tell whether you're in a modern office building or a resort hotel." Eero Saarinen said,*

"Gordon Bunshaft, who is chiefly responsible for the design, should be covered with laurels because he has created one of the finest buildings of our times."

In 1964, the architectural historian John Jacobus assessed Lever House as "so successful that by the end of the 1950s, imitations of this specific office block could be found in London, Copenhagen, Caracas, and elsewhere."[1]

Lever House • New York City

In 1952 Lewis Mumford wrote, with uncharacteristic praise, about a newly opened glass and steel corporate office building:

" . . . throngs of people, waiting patiently in great queues in the lobby, demanded admission so insistently that the elevator system, designed to handle only Lever Brothers' office staff of twelve hundred employees and a normal complement of visitors, was severely overtaxed. People acted as if this was the eighth wonder of the world, this house of glass approached through an open forecourt that is paneled with glistening marble, punctuated by columns encased in stainless steel, and embellished by a vast bed of flowers and—last touch of elegance against the greenish-blue windows and the bluish-green spandrels of the glassy building that rises above it—a weeping-willow tree."[2]

Writing five months earlier, Aline Louchheim said of Lever House,

"This building, which carries to a new point of refinement the Le Corbusier-Mies van der Rohe style of steel skeleton with glass curtain wall, is the most handsome and best example of modern architecture in New York."[3]

Why were these discriminating critics expressing such adulation for the type of structure that would later be disparagingly labeled a glass box?

Louchheim gives her answer in her very next sentence: "Standing luxuriously in space and sparkling like some sea-colored jewel, it is our one building which takes full esthet-

The stainless steel and blue-green glass Lever House was considered daring in 1952 in that it occupied only 25 percent of the space allowed by New York City's building code. Another one of its innovative features is the shopless plaza at street level made possible by raising the first floor of the building on thin columns.

SOM

Louis Skidmore and Nathaniel A. Owings joined forces as consultants for the Chicago World's Fair in 1933 and formalized their partnership in 1936. Skidmore set up the New York office the following year and worked on the New York World's Fair in 1939. That year they invited architect-engineer John O. Merrill to join them. Early on they offered clients a diversity of services on a very large scale.

Other partners were added in 1949 including Gordon Bunshaft. Together they perfected a new building type—the modern, all-glass corporate headquarters—a style for which the firm would become internationally renowned.

Lewis Mumford praised the company that could finally master the promising possibilities of glass:

" . . . among the architects who have done most to put the idea [of building in glass] to practical use—Philip Johnson in his own house, in New Canaan; Mies van der Rohe in the Lake Shore Drive Apartments, in Chicago; Frank Lloyd Wright in the S.C. Johnson & Son's Laboratory, in Racine, Wisconsin—none has done more than the firm of Skidmore, Owings & Merrill. In the Manufacturers Trust, they have followed up their Lever House with a quite different mode of design, and in the course of executing it they have pointed up many of the possibilities of glass, both structurally and aesthetically."[4]

ic as well as practical advantage of modern means of construction." And, Mumford says, " . . .it is the first office building in which modern materials, modern construction, modern functions have been combined with a modern plan."

As with any innovative project, Lever House depended on a client willing to take risks. In this case the client was Charles Luckman, an architect who during the 1930s had practiced with some distinction in the Midwest as partner of William Pereira before becoming a Lever salesman during the Depression; he was now President of Lever Brothers. Jervis J. Babb, a Lever executive, and eventually Luckman's successor, was also sympathetic to the project and played an important role in its development. Babb had been drawn to modern architecture while serving as Vice President of the S.C. Johnson Company, in Racine (page 38).

From the beginning there was discussion about a glass slab—something clear and clean. SOM showed Luckman a transparent plastic sketch model for a site Lever Brothers was considering in Chicago. Nathaniel Owings might have also shown his 1947 drawing for a slab building on a plaza. Luckman himself made no design proposals. He simply asked for a distinguished building devoted entirely to 800 to 1,000 Lever employees and their services. He wanted something that looked new, clean, spectacular, and American; in other words, like Lever's products.

New York was eventually chosen for the company headquarters since, according to Lever officials, "the price one pays for soap is 89 percent advertising . . . and the advertising agencies of America were there."

Once in New York the architects had to follow the zoning regulations, which required office buildings that occupied more than 25 percent of their sites to be set back according to a formula that produced the city's famous "wedding cake" skyscrapers (page 144).

The architects really wanted to avoid setbacks. After several months' study of the client's requirements, Gordon Bunshaft, the associate now in charge of the project, proposed something remarkable: a rectangular slab that covered

above: Nathaniel Owings, John Merrill, Loius Skidmore, J. Walter Severinghaus, Gordon Bunshaft, and Walter Hartman at an SOM partners' meeting in 1953.
left: Lewis Mumford's comment about Bunshaft's Manufacturers Trust Building [New York, 1954] is equally true of the best glass boxes: "This building is essentially a glass lantern, and, like a lantern, it is even more striking by dark than by daylight."

only a quarter of the site, rising above a second floor element that rested on stilts and surrounded the perimeter of the site at the south.

Had the site been developed in a conventional fashion, it could easily have supported a bigger building: as built, Lever House was equal only to an eight-story building covering the entire site. The proportions of the slender, 53-foot-wide slab took advantage of the provision in the zoning ordinance which stipulated that a tower of unlimited height could be built without setbacks provided the footprint of the tower occupied no more than one-quarter of the site's area at the tower's base. The relatively small size of the tower floors was much more humane for the workers, who had unlimited access to light and views. In fact, the building is narrow enough inside to enable one to see from one side to the other. This was in marked contrast to postwar trends. SOM could only pull this off because Lever Brothers chose to be the sole tenant in its building.

As *Architectural Forum* explained when the design of Lever House was released:

> "With space-starved tenants ready to pay $5 a ft. for offices 90 ft. deep, why worry whether the deepest areas were really worth building and paying their way? . . . Overnight New York forgot the vision given substance by Rockefeller Center . . . . Promoters bade their architects fill every inch of the city's lop-sided zoning envelope in typical pre-Rockefeller Center fashion. . . . Now at last [with Lever House] New York is getting a fine office building that carries on from Rockefeller Center, a tower built on pride and the desire to build a name rather than the chance for a quick profit."[5]

Equally remarkable was the client's insistence that there be no retail shops at the street level. During the planning stages, Louis Skidmore, doubting the owner's willingness to forgo tenant income, prepared an alternative design with some shops. Luckman rejected the scheme immediately, saying that Skidmore had destroyed the project's best idea.

The Garden That Never Was
When Gordon Bunshaft commissioned Isamu Noguchi to design a garden for Lever House the building was already under construction and a design for the ground floor existed. Noguchi presented a concept of a "marble stage" that would "float" above the courtyard with planting beds flush with its surface, a reflecting pool, and sculptures rising from it. The whole was conceived as a freestanding sculpture. The remainder of the ground floor was to be treated as an informal seating area. The group of three columns he conceived as a "family," an idea he would later realize in his garden for the Connecticut General Life Insurance Company Building (SOM, 1956–57). The design was rejected. He submitted revision after revision, including a proposal that used one of his studies of Brancusi's "Endless Column." Although Noguchi's efforts came to nought on this project, he managed to recycle some of the ideas in later works. And, while the project went unrealized, it established the groundwork for an ongoing collaborative relationship between Noguchi and Bunshaft.

above: Lever Brothers Garden, unrealized project by Isamu Noguchi, model, 1952. When a garden design by Isamu Noguchi was abandoned, Aline Louchheim was disappointed: "This spectator longs for some organic enlivening shapes to play a counterpoint with the rectilinear regularity of the building and to make dynamic transitions from arcade to lobby and from the street level, through the open well, to the cafeteria terraces."[6]

Packaging Lever's Interiors

Raymond Loewy's interiors met with mixed reactions. Critics were particularly divided over the use of color.

Whereas Lewis Mumford said:

"To offset the bluish light from the exterior, a grayish beige was chosen as the basic color for desks and floors. (Even the elevator boys are dressed in dark beige.) But against that background a great variety of colors has been introduced. Each floor has its own color scheme, from brisk yellows and delicate blues to a combination-on the floor devoted to the firm's cosmetics-of boudoir pink and eyeshadow lavender. I don't know any other building in the city in which so much color has been used with such skill and charm over such a large area. Both our school architects and our equally timid hospital architects have something to learn from this."

Aline Louchheim said,

"The interiors were designed by Raymond Loewy, long associated with Lever Brothers and responsible for its commercially successful product packaging. For me the interior décor is too obtrusive for a building where the view is an insistent and fascinating feature. Moreover, I found some of the thirty-one color accents which play against the pleasant tan of the walls and standard office equipment disturbingly intense and frequently used without apparent decorative, much less architectural, logic."

The decision to keep the ground floor of Lever House open was carefully considered in both architectural and in public relations terms. When asked about this decision by a writer from *The New Yorker*, a Lever Brothers spokesman stated that "the trees and flowers were more important than any quick return on some shops." Not only was the ground floor largely reserved for public use—even the glassed-in lobby was to function as an exhibition hall during building hours—but, the planted rooftop of the horizontal slab was also to be a recreational and visual amenity for the building's workers.

Everything made good economic sense, too. According to Lever Brothers, the building returned 4 million dollars worth of advertising when the building cost 7 million. Lever House became a model for new commercial buildings. Meanwhile, the architects assumed the leading position in the area of corporate architecture.

The shopless lobby emphasizes the building as Lever's alone and preserves the illusion of a floating form, one of the design's most appealing features. The glass-enclosed lobby, with a planter bed that runs from the courtyard through the wall, blurs the distinction between the inside and the outside. The flow of space from enclosure to openness is reinforced by continuous pavement lines from lobby to courtyard and to the surrounding sidewalk, a formula widely adopted elsewhere since. The columns appear to be especially slender since, other than insulation and crisply contoured stainless-steel cladding, no ductwork surrounds them. With 75 percent of its area devoted to pedestrian passage and planting, the ground floor made a strong impression on the public.

Lever House is notable for several technological innovations. It was one of the first office buildings to

Lewis Mumford said, "Just as a sensible farmer designs his cow stalls around his cow, the fundamental unit around which Lever House's hundred and thirty thousand square feet of floor space was designed was the desk." The light wells resemble Loewy's soap designs. In India and Pakistan the vivid green and yellow of Rexona toilet soap is as widely recognised as the red of Coca Cola.

offer a complete air-conditioning system in an entirely sealed building in a very thin envelope. To cut down on the use of elevators and office boys, a vertical and a horizontal correspondence conveyer which links all floors was installed. To accommodate the need to keep the building sparkling a new apparatus for cleaning a sheer glass wall with no access from the inside was invented.

Lewis Mumford couldn't resist extolling the ingenuity of the window-washing machine and the public relations value of an all-glass building:

> "For a company whose main products are soap and detergents, that little handicap of the sealed windows is a heaven-sent opportunity, for what could better dramatize its business than a squad of cleaners operating in their chariot, like the Zeus ex machina of Greek tragedy, and capturing the eye of the passerby as they performed their daily duties? This perfect bit of symbolism alone almost justifies the all glass facade."[7]

Referring to the intriguing window washing apparatus in a magazine interview just after Lever House opened, a company represenative said, "We're in the soap business and we wanted our building to be a symbol of everlasting cleanliness." He said that this was the first of two fond hopes of Lever Brothers. The second hope was "to put up a building that women would enjoy working in, after all, most of our twelve hundred employees are women, as are most of our customers. Raymond Loewy did the interior design, and the girls are crazy about it. . . . Note the gray-beige color of the floor . . . Loewy has named it Lever House beige."[8]

Raymond Loewy (1893–1986), the first designer to appear on the cover of TIME magazine (1949), designed products, interiors, textiles, furniture, and graphics and was renowned for the streamlining style which he introduced to numerous American cars, trains, and machines. He stands astride his 1937 bullet-nosed Pennsylvania Railroad S-1 locomotive.

Man of the Year

It was Raymond Loewy's lifelong crusade to "rid the world of so much junk . . . and contribute a little beauty."

The Lever House commission demonstrated Loewy's range, as he expanded his studies for Lever's packaging to the design of interiors for the headquarters. In a 1962 company brochure, Loewy wrote that Lever House was little more than "a design problem of moving a complex corporation into pre-determined architectural space intended primarily as corporate and public relations . . . in all office design, the interior 'announces' the type of business, implements operational, client, and staff working methods, and—without shame—advertises the business' pride in itself."

Loewy and SOM achieved harmony around the architecture's four-foot, eight-inch module. The open plan, the orderly rows of metal desks and the factory-like standardization resulted from the popular conviction that time-motion studies of the period were a rational science.

These were concepts that emerged in the 1910s when Frank and Lillian Gilbreth applied Henry Ford's assembly-line techniques to business by proposing ways to maximize the efficiency of office procedures. After World War II, this image of the corporate office was solidified as the country's successful military organization was translated into postwar America's management model.

lever house

Philip Johnson (second from left) and Mies van der Rohe testing a model of a fountain for Seagram Plaza at the laboratories of M. I. T. Phyllis Lambert is to the right.

The architect's work-methods were quite interesting. In a letter to a friend Phyllis Lambert wrote,

"I can't wait to see what Mies comes up with for this building—he has a cardboard model made of Park Avenue between 46th and 57th streets with all the buildings on the Avenue and some going in the blocks and then he has a number of towers for different solutions that he places in the empty place of the old 375 and this model is up on a high table so that when sitting in a chair his eye is just level with the table top which equals the street—and for hours on end he peers down his Park Avenue trying out the different towers."[1]

It quickly became clear to Mies that the half-acre pocket of open space which would result if his building were set back 100 feet from the avenue would contribute in many ways to the project, as well as to the city. The open space established a point of reference amongst the other buildings. Mies knew that it would give an undeniable identity to the whole enterprise.

Seagram Building • New York City

The Seagram Building is without question one of the most important tall buildings built in the post-World War II period. Lewis Mumford called it a "Roll-Royce" of buildings with "the aesthetic impact that only a work of art"[2] enjoys. Its magisterial beauty has only improved with time.

As early as 1954 Seagram and Sons began planning a building in anticipation of its hundredth anniversary in 1958. Board chairman Samuel Bronfman requested a proposal from Luckman & Pereira (Charles Luckman having left Lever Brothers was now in practice in California). When their design was pictured in model form in the international press, it was seen by Bronfman's daughter Phyllis Lambert, who was studying in Paris and had well-informed opinions of her own about art and architecture. She made it clear to her father that she was unimpressed by the design, and he generously responded by granting her full authority over the selection of the final architect.

Lambert sought the advice of Philip Johnson who was just about to leave his position as director of the Department of Architecture at the Museum of Modern Art in order to set up his own architectural practice. Although he lacked the reputation to be a candidate for the job, Johnson proved generous with his time since he recognized that Seagram's plan to hire the best possible architect and treat him to a lavish budget would to some degree offset the sorry abundance of second rate building in New York in the boom of the mid-1950s.

Johnson drew up a list of the top dozen architects in the United States for Phyllis to visit. Interviewing each in turn, she asked a basic question: "Given the problem of an office

The glass skyscraper as envisioned by Mies van der Rohe in his projects of the 1920s had been a stimulus to others, but it wasn't until the 1950s that Mies himself had the opportunity to realize the practical possibilities of his early concepts. The commission for the Seagram Building enabled him to develop his ideas on a scale and in a manner that had not been previously available to him.

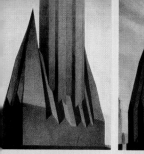

No More Wedding Cakes

The New York Zoning Law of 1916 required that adequate light and air and proper building density be maintained by designing new buildings to fit an imaginary "envelope" determined by the size of their lots and their location on a block. In order to maintain a modicum of light and air in the city's canyons, the new code dictated that after a fixed vertical height, a building had to be stepped back (like a wedding cake) in accordance with a designated angle drawn from the center of the street.

An article in the New York Times *from 1923 stated that "the buildings of the future will take the form which has resulted from the establishing of the New York zoning laws. Its most distinguishing feature is the setback roof. It is a wall architecture, depending for its effect on surface decoration, on the proportion of the windows, and on the mass of wall space formed in accordance with the setback style."[3]*

Though no one dared to build such a structure until 1952, under the code a tower covering no more than one-quarter of the site could conceivably rise to an unlimited height.

The "Plan for Re-zoning New York" (1950) called for changes that were finally adopted in 1961. The acclaim that the Seagram Building received prompted the city to pass the resolution which encouraged the construction of office buildings with amenities such as plazas.

building in New York, who is going to make the greatest contribution?" When she discovered "everybody seemed to be talking in Mies's terms or denying him," her search was ended.

Lambert later justified the choice, observing that,

"the younger men, the second generation, are talking in terms of Mies, but a measure of the Seagram decision to award him the commission derived from the suspicion that both Le Corbusier and Wright would have proven temperamentally too difficult to work with. Mies, by contrast, was the least likely to force his ego on the project—in short, the most trustworthy, the most predictable."[4]

While one of the factors that won Mies van der Rohe the commission to design the Seagram Building was his perceived single-mindedness verging on predictability, the solution he came up with was among the most inventive and original of his entire career. As little as a glance is all that's required to recognize Seagram as a building by Mies, yet further inspection reveals features not only unique to Mies, but vital to the exceptional quality of the finished product.

While critics have often accused him of indifference to the surroundings of his buildings, that criticism has little merit. In the Lake Shore Drive Apartments, the relationship of the two towers to each other and to the Lake Michigan shoreline is one of the most winning aspects of that design, and in New York Mies's response to the context of the Seagram Building is even more impressive.

Among the earliest of his self-imposed duties was a careful, characteristically deliberate study of the area adjacent to the chosen site. There he found the buildings facing Park Avenue built consistently close to the sidewalk in deference to local zoning laws.

"My approach to the Seagram Building was no different from that of any other building that I might build. My idea, or better "direction," in which I go is toward a clear

above: *Study for Maximum Mass Permitted by the 1916 New York Zoning Law, Stages 1-4,* drawn by Hugh Ferriss, 1922.
The zoning laws literally determined a look. The setback style, or the "wedding cake" skyscraper as it was called, was championed particularly by Harvey Wiley Corbett. These now iconic images resulted from a collaboration between Ferriss and Corbett.

structure and construction—this applies not to any one problem, but to all architectural problems, which I approach. I am, in fact, completely opposed to the idea that a specific building should have individual character. Rather, I believe that it should express a universal character, which has been determined by the total problem which architecture must strive to solve. On the Seagram Building, since it was to be built in New York and since it was to be the first major office building, which I was to build, I asked for two types of advice for the development of the plans. One, the best real estate advice as to the types of desirable rentable space and, two, professional advice regarding the New York Building Code. With my direction established and with these advisers, it was then only a matter of hard work."[5]

Among the ideas Mies considered for the tower were one square in plan and another in rectangular slab form that would have been set perpendicular to the avenue. Both of these he discarded in favor of a third possibility, borne out in the structure that now stands parallel to the street. Mies pushed the building back far enough on its site to leave a 100 foot deep plaza with fountains. So conceived, it proved a very clever way of bowing to the zoning laws while opening up a space that was at the time unprecedented on Park Avenue. Its 39 stories ascends to a height of 516 feet, the loftiest of any high-rise he ever completed, yet there is ample room to view the building equally well from both sides of the avenue.

Despite the building's height and size, the design had sacrificed a significant amount of floor space to accommodate the plaza. Mies then devised a deftly inventive way of providing that space while remaining true to most of his customary habits. To the rear of the slab he attached a one-bay deep spine that rose the full 39 stories, and added to it another three-bay-deep, ten-story-high structure flanked in turn by two three-bay-deep, four-story-high wings. Thus he managed to add an enormous amount of floor area to what had

top: Office Interiors, c.1958. The lighting panels in the ceilings of all the outer offices of each floor remain lit 24 hours a day. The Seagram logo on the travertine wall was designed by Herbert Matter who also painted a mural of the distillation process.
above: The lobby, c. 1958.
right: The plaza, c. 1958. No poor imitations have encroached as yet.

Matchless Detail

Mies's use of materials was of perpetual importance to him. The generous budget at Seagram enabled him to treat everything inside and outside the structure with exceptional refinement. The plaza is paved in a high-grade pink granite. The foyer features four banks of elevators clad in quality travertine; the soffit above them is lined with glass mosaic in pinkish-gray, a color akin to that used in all the windows.

But, the material most associated with the understated opulence of the Seagram Building as a whole is the bronze of the curtain wall, a substance whose warmth is matched by its connotations of historic age. Mies's own respect for the material, not to mention his authority over it, is evident from the treatment to which he subjected the exterior vertical I-beams, a standard part of the Miesian vocabulary since the Lake Shore Drive Apartments.

As with 860, Mies carefully balanced the relationship of the mullions in their length and width. This was the only way to preserve the illusion of moving the skeleton to the outside while separating the shell and the supporting structure. Philip Johnson forever marveled at Mies's determination to widen the edge of the flange, just enough to keep it from looking insubstantial, but executed subtly enough to escape all but the most scrupulous notice.

become a complicated overall form, without surrendering the splendid simplicity of the main slab, which remains the dominant element of the building. People are clearly divided on the addition of the "bustle," as it is disparaging called. For some, it was a kind of cheating; for others, it goes wholly unnoticed. At the very least one can say that the building has such a strong sculptural frontality that the goings on at the rear are like looking at the back of the statue.

Bronze sheathing for the exterior appealed to Mies because "it is a very noble material and lasts forever if it is used in the right way." To avoid the natural patination, or even its weathering to a darker shade, the bronze is hand wiped from top to bottom with lemon oil on a regular basis—until this day.

Around the perimeter offices of all 38 floors is a band of luminous ceiling panels 20 feet in depth. In the daytime, this band, which provides upwards of 100-ft. candles of illumination, effectively counteracts the brightest glare inside. While minimizing the contrast between ceiling and sky, the lighting has the curious effect of making New York City seem like a photographic mural mounted on the other side of the glass. At night, fully lighted by a secondary wiring system at one-fifth of the daytime intensity, the panels not only provide a uniform glow, they silhouette the bays of the structural steel frame along with the mullions—giving the pedestrian the impression of a kind of "x-ray" of the building's structure. This auxiliary illumination is operable only by the building management, so that the continuity of the display cannot be interrupted at any section of the façade.

Venetian blinds in the offices have been altered so that the slats can only remain in their open positions. The blinds themselves can only be raised at one-third, one-half, or two-thirds marks. The exterior aspect of the building, therefore, is never marred by a chaotic lack of proportion.

The lobby is uniformly and brightly lighted by sunken canisters that wash the travertine walls. Astronomical and numerical clocks together adjust the balance of brightness relative to midday sun, twilight, and night blackness as well

above: Looking west towards Lever House.
The care with which the bronze mullions are joined can be seen here.
The venetian blinds are either fully opened, fully closed, or locked at their half-way mark.

as the density of usage.

The lighting scheme is such an essential feature of the building that it was included in the description of the building's exterior in its citation as a Landmark. Tenants are prohibited from indiscriminately fiddling with this or any other permanent feature of the building.

Philip Johnson arranged and detailed the lobby to coordinate with the overall character of the building. This includes, among other items, travertine floors and walls, bronze mullions, and specially designed elevator cab interiors. All details, including square serif lettering and special door hardware, were painstakingly designed to harmonize. Great care was taken in selecting cladding materials, to assure among other things, that appearances would improve as the building aged.

To accommodate slight changes in level which were present on the Park Avenue frontage and towards Lexington Avenue, the broad, pink granite-paved plaza was raised a few steps above the pavement. As a result, the plaza (which has a radiant heating system to keep it ice-free) is detached from the noise and bustle of traffic. At the same time the plaza essentially becomes a classical plinth upon which sits the latter-day temple of the Seagram Building.

The westward view from the plaza discloses another success in the total design package. On the other side of Park Avenue parallel with the façade of the Seagram Building is a a neo-Florentine Palazzo, the Racquet and Tennis Club, erected in 1918 by the firm of McKim, Mead & White. The differences between the two buildings consists of more than a chronology of forty years. The older structure is noble, solid masonry, historicist in style; the newer, by contrast, is open, vitreous, and equally assured in its modernist abstraction. Yet they are joined beneath their surfaces by an underlying commitment to classicism.

The Seagram Building is a tribute to Mies van der Rohe's masterful craftsmanship and a revelation of his consummate understanding of classical sources—sources that are never allusions, but are ingrained in his very art.

above: *View From the Main Staircase of the Altes Museum*, 1843, Carl Daniel Freydanck, oil on canvas.
Ironically, since glass doors have been added to the museum entrance, it now bears a resemblance the Mies lobby, pictured at right. The McKim, Mead & White Raquet Club is visible directly across Park Avenue.

Where Two Classicists Meet

A favorite architectural gesture of Mies was to blur the distinction between the idea of inside and outside at the point of entry to a building. This is something he often referred to as having been influenced by his idol Karl Friedrich Schinkel (1781-1841). Schinkel was one of the most influential architects, not only in his native Germany, but in the western world. His neo-classicism reflected the influence of Durand (page 14) as well as a reverence for both antiquity and the Middle Ages. Schinkel believed that the social nature of the architect's endeavor gave him more responsibility than other artists to bring clarity to the forms of public institutions.

The painting, above, of the main, open staircase of the Altes Museum of Schinkel in Berlin places the viewer inside looking out. The museum staircase is a brilliant combination of interior and exterior spaces and is an essential feature of Schinkel's design.

By raising the Seagram tower above the first-story glazed exterior wall, Mies united the plaza with the lobby. This unity is enhanced through continuous travertine paving and a slab marquee, which is, in effect, an exterior extension of the lobby ceiling. Outside and inside flow into one another. The building "floats" free from the ground, especially at night.

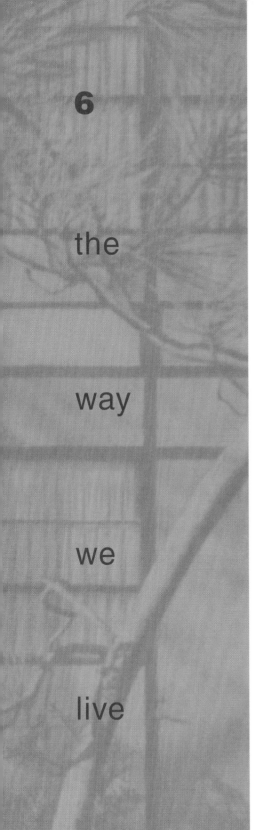

6

the

way

we

live

Eames House
The Glass House
Farnsworth House
Vanna Venturi House
Smith House

Contrary to what one might imagine, modern architecture was being seen while it was being made, by a fairly broad audience, very often outside the context of a museum. For example, the Museum of Modern Art's *International Modern Architecture Exhibition*, from its closing in New York at the end of March 1932 to the end of 1933, toured sixteen American cities, often in non-museum settings. Lucid press releases informed local critics about the principles upon which the exhibition was based. In many cities progressive art critics joined MoMA in its evangelistic fervor; others, knowing little about modern architecture were content to simply reproduce the museum's statement. In Chicago, where the exhibition was shown in the Sears Roebuck department store, a columnist described the new architecture as "a banding together of architects of many lands, men of vision and imagination who recognize the urgent need of building to fit the requirements of modern life."

Opinions were strongly expressed one way or the other. Much about modernism was thought to be as foreign to America's spirit as it was to its shores. A newspaper critic in Cleveland appealed to the patriotism of the readers: "Though America, because of its youth, its perfection of the means of mass production meth-

" . . . *every improvement in the abodes of men which renders them more neat, comfortable, and pleasing, contributes not only to physical enjoyment, but to mental and moral advancement.*"[1]
— *Henry William Cleaveland, Village and Farm Cottages 1854*

Glass Architecture, New Era

In 1914, the German poet Paul Scheerbart wrote: "In order to raise our culture to a higher level, we are forced, whether we like it or not, to change our architecture . . . [to] a glass architecture, which admits the light of the sun, of the moon, and of the stars into the rooms, not only through a few windows, but through as many walls as feasible, these to consist entirely of glass—of coloured glass."

The text of Scheerbart's Glasarchitektur was dedicated to Bruno Taut, whose Glass Pavilion was inscribed with Scheerbart's aphorisms: "Light wants crystal;" "Glass brings a new era;" "We feel sorry for the brick culture;" "Without a glass palace, life becomes a burden" "Building in brick only does us harm;" "Colored glass destroys hatred."

Light filtered through the pavilion's faceted cupola and glass-block walls to illuminate an axial seven-tiered chamber, lined with glass mosaic.

According to Taut the crystalline structure had been designed in the spirit of a Gothic cathedral. It was in effect a Stadtkrone or 'city crown', the pyramidal form postulated by Taut as the universal paradigm of all religious building, which together with the faith it would inspire was an essential urban element for the restructuring of society.

ods and the pioneering of Wright in architecture, is the logical nation to be leading the movement, it has abandoned the leadership to Europe."

None of these ideas were foreign to America's architects. Besides, there was an American strain of modernism that ran deep and wide. While the exhibition toured the country, its curators, Henry-Russell Hitchcock and Philip Johnson, put together a show entitled *Work of Young Architects in the Middle-West,* which opened in New York City in April 1933. The show was mounted that June in the Home Planning Hall at The Century of Progress International Exposition in Chicago. George Frederick Keck assisted in the installation, and was among the architects included in the exhibit. He and Robert Schweikher showed their model of a Chicago Housing Project, a design that used "prefabrication, duplication, standardized parts, rapidity of construction, available materials and facilities, structural steel frame, and site orientation so as to attain the utmost advantage of sunlight." These are some, if not all, of the tenets of Modernism.

Notwithstanding frequent exhibitions and its appearance in popular publications, modern architecture was financially out of reach for the majority of the population—82% of the wage-earning population made less than $1,949 a year in 1933. Construction was also slow—137 private houses were built in Chicago during 1933 as compared to 42,932 in 1926.[9] Conservative lending institutions in a Depression economy made building extremely difficult. In 1935, the editors of *Architectural Forum* and *Fortune Quarterly* surveyed the American public on preference of style in residential design; 35% preferred modern, 42% wanted early American, and 17% chose English. A year later the clientele for modern design dropped by two-thirds. A 1936 *Architectural Forum* questionnaire revealed that only one institu-

left: Bruno Taut, Interior of Glass Pavilion at Werkbund Exhibition, Cologne, 1914. For a picture of the exterior, see page 73. The Gropius and Meyer Model Factory Building (page 118) was exhibited at the same time. In some ways these structures represent two diametrically opposed points of view—everpresent, yet never reconciled —in 20th Century architecture.

tion out of 170 surveyed consistently financed modern homes.[10] Mortgage associations simply refused to invest in modern residential architecture.

More than a touch of naiveté attended modernist visions of utopia, anyway, since they were often projections of upper middle class or affluent values. For instance, though Fred Keck adhered to the guidelines of the Home Planning Division of the 1933 fair that required durability, convenience, livability, and cost-efficiency, his House of Tomorrow was furnished with handwoven Moroccan area rugs and pigskin-cushioned Tugendhat chairs. And it came with a Silver Arrow automobile and a Curtiss-Wright Sport Biplane as standard equipment: we were all meant to fly to work.

As much as they differ from each other the houses in this section are all decidedly modern in style. And, it is an undeniable fact that modern houses have never been the way any but a small minority have pictured themselves living. But, it is the broader concepts, the design, technology, efficiency, and the flexibility, that make these houses inspiring to the present day.

What's important is that the ideas about durability, convenience, livability, and cost-efficiency that were brewing before the war were played out immediately afterwards. Chief among the concerns of the modern architect, after ease of fabrication and cost, is the health and emotional well-being of their buildings' inhabitants. For some architects the mention of new materials and technology simply meant air-conditioning, easy-to-clean surfaces, and labor-saving devices in the traditional home. For others, especially the architects in this section, new materials and technology meant nothing short of transforming the way we think of the house—the way we live.

An Enduring House of Cards

The house Charles and Ray Eames built for them-

True Deco

The Arts Decoratifs exhibition in Paris in 1925 focused the world's attention on over 300 pavilions built to demonstrate the latest ideas of comfort and taste in the domestic interior. One diminutive, white cube with the letters EN painted on its side, designed by the cousins Charles-Edouard and Pierre Jeanneret, represented their new magazine, L'Esprit Nouveau. Charles-Edouard would soon make a reputation for himself under the name of Le Corbusier. Hardly noticed at the time, their simple, unadorned pavilion went on to become, in retrospect, the most influential of all the exhibits.

Pierre Chareau (1883-1950) remodeled an old building in the center of Paris to create a doctor's consulting rooms and apartment. In the process, he entirely dismantled the first three floors of the courtyard building and introduced structural steel to support the fourth floor which he left intact. The new structure gave him the freedom to reconfigure the interior and enclose the new façade in glass block which floods the interior with light. Chareau designed all the industrial looking details as well as the contrasting art deco furniture.

above: Le Corbusier, L'Esprit Nouveau Pavilion, Paris, 1925. The *Arts Decoratifs* exhibition came to be known as *Art Deco* for short. Notice the tree growing through the building.

right: Pierre Chareau and Bernard Bijvoet, Le Maison de Verre, Paris 1932. Compare the painting on the easel with the photos of the Glass House at top of page 165.

Tomorrow's Houses Today

The House of Tomorrow (under construction above) was one of twelve experimental houses built for the Home and Industrial Arts Exhibit of Chicago's Century of Progress International Exposition of 1933. The form and the engineering of Fred Keck's structure may be compared with Buckminster Fuller's Dymaxion House which Keck may well have seen at Marshall Field's department store in 1929 when it was unveiled to promote modern furniture. It was shown again at the Chicago Arts Club a year later.

Keck built the Crystal House (below) when the Century of Progress re-opened in 1934. A re-circulating air-conditioning system used window-base vents to heat, humidify, and filter the air of the Crystal House. Venetian blinds were installed in a recessed channel along the upper inside edge of the glass. Curtains helped soften the mechanical appearance of the external trusses, and shades afforded privacy.

Compared with the other Century of Progress houses, the House of Tomorrow and the Crystal House were radical designs. They are also singular in Keck's career. The model houses were not intended to be merely symbolic, however. They were attempts to solve contemporary construction problems, explore concepts of prefabrication, and provide greater flexibility in spatial planning and family living conditions. As such they are unique in the history of early 20th Century American residential architecture.

selves in Pacific Palisades, California, was part of *Arts & Architecture* magazine's Case Study House Program. It is also the embodiment of their singular vision. The Eameses really lived in their house—it grew while they were alive. Even now, with both of them gone, their presence can still be felt.

They decided to set a two-part challenge for themselves: first, to build an entire house from industrial materials—prefabricated, off the shelf, ordered from catalogues. Second, to put it all together so that it would be warm, inviting, comfortable—even beautiful—and make the house a home. They succeeded admirably on both counts.

Whereas people adapt, more or less, to their houses, the Eames's house adapted to them. Everything that surrounds and fills the house has been as transformed by it as much as the other way around. Consequently, the particulars of the house are not repeatable, except in the abstract. As Ray put it, "the fact that it's metal, you know, steel frame, I think is less important than the idea that its form can be adapted to a person's needs rather than a person's needs being a part of every little connection."[2]

Room With A View

From the very moment it was finished representatives of the press and students came to marvel at the house of glass that Philip Johnson built for himself in New Caanan, Connecticut. It even attracted the likes of Mies and Frank Lloyd Wright.

Wright walked through the front door and asked whether he should take his hat off or leave it on. Mies disapproved of the fact that the ceiling joists were made of wood. "Mies thought the workmanship was bad, that the design was bad, that it was a bad copy of his Farnsworth house, which had inspired me," says Johnson. "He thought I should have understood his work better."

The Home Planning Division of the 1933 fair had four qualifications for demonstration houses: durability, convenience, livability, and cost-efficiency. Fred Keck met them all.
above: It took only 48 hours to assemble the frame for the House of Tomorrow, 1933, which was then sheathed in fixed, tinted, storefront glass.
left: Buckminster Fuller's Dymaxion Car was exhibited as part of the Crystal House, 1934.

These two houses, which are so frequently compared starting with Johnson himself, really ought not to be. As Peter Blake wisely points out:

" . . . Johnson is unnecessarily modest in crediting Mies with all the qualities of his own house, for the Johnson and the Farnsworth houses—apart from being all steel and glass—are completely different in character. Johnson's house is symmetrical in its elevations; the Farnsworth house . . . is quite dynamically asymmetrical. Johnson's house sits on the ground like a delightful little classical temple; the Farnsworth house is virtually airborne. . . . the Johnson house has a strong post-and-beam look, a feeling of compression in the columns; whereas the Farnsworth house has a sense of tension, of steel being stretched out to its ultimate potentials."[3]

And, there is more than a structural difference between the two houses; their intentions are entirely different. Johnson built his house as a showpiece for all the world to see. It literally focuses the spotlight on his interior, and on his property, and ultimately on himself. Mies built a house for the ages.

A House For All Time

The kind of house that Charles and Ray Eames built adapts to the people who live in it. On the contrary, one adapts to a house such as the one Mies van der Rohe built for Dr. Farnsworth in Plano, Illinois. In spite of their common sources, you probably won't find two more dissimilar houses. In one the universal is personalized; in the other the personal is universalized.

The Farnsworth house is the embodiment

Freedom to Build

In September 1945, House & Garden told its readers that modern architecture is part of "a continuing struggle for growing liberty."

George Nelson and Henry Wright in their popular 1945 book, TOMORROW'S HOUSE, wrote: "Where people were afraid of freedom, they try to give it up." The authors said that only through open-mindedness, and open planning in the design of American houses, could the ideals for which the War was fought be fulfilled.

Elizabeth Mock wrote in her catalogue to the MoMA exhibition, IF YOU WANT TO BUILD A HOUSE, " . . . only the modern architect is free to use every inch of space to your greatest advantage, free to use new and more efficient materials and structural techniques, and free to give you at least a feeling of spaciousness if the actuality is unattainable."

In its January 1945 issue House Beautiful presented a house in Beverly Hills it said was the house to which Johnny dreams of marching home. "All of these plusses add up to the American ideal of good living," the magazine concluded, "one of the ideals these veterans have fought for and which they can now look forward to attaining."

above: "A Proper Dream House for Any Veteran," a *House Beautiful* article from January 1945.
right: Aimed at returning G.I.s and their families, *Tomorrow's House* was published by the editors of Architectural Forum in 1945.
far right: Catalogue for an exhibition at MoMA, New York, 1946.

Freedom Endangered

Elizabeth Gordon's April 1953 editorial in HOUSE BEAUTIFUL, *entitled* The Threat to the Next America, *was a call to arms for those who feared, along with her, that* "the much touted all-glass cube of International Style architecture is perhaps the most unlivable type of home for man since he descended from the tree and entered a cave. You burn in the summer and freeze in the winter, because nothing must interfere with the "pure" form of their rectangles . . . ."

"There is a well-established movement, in modern architecture, decorating, and furnishings, which is promoting the mystical idea that 'less is more.'

"They are promoting unlivability, stripped-down emptiness, lack of storage space and therefore lack of possessions."

These purists endangered everything Americans hold dear, especially their privacy. "You can recognize the International Style by a combination of these characteristics . . . Flat roofs. Smooth surfaces. Walls that look like Mondrian compositions. Abhorrence of ornamentation and decoration. Elimination of partition walls so that a house tends to be one public room with open areas for sleeping, playing, etc. Maximum use of glass without any corrective devices for shade or privacy."

of an idea—not so much the archetypal *house* as the archetypal *structure*. Mies single-handedly changed the concept of post-and-beam construction with his clearspan structure. There's the idea of roof and floor planes, the near dematerialization of the walls, the passage of exterior to interior, and visa versa. The overarching principles of the Farnsworth house are transferable to a school (IIT), a museum (the New National Gallery in Berlin), as well as to a factory or any other conceivable building type.

For Mies the concept of universality in architecture implied the highest possible degree of freedom. As he saw it a structure reduced to "almost nothing" represents the ultimate in noninterference on the part of an architect with the lives of his clients. For Mies, this platonic ideal, or perhaps more accurately, this zen-like quality of "nothingness," provides a maximum opportunity for free expression for those who use the building: they can furnish it in any way they like, use it for anything they like, change its interior spaces in any manner that seems most suitable.

Complex and Contradictory

Chestnut Hill, Pennsylvania, is a quaint village of vernacular stone houses mixed with structures that look like farmhouses from Normandy. Robert Venturi built a house for his mother in Chestnut Hill and used the opportunity to thumb his nose at modernist propriety. When style and taste change, what's proper and improper change along with it. Venturi himself has expressed surprise at how classic the house now seems to appear. Intended to be an anti-icon, the house is an icon nonetheless.

However, it's not as a model of anything new that the house is important, but rather as an emblem of change itself. The house is a symbol of Venturi's disruption of what had become a monolithic stronghold on art, architecture, and culture in general. That

The strident tone of this article sounds as if Frank Lloyd Wright were in the background. He's quoted at the very end—"These Bauhaus architects ran from political totalitarianism in Germany to what is now made by specious promotion to seem their own totalitarianism in art here in America . . . " Gordon ends by advising her readers, faced by an "elite who are telling us . . . how we should live," to use common sense. "Don't let them take it away."

stronghold was not the legacy of the actual works of modernism so much as what had become of those ideals in academia and in the marketplace. Stripped-down and spare became the *only* order of the day. So, whereas Mies had said, "Less is more," Robert Venturi said, "Less is a bore." At the very least, this was a much needed breath of fresh air.

With his mother's house Venturi began to build with "complexity" and "contradiction." The complexity and contradiction that Venturi called for in his house can only be matched by that of his prose:

> "This building recognizes complexities and contradictions: it is both complex and simple, open and closed, big and little; some of its elements are good on one level and bad on another; its order accommodates the generic elements of the house in general, and the circumstantial elements of a house in particular. It achieves the difficult unity of a medium number of diverse parts rather than the easy unity of few or many motival parts."[4]

Ideal Shelter

Richard Meier considers the Smith House his first real building. "It was there, working on the Smith House that I was first able to develop and test a number of design issues that I had been preoccupied with. In fact, those issues still preoccupy me: the making of space, the distinction between interior and exterior space, the play of light and shadow, the different ways in which a building exists in the natural or urban world; the separation of public and private space."[5]

In the Smith House, Richard Meier accepted the new as classical. It nods in Le Corbusier's direction without strict adherence to doctrine. There is nothing dogmatic about his decisions. There are, in fact, many witty departures that are every bit as complex and contradictory as any so-called post-modern design.

above: Lambay Castle, Ireland. Sir Edwin Lutyens (1869-1944). Venturi used this image in the catalogue to his ground-breaking exhibition *Complexity and Contradiction*.
right: Vanna Venturi House, Robert Venturi.
opposite top: Cartoon drawn for *Architectural Record* by Alan Dunn, 1947.
opposite bottom: Sleeping area of the Glass House of Philip Johnson.

A Flair for Inflection
Though Sir Edward Lutyens (1869-1944) began his career designing in the Arts and Crafts style, he was attracted early on to the fashionable grandeur of the Edwardian era. The restrained clarity in his original use of classical forms, as structure rather than as mere decoration, was later overlooked as his work fell more and more outside the European mainstream.

By the 1960s Robert Venturi and others began reassessing the value of architects such as Lutyens. Venturi says of Lambay Castle (above) that it "abounds in dualities. The duality of the entrance façade . . for instance, is resolved by the inflecting shape of the opening in the juxtaposed garden wall."

Among Venturi's many favorite words is "inflection." If inflection means turning or bending away from a course or position of alignment, then might it just as easily be applied to Robert Venturi's moving away from the position of Modernism as it is to his aligning a chimney?

Does Venturi place the chimney where he does in Vanna's house because it suits his mother's purposes (or the town planning board for that matter), or because it breaks the rules? Or, is the chimney positioned against the accepted norm and its place in history?

the way we live 155

Eames House • Pacific Palisades, California

The Eames house was one of several experimental houses commissioned by the publisher of Arts & Architecture magazine to show a post-war public, hungry for ideal new homes, that modern architects could offer more for their money than conventional house builders.

The Case Study House Program, as it was called, was not a search for ideal solutions. "These houses must function as an integral part of the living pattern of the occupants and will therefore be completely 'used' in a very full and real sense. 'House' in these cases means center of productive activities."[1]

The project was a resounding success: the first six houses, completed by 1948, attracted 370,000 visitors.

In 1943, John Entenza, editor and publisher of *Arts & Architecture,* organized a competition entitled "Designs for Postwar Living," and dedicated an entire issue of the magazine to the results. The issue "was devoted to the prefabrication, mass production and industrialization of residential construction" and contained an article by Charles Eames and Entenza entitled "What is a House?". Reacting to a projected housing shortage in the postwar period, the authors explored the possibilities of using industrial technologies originally developed to meet wartime needs to approach "the impending shortage with the same urgency and energy that was employed in meeting wartime challenges." The article "reflected the general optimism of planners and designers that the postwar world would bring with it qualitative changes in the way people live and think about their environment."[2]

This initiative was expanded in January 1945 into an ambitious program of Case Study Houses, intended to utilize the products of industrialization for domestic purposes while promoting the ideals of modernism. Entenza selected eight architects, or firms, who were given a mandate to identify and express the salient characteristics of a new life-style that was seen to be desired by postwar families in southern California. Details of the first eight houses, along with a ninth for Entenza himself, were presented in *Arts & Architecture* following the announcement of the program.

Case Study #8, later known as the Eames House, was designed for a three-acre plot in Pacific Palisades at the top of a 150-foot high cliff, overlooking the Pacific. It, and three other Case Study houses, were planned as part of a five-acre

" . . . the idea of our house was more linked to the furniture, I think than anything else. We were concerned about the use of time, people's labor, for the greatest result, so that one person could spend a long time making one chair and he would have made that nice chair, and then other people would not have that result, they would have something much less. But if that effort went into production, it would be at a higher level."[3] — Ray Eames

Case Study Program

In October, 1945, within two months of the close of World War II, Arts & Architecture announced "The Case Study Program" to its readers:

"Because most opinion, both profound and light-headed, in terms of post war housing is nothing but speculation in the form of talk and reams of paper," the article begins," it occurs to us that it might be a good idea to get down to cases and at least make a beginning in the gathering of that mass of material that must eventually result in what we know as 'house—post war.'

"Agreeing that the whole matter is surrounded by conditions over which few of us have any control, certainly we can develop a point of view and do some organized thinking which might come to a practical end. It is with that in mind that we now announce the project we have called THE 'CASE STUDY' HOUSE PROGRAM.

"The magazine has undertaken to supply an answer insofar as it is possible to correlate the facts and point them in the direction of an end result. We are, within the limits of uncontrollable factors, proposing to begin immediately the study, planning, actual design and construction of eight houses, each to fulfil the specifications of a special living problem in the Southern California area. Eight nationally known architects,

parcel Entenza had purchased on behalf of the magazine from the Will Rogers estate in Santa Monica canyon.

The first design, for Case Study #8, was by Charles and Ray Eames, and Eero Saarinen, with structural consultation by Edgardo Contini.

While the first houses in the Case Study program, all built in wood, were being completed and prepared for public tours, Charles visited New York City where he saw an exhibition of the work of Mies van der Rohe at the Museum of Modern Art. He was familiar with the architect's work, having traveled to Europe in 1929 specifically to see it, along with buildings by Le Corbusier, Walter Gropius, and Henry Van de Velde.

After the Mies exhibition the plan was substantially altered. Similarities between the original scheme and one of the sketches in the exhibition (top of page 170) might indicate that Charles was concerned about being derivative, and changed the design to avoid this criticism.

The new design, now solely the work of Charles and Ray, still took certain cues from Mies, but is more original in its massing and proportion, as well as in the treatment of the exteriors; they simplified things considerably. The living component of the house was pulled back in line with the studio. A retaining wall, which had only been necessary as part of the studio, was now extended along the hill, becoming a support along that entire side of the house at ground floor level.

As a result of the modified plan the sight lines from the interior were now redirected obliquely away from the sea and directly towards the Entenza house next door. To offset this, the fill from the excavation for the retaining wall was placed between the two houses, forming an elongated

In alphabetical order, the architects chosen were: Thornton Abell, **J R Davidson**, **Charles Eames** and **Eero Saarinen**, Richard Neutra, **Ralph Rapson**, Whitney Smith, **Spaulding** and Rex, and **Wurster** and Bernardi. (Those in bold are pictured at left.)

mound that was then planted as a screen.

Unlike typical modern LA homes that open out and merge their private space with the public, the Eames house and property turns inward for intimacy and privacy. Additional privacy was obtained by giving the mound the slighly unkempt quality of a natural meadow (they only cut it once a year). The eucalyptus trees that line the walk in front of the house have matured and are now a integral element in the façade.

The Eames house is really two structures—a two-story living space and a studio—connected by a brick-paved patio. A pathway, beginning at the drive, leads up to the main entrance of the residential side. The front door is directly opposite a spiral stair—the only means of access to the upper floor. A conventional stair leads to the upper section of the studio which is more like a loft.

The house and studio are two rectangular steel cages, each 20 feet wide. The living quarters, the larger of the two, is 51 feet long; the studio is 37 feet long. The structural members, which are left exposed, are surprisingly delicate—4-inch columns sometimes rising as high as 17 feet.

More than any of the Case Study houses built prior to it, the Eames House fulfils the intention of the program in that it only uses prefabricated, standardized parts, and industrial materials. In the words of Edgardo Contini, "the Eames house is poetry expressed with high-tech vocabulary."

The exterior is configured very much as if the elements were toy mechano pieces snapped in place. The infill panels emphasize the structure rather than disguise it. The ready-made panels include transparent glass, security glass, fiberglass, plywood, gray asbestos, and aluminum painted red, blue, ochre, black, or covered with gold leaf (over the front door). The color provides a lively contrast to the dark grid of the steel frame. The Eameses used ordinary house paint thinking that they might easily change their minds—they never did.

Rather than denying the surroundings of the house, Charles saw these inorganic materials as being complementary to

chosen not only for their obvious talents, but for their ability to evaluate realistically housing in terms of need, have been commissioned to . . . create 'good' living conditions for eight American families. They will be free to choose or reject, on a merit basis, the products of national manufacturers offering either old or new materials considered best for the purpose by each architect in his attempt to create contemporary dwelling units. . . ."

The article ended with:

" . . . We of course assume that the shape and form of post war living is of primary importance to a great many Americans, and that is our reason for attempting to find at least enough of an answer to give some direction to current thinking on the matter. Whether that answer is to be the 'miracle' house remains to be seen, but it is our guess that after all of the witches have stirred up the broth, the house that will come out of the vapors will be conceived within the spirit of our time, using as far as is practicable, many war-born techniques and materials best suited to the expression of man's life in the modern world."

above, opposite: Ray Eames did a number of covers for ARTS & ARCHITECTURE magazine including this one from April, 1942. The magazine became a vehicle for modernist ideas and a platform for the avant-garde of California. It took a liberal stance on issues of race, human rights, and child care, and it advocated equality among the arts, regularly featuring painting, sculpture, architecture, design, photogtaphy, dance, and film.

Prefabrication

In an ARTS & ARCHITECTURE article from July 1944 entitled "What is a House?" Charles Eames and John Entenza explain how we can now benefit from prefabrication:

"Prefabrication in the truly industrialized sense is a very special approach to the problem of the 'house'-an approach made possible NOW, for the first time, when industry, research and material exist in the right relationship to one another, making possible an intelligent application of these resources to the needs of housing.

"Prefabrication

IS NOT Just a trick to save labor in the building of a house

IS NOT a super-industrialized method to be used for the reproduction of the architecture of the past

IS NOT merely an ingenious mechano-set of parts which, when put together, form walls, roofs, shells of buildings

IS NOT the use of the factory as a catch all for obsolete building crafts

IS NOT a new sales promotion package for the purpose of marketing streamlined versions of old products

"BUT modern industrialized prefabrication, by its very nature, cannot be disassociated from any of the functions of living related to the house. It is, then, the complete use of all the facilities of mass production aided by the best research, the best techniques and the best materials available, to the end that every living activity will receive the benefits of our enormous industrial energies. It is through the complete integration of all these forces that we will arrive at the form of the product. Form, then, will be the by-product of the end result of our best intellectual and industrial energies rather than a point of departure."

them, because, as he said, "the texture of the ceiling, the metal joists, the repetition of the standard sash, the change of glazing from transparent to translucent . . . all add to the architectural relationship of house to nature."

The Eameses understood their materials well enough to subordinate them to their overall personal needs and aesthetic; they didn't allow them to restrict their sense of visual and spatial play. "The structural approach," Eames stated, "became an expansive one in that it encouraged use of space as such, beyond the optimum requirements of living. However, the actual plan within the system is personal . . . it is interesting to consider how the rigidity of the system was responsible for the free use of space and to see how the most matter-of-fact structure resulted in pattern and texture."

The interior is spacious, light, and flexible. The main living area (23 by 20 feet) utilizes the entire height (17 feet). The ribbed underside of the ceiling is painted white but left uncovered, as are the steel beams running across it at bay intervals. Nothing is concealed in the Eames house: it is faithful to the modernist dictum that materials be used honestly, their functional roles articulated.

The glass panels used in the window sash—ranging from completely transparent to translucent—screen or reflect the sunlight and the shadows of the trees to create dappled patterns of light and shade inside the house. In the sleeping loft translucent Japanese-style shoji panels of glass cloth laminate can be slid back and forth across the outer wall to regulate the amount of light.

The stripped down interiors of the Case Study series, offered as a modern alternative to the cluttered and compartmentalized pre-Second World War American house, were meant to allow returning veterans and their families a more casual lifestyle, in a climate that is most conducive to it. The idea, however, was not new, since, even before the end of the 19th Century, Californians were aware of how much the

above: The Eames's furniture is of a piece with their architecture. Charles and Ray made room within modernism for a more personal idea of the house. Ray, who had as strong and understanding of structure as Charles, truly collaborated with him on the house—inside and out. She is still pictured as the artist-wife interior designer.

Japanese valued restraint over the ostentation of late-Victorian and Edwardian taste. Their use of natural materials, simple forms, and light and shadow to induce calm and contemplation, was widely admired.

The effect of the Eames House, inside and out, is not unlike that of Japanese architecture. There are qualities of simplicity, elegance, lightness, and a rectilinear geometry. The Edo ideals of purity, humility, and oneness with nature that captivated Greene & Greene (page 196) and Frank Lloyd Wright are distilled most recently in the Eames House, making it a bench-mark of that tradition in the city.

Charles started out as a photographer and continued along with Ray to photograph and film everything including the house. With the eyes of filmmakers they looked at the house as if it were a series of scrims and screens, behind and in front of which moving tableaus take place. Light and shadows from the natural and man-made worlds interplay with each other in a dazzling tapestry of texture and color.

John Entenza said the Eames House "represents an attempt to state an idea rather than a fixed architectural pattern." The Eameses' particular gift as designers was the singular, magical way that they put things together. They didn't create a rarified or codified style. Instead, they conveyed a wondrous vision in which forms, spaces, light, and objects were playfully transformed or rearranged in fresh and surprising combinations. They were able to present things to us as if we'd never seen them before.

They used their off-the-shelf building materials in much the same way they did everything, with a combination of childlike wonder, transformative power, and consummate skill. Their collected objects, the furniture they designed, everything that decorates—almost populates—the house, is of a piece with it. The interior is as dense, as rococo a mix of colors and textures as those assembled on the exterior. There are no anomalies in the combinations as far apart as they can sometimes be. Their house is as cozy as any Victorian parlor.

Have we simply grown used to this kind of thing? Or, have the Eameses re-informed our vision?

The Eames House is immediately recognized for what it is.

It has grown ever more comfortable in its setting.

The interior is particularly spacious, light, and flexible.

As Philip Johnson sees it, the site of his glass house is history itself as much as it is the bluff on which it sits. And, he was as responsible as anyone for making it so. Within a year of completing the house he began writing about it and other work on the principle that texts as well as projects are to be taken together as a whole. He began a lasting trend which he now bemoans.

In September 1950 Johnson wrote in Architectural Review:

"Although I had forgotten the Malevich picture, it is obviously the inspiration for the plan of the glass house. Malevich proved what interesting surrounding areas could be created by correctly placing a circle in a rectangle.

"Abstract painting of forty years ago remains even today the strongest single aesthetic influence on the grammar of architecture."[1]

Looking at the Malevich above and the photo of Johnson's house to the right is bound to create an indelible impression.

The Glass House • New Caanan, Connecticut

"I was brought up on a sleeping porch, so I'm used to this," says Philip Johnson referring to the all glass house he built for himself over 50 years ago. "It's very livable because, like anything else, you adapt to it. When it's too hot you eat or sleep outside. In a house like this you live in the weather—it's a changing shoal."[2] On close reading, this typically wry comment says little about the house. In fact, it ignores or dismisses any merits it might have.

The Glass House, as it is popularly called, can only be understood as one element, perhaps the most important element, in a larger tapestry which is the property that Philip Johnson has cultivated and built on since the late '40s. If not taken in this context, questions regarding the success of the house as a house are misplaced. Johnson himself often dismisses the houses's value, but never fails to mention its importance in the way he regards and fashions his property. While the Glass House never changed, everything around it did—the property became his canvas and laboratory. "I learned that a pavilion in the woods is suffocated by the trees," he said. "They close in. The wallpaper needed pushing out."

In an article in the *Architectural Review* written in 1950, Johnson outlined his views on the relationships between the compositional principles seen in his work at New Canaan and various historical examples. In that same article he acknowledged his indebtedness to Mies van der Rohe for the very idea of the Glass House: "Mies had mentioned to me as early as 1945 how easy it would be to build a house entirely of large sheets of glass. I was skeptical at the time, and it was not until I had seen the sketches of the Farnsworth

"In order to live successfully in Philip Johnson's new house one would have to be Philip Johnson, or at least a reasonable facsimile. In its time Versailles must also have been a little problematic, to the peasants outside, but after one has admitted that several Louis's were able to stand the pace without undue strain, one is free to enjoy the architecture."[3]
—Arthur Drexler, October 1949

Good Company

House that I started the three-year work of designing my Glass House. My debt is therefore clear, in spite of obvious differences in composition and relation to the ground."

A great fuss has been made over the years about lack of privacy in a glass house—but, there's plenty of privacy if one looks at Johnson's site as if it were a large room. On one side a screen of trees conceals the "room" from the public road. The land slopes down past the guest house to a broad, clear lawn, with the glass pavilion placed at its western limit. Immediately beyond the house is an abrupt drop into a valley, out of which appear only the trimmed tops of trees.

The floor of the house appears to extend to the low concrete rail so that, from inside, it is defined only by the boundary of the ample terrace; the view extends beyond this to trees and rolling landscape, or downward to the lake.

"With the lights out and the snow failing," says Johnson, "it is almost like a celestial elevator." Living in the house one is in a controlled, slightly detached communion with nature, an observer rather than participant.

In terms of the architectural vocabulary used the glass house is the most economical expression of a volume. In fact it is less like a house than like a diagram drawn in the air to indicate a quantity of space. And so, in several ways, it might be said of this small and simple building that its simplicity is really only skin deep.

The brick used on the floor/platform is laid in a herringbone pattern, and, as elsewhere in the house, is Pennsylvania Ironspot. Its color ranges from a deep, orange-flecked red to dark brown, and it has been heavily glazed with wax to bring out a cold, purple overtone.

The most dominant element, and the only internal one that cuts through the ceiling plane, is a 10-foot in diameter brick cylinder housing a leather-tiled bathroom, and a built-in fireplace for the living areas. Its round mass thickens the space around it, drawing attention to the fireplace.

The roof, and the steel columns by which it is supported, seem dropped over the platform like a kind of glass bell. The brick cylinder projects through the roof and reappears on top

left: The Casino, Schloss Glienke, 1825, architect Karl Friedrich Schinkel (1781-1841).

The Casino, Schinkel's first work for Prince Karl at Glienke, is a villa in the best classical sense, with admirably harmonious proportions.

of the house emphasizing the relative weightlessness of the steel cage.

The floor and the ceiling are radiant heated. The furnace is located in the guest house across the lawn, and from there the pipes move out under the gravel path towards the glass pavilion. As the pipes run under the gravel they automatically melt the snow keeping the path clear all winter.

In plan the house is a rectangle 32' x 56'. The long dimension is divided into three equal bays, and the steel columns are placed to emphasize the extremities of the total volume. The height from floor to finished ceiling is 10 feet 6 inches, with a door rising uninterrupted to the full height on each facade, a simple way to establish the grandiose scale.

The facades, entirely of glass, are the minimum interference between the area they enclose and the surrounding view. Because the individual panels of glass are so large, interest is automatically shifted away from the glass itself to the divisions made by the steel columns. When the sun splashes through the trees, the glass and the house with it seem to disappear in a reflected mobile of foliage and clouds. Protection from this sometimes dazzling barrage of sunlight is achieved without benefit of curtains.

There are 176 running feet of glass wall, each of which has been equipped with a set of cloth shades. These are like flat, narrow scrolls, permanently unrolled. They can be spread out to cover a long expanse of glass, or banked one behind the other, by sliding them along a track in the ceiling.

There are only two major area divisions in the entire room. The most important, in terms of the amount of space it conceals, is the line of cabinets marking off the bedroom. These cabinets are only six feet high, and the basic shape of the house is maintained because it is possible to see the intersection of ceiling and glass wall behind them.

In his inimitable style, Johnson shrugs the house off saying, "I'd never do it again—I'm numb when I think about the Glass House," Johnson said. "I feel now it's a vacuum. I never think of the house except for repairs; the most interesting house is the one I'm going to do next."

Doors hung on a double axis, columns symmetrically aligned, a floor that is really a podium (but for the steps)—everything suggests a highly refined Greek temple.

All the furniture in the Glass House was designed by Mies van der Rohe. In the living area are two of the famous chairs designed originally for the German Pavilion in the 1929 Barcelona Fair, a glass and metal coffee table which first appeared in the Tugendhat house, and an elegant leather-cushioned stool. Each of these modern classics is placed with a meticulous precision equivalent to that which went into its design.

A 17th Century painting by Poussin sits on an easel as if it were hanging on an invisible wall. It's lit by a single spotlight.

The arrangement is so completely and irrevocably formal that it frees people from the need to be formal.

In America Mies devoted himself to three basic building-forms: the high-rise skeleton structure (skyscraper) with identical floors behind a seemingly unbroken glass surface; the low-rise skeleton construction (such as the secondary IIT buildings); and the pavilion, a support-free interior, which in its ideal form was a floating volume of "air between two plates."

The Farnsworth House represents the latter—the perfect resolution of the pavilion—the embodiment of simplicity itself.

Mies's work is inadequately described by phrases such as "almost nothing," or "less is more." These terms belie the careful attention he paid to quality of materials, and quantity of detail, which are as much the hallmark of his buildings as their classical simplicity.

Farnsworth House • Plano, Illinois

D r. Edith Farnsworth commissioned Mies van der Rohe to design a weekend retreat for her in rural Illinois in 1946. The result is a structure of light in the midst of nature —transparent, taut, and weightless. Pure to the point of austerity, the house is truly sublime.

The most obvious thing to say about the Farnsworth House is that it is a single space walled from floor to ceiling in glass. But, there is nothing obvious about this house. Most visitors are awestruck by their initial perception—a feeling that doesn't go away. The simple rectilinear geometry of its piers and slabs, the transparency of its walls creates an impression, which Mies fully intended, of architectural structure reduced to its very essence. The image is all the more striking in a wooded natural environment.

The floor of the house hovers some five feet above the ground. One reason is that the house is in the flood plain of the Fox River, which flows westerly a few yards away from the south elevation; the house is set high enough to ride above encroaching water. The river tends to rise and overflow its banks in the spring, so that the house can look like a pier or a boat.

Another reason that the house hovers is that Mies wanted a quality of airiness, of space-in-motion, that an earth-bound house would not have had. Visually heightened by the white of the painted steel, the house seems in a state of levitation, prompting one to conclude that Mies was moved as much by esthetic as by functional considerations in siting and constructing the building as he did. That this was intention is further reinforced by the contrast between the sturdiness of the steel structure and the apparent immateriality of the glass

Mies's concept of a clear-span structure allows for almost any function relative to the magnitude of a structure.

The Farnsworth House provides a single column-free volume where optimum flexibility is possible. It is, in fact, a universal space.

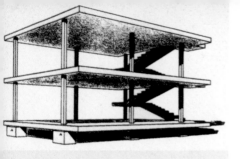

Universal Space
In 1914-15, the young Charles Edouard Jeanneret (later known as Le Corbusier) designed a concrete system—a veritable housing kit—to help with the rapid reconstruction of war-ravaged Flanders. The Dom-ino system, as he called it, was a set of basic, mass-produced components that made up a simple six-point-support concrete skeleton with cantilevered slabs. The framework of the dwelling could be assembled in less than three weeks; rubble walls made from ruined buildings could be used as an infill. The name 'Dom-ino' implied both the Latin word for house (domus) and the game of dominoes.

As the weight of the building is borne by the skeleton, the external cladding can be arranged without concern for the load on it and without interruption to its frame. The outer walls become a membrane to be punctured as functional necessities or compositional instincts require. In the drawings for Dom-ino houses, glass was often placed at the corners, just where a traditional masonry structure would have been structurally most solid.

The system reflect Le Corbusier's admiration for the unadorned dwellings of the Mediterranean, with their flat roofs and cubic shapes modelled by light. Indeed, the Dom-ino houses were the first of a number of his attempts at founding a modern, industrialized equivalent to the vernaculars of the past.

walls it frames.

Four simple steps bring one to an open rectangular terrace of travertine nearly as large in plan as the house. Five more steps and you're on the porch, another travertine plane that is a continuation of the floor of the house. You turn 90-degrees to enter the house itself.

Painted steel columns, resting on concrete footings, are welded flush to the fascias of the floor and the roof, which are made up of girders crossing laterally, with diagonal bracing, and filled in with concrete.

The Farnsworth House is one of the first completed buildings in which the architect made use of the wide-flange steel beam that became so much a part of his architectural vocabulary. Mies appreciated the beam not just for its strength—a tube would have been just as strong—but for its sculptural appearance and the tectonic character its placement on the exterior of the slabs added to the structure. In short, the I-beam undoubtedly appealed to his esthetic sense as much as it represented the steel technology he so often claimed as a point of departure in his work.

Mies relied on the services of local craftsmen to fabricate all the building's elements to his scrupulous specifications. The frame of the house was carefully polished before the coats of white paint were applied: first, all the welding marks at the connections between columns and beams were ground down; next, Mies had the steel sandblasted to get rid of the rough texture of the rolled, structural sections; then he had a coat of zinc sprayed over the sandblasted surface to prevent rust; and, finally, white paint was applied with such care that the finished surfaces look almost baked on.

Son of a stonemason, Mies devoted himself to no single task more diligently than the selection of the 24-by-33-inch slabs that make up the modules of the floor of the house and terrace. Travertine was one of Mies's favorite stones, and he employed it with singular effectiveness in the Farnsworth House. Even now, the slabs, white tinged with gray and all of them original, remain among its most striking features.

The house is a rectangular structure of eight steel columns,

above: The Dom-ino skeleton, Le Corbusier, 1914-1915. Included are principles—the free plan, the free façade, the flat-roof terrace—that would be of later importance to Le Corbusier. left: IIT's Crown Hall was the first large-scale realization of Mies's concept of the clear-span structure. Housing the School of Architecture, the building consists of a 120-foot-wide, 220-foot-long, 18-foot-high column-free hall.

set in two parallel rows some 28 feet apart. In the long direction of the plan the steel columns are spaced 22 feet apart. The floor slab is about four feet above the ground, and the ceiling plane is about nine feet above that. At each end the floor and roof slabs cantilever out six feet beyond the last row of columns.

Just as the visible exterior form is minimally expressed, the space within is maximally open. The interior is a single space asymmetrically subdivided by a freestanding core of wood, with a fireplace facing the larger living area, a utility room flanked by two bathrooms east and west, and a kitchen in the narrow space to the north. There is a dining area west of the core. A freestanding teak-clad storage closet serves a sleeping area east of the core. The living area faces south with an unimpeded view of the river. The house is sheathed entirely in 3/4-inch thick plate glass.

Plumbing, wiring, and circulation fans are embedded in a cylindrical stack inside the utility room. The floor platform is deep enough to hold a radiant-heating system as well as all the plumbing.

The solution of the problem of drainage, especially as it affected the floor of the deck and the terrace, is credited mostly to Mies's chief assistant on the Farnsworth project, Myron Goldsmith, who later went on to a distinguished career of his own. Most of the water simply runs off the travertine surface of the terrace. Whatever infiltrates the porous marble drains into a system of gravel-filled, sheet-metal pans welded into an inverted pyramid and then out through pipe openings to the ground. The flat roof, in turn, is bordered by low, single-beveled coping that water cannot overflow. The roof slopes slightly from the edges towards the center where water runs through a drain into a central pipe, directly above the core, that is connected to the utility room stack, where it runs into the ground.

One missing convenience was air conditioning. It should be remembered that even wealthy people of the Middle West in the late 1940s were long accustomed to enduring summer heat in their homes. Air-conditioning in private dwellings

A Higher Unity

With each project Mies came closer to realizing his ambition—to build a totally wide open structure with transparent walls and a nearly free-floating roof—a structure that would, as he put it, "bring Nature, man and architecture together into a higher Unity."

The Farnsworth House came as close to realizing this ambition as is practically possible. Two earlier structures with similar intentions are now also regarded as landmarks in 20th Century architecture.

Mies brilliantly synthesized the classical and the modern in the temporary German pavilion that he designed for the International Exhibition in Barcelona in 1929. He created a luxurious, almost opulent structure while he liberated the wall planes of glass and polished, colored travertine from their customary role of supporting the roof. The thin concrete roof slab is balanced on eight chrome-plated columns. Sunlight reflects from the twin pools and dapples the ceiling and the walls inside and out.

The Tugendhat House, built in Brno in 1930, is sited on a hill. The north side, off the road, is closed and demur; the south side is open and transparent. The true revelation in this house is the open livingroom/diningroom/study at the lower level.

above: Mies van der Rohe, German Pavilion, Barcelona, Spain, 1929. The chair Mies designed for the pavilion has become well known as the Barcelona chair.
right: Mies van der Rohe, Tugendhat House, Brno, Czechoslovakia, 1930. The chair designed for this house has become well known as the Tugendhat chair. There are Barcelona chairs here as well.

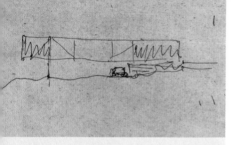

Pure and Simple

It is not obligatory to reveal structure in architecture any more than it is to conceal it; it is a matter of choice. Buildings will certainly stand up regardless. For many years after the advent of the cast-iron and steel skeleton buildings were clad in masonry, because architects were committed to regard massing and ornament as a primary architectural concern.

It's only after a reductive philosophy of abstraction took hold in the arts, with Mies as its chief proponent in architecture, that the expression of structure pure and simple achieved primacy.

The time was ripe at the close of the Second World War for modernism to shine forth after being eclipsed for a decade or more by the Depression and international totalitarianism. Most of the architects and designers who had emigrated to the U.S. before the war were teaching by now and bringing abstraction to the fore as the favored expressive language.

It is when architecture expresses itself, rather than points indirectly to a metaphorical, symbolic, or literary meaning, that it is referred to as formalist. This is one of the oft-talked about modernist ideals.

In good design, however, all this should merely be a shift in emphasis rather than a difference in intentions. Many of the same criteria of judgment should hold true if one is able to see past the surface. It might even be argued that when a building succeeds it is always for the same reasons.

was as much a rarity as it was a luxury. So far as is known, Dr. Farnsworth was not troubled by the lack of it.

Heating and drainage were more unconditional necessities, and in both respects the Farnsworth House was and remains quite adequately equipped. Hot water pipes in a coil system embedded in the floor not only radiate heat throughout the interior but provide special comfort to feet chilled by the winter cold. The slowness of such a system to make itself felt to anyone entering the house when the heat has been turned off is alleviated by a small forced-air furnace in the utility room, whose fan blows a measure of warmth directly into the interior.

The full impact of Mies's objectives is clearly felt from the interior of the house. Here the dialogue of tangible, reductivist structure and intangible, open space, each dependent on the other, is lucidly asserted; his intentions are evidenced by the spectacular view of the outdoors. Alluring to behold, the view constantly shifts according to weather conditions, time of day, or the changing seasons. The house provides shelter by filtering nature rather than by walling it off. Mies's own reflections confirm this: "When one looks at Nature through the glass walls of the Farnsworth House," he once said, "it takes on a deeper significance than when one stands outside. More of Nature is thus expressed—it becomes part of a greater whole."[1]

Nature is integral to the viewer's appreciation of the architecture. The seven acres of the original narrow strip of land on which Mies was commissioned to build are themselves laid out in an east-west direction bordering the low banks of the river. In choosing the exact site for the house, Mies was moved to situate it behind and in the shade of the district's most venerable black sugar maple tree, once, at the turn of the 1950s, resplendent and now slowly dying, but still majestic, a foil to the geometry of the architecture and a screen through which the river is visible. During the autumn it turns a radiant gold, underscoring further the contrast of the flat white of the house with its variegated setting.

Mies supervised the selection of materials, especially the

above: Glass House on a Hillside: Sketch Elevation, Mies van der Rohe, 1934. A gap of 15 years separated this conceptual sketch from its realization. Exhibited in the first major retrospective of Mies's work at MoMA in 1947 (page 9), the drawing had a profound effect on Charles Eames (page 158).
left: The kitchen side of the Farnsworth House at dusk.

travertine, and insisted on the highest quality and finest tolerance in the joinery. In spite of the fact that components such as the I-beams were drawn from industrial sources he exerted his influence over the construction crews so that everything was lavished with care and the highest level of craftsmanship possible. There is the same kind of concern for detail as in any traditional structure.

While Mies's longstanding reputation as a classicist is borne out in early and late stages by the axiality of the glazed enclosure and deck, he could deviate at will from doctrinaire classicism—much the way his hero Schinkel freely employed asymmetries in his Italianate villas in Potsdam near Berlin. The very location of the Farnsworth terrace ajog of the house attests to this. A similar informality in the interior is evident from the outset, with the core invariably shown closer to the northeast corner of the house than to the lateral axis.

Mies's house was a very American sort of statement—dynamic, cantilevered, almost in motion. Mies's responsiveness to North America—a continent of motion—began long before he came to Chicago; indeed, this quality of motion is already quite apparent in the Barcelona Pavilion (although the Pavilion did sit on a pedestal), and it is the quality Mies undoubtedly derived from Wright's Prairie houses.

Mies accomplishes his goal admirably. He is able to create a dematerialized architecture that is the expression of a transcendental order at the same time that he gives over to nature that which is its due: the ability to demonstrate in full glory the ever-changing light of day and the seasons of the year. The alleged "nothingness" that went into the house draws in its environment so that it is an integral part of the experience.

As the architect and critic Peter Blake wrote:

"The Farnsworth house is, in all likelihood, the most complete statement of glass-and-steel, skin-and-bones architecture Mies or anyone else will ever be able to make. It is, also, the ultimate in universality, the ultimate in precision and polish, the ultimate in the crystallization of an idea."[2]

Everything Mies ever strove for is present in the Farnsworth House: a clear-span structure, minimal support, luxurious materials, impeccable details. Complexly simple, the house gracefully embraces the landscape.

In the detail at right, the distinction between inside and outside is truly blurred.

One important benefit of Robert Venturi's rebelliousness is that he made it possible to look favorably once more upon certain architects who had been ignored or dismissed over the years. One such architect is Irving John Gill (1870-1936) whose Scripps House, 1916, is pictured above. Venturi says that he has "spent some time thinking about Gill . . . he is many things at once."

Gill, who trained under Louis Sullivan in Chicago, set up his own practice in San Diego in 1896. Although his early work belongs to the Arts and Crafts Shingle Style, he soon created his own cubic, concrete-block vocabulary inspired by the Spanish Mission Style of California.

Vanna Venturi House • Chestnut Hill, Pennsylvania

Thirty-five years ago Robert Venturi "called for an architecture that promotes richness and ambiguity over unity and clarity, contradiction and redundancy over harmony and simplicity."[1]

Venturi's first built project was a house for his mother Vanna. She didn't want an ostentatious house, she didn't want an expensive house, and since she didn't drive, she didn't want a garage. Beyond these simple requests, she gave her son freedom to do as he wished. Throughout six years of design and construction, Robert Venturi developed six different schemes for the house.

Things "started out more like [Louis] Kahn," he said but his intuition, he added, eventually "took control of my hand." The result was a house that was at once "modern and not modern."

The Vanna Venturi house is arguably the most renowned house designed in recent times. In its combined use of classical and vernacular elements, and its embrace of architectural iconography, it set the stage for Venturi's long and important career. Years later, he looked back at the house and commented that "what seemed extraordinary then seems ordinary now—and vice versa."[2]

It is a simple house made complex because its elements are oversized and its spaces are skewed and shifted in unexpected ways. None of these things is discomfitting—they are, in fact, witty, even whimsical gestures. The front façade seems more or less symmetrical at first. But the symmetry is broken by the placement of such elements as the windows and the chimney. One side of the enormous split gable has two square windows, a larger mullioned one and a smaller

above: In 1996 Venturi, Scott Brown and Associates redesigned the Museum of Contemporary Art, San Diego, around the Irving Gill-designed home of Ellen Browning Scripps.

right: Vanna Venturi, who died in 1975, sits outside the house her son built for her.

A Villa for Mom

The following are excerpts from Robert Venturi's Nonstraightforward Architecture: A Gentle Manifesto *which appear in the catalogue to the ground-breaking exhibition,* Complexity and Contradiction, *that he curated for the Museum of Modern Art in 1966:*

"I like complexity and contradiction in architecture. . . . I speak of a complex and contradictory architecture based on the richness and ambiguity of modern experience, including that experience which is inherent in art. . .

"But architecture is necessarily complex and contradictory in its very inclusion of the traditional Vitruvian elements of commodity, firmness, and delight. And today the wants of program, structure, mechanical equipment, and expression, even in single buildings in simple contexts, are diverse and conflicting in ways previously unimaginable. . . . I welcome the problems and exploit the uncertainties. By embracing contradiction as well as complexity, I aim for vitality as well as validity. . . .

"Architects can no longer afford to be intimidated by the puritanically moral language of orthodox Modern architecture. . . .

"But an architecture of complexity and contradiction has a special obligation toward the whole: its truth must be in its totality or its implications of totality. It must embody the difficult unity of inclusion rather than the easy unity of exclusion. More is not less."

one; the other side has a horizontal window composed of five connected squares. The chimney rises behind the gable, set off center. The door is centered and sits under an applied ornamental fragment of a circle. One of the most delightful maneuvers occurs when following this arc from left to right—one expects another window, but it's "missing."

On the façade, Venturi applies conventional elements unconventionally, emphasizing the classical and domestic symbolism of the house. The conversation between the classical and the domestic has remained central to Venturi's architectural philosophy through the years. His work has involved both sign and symbol, and this house was the springboard for his philosophy. It was a moment for fresh beginnings. "With its gable roof, central door, ordinary windows and chimney, it looked like an elemental house, like a child's drawing of a house," Venturi reflected years after the house was completed.

The interior elements are also familiar and unfamiliar, "complex," says Venturi, "in both shapes and relationships." There are numerous twists and turns that reflect the outside on the inside—this is no decorated shed. One of the most beautiful moments occurs in the intersection of the vault that follows the arched window and the otherwise flat ceiling (photo, upper right). It's as if there are two ceilings.

The house is ultimately an act of rebellion. An act of rebellion is meaningful if it gives the rest of us permission to see and think about things differently. Whatever is novel about the act itself may wear off with time, but its legacy may be more important than we realize because with time the liberty is invisible and we take it for granted. Our approach to examining buildings critically would probably not be the same now if it were not for Robert Venturi's manifesto, "Complexity and Contradiction," and the house that he built for his mother. The house also paved the way for a new style, but it is no more responsible for the vagaries of that style than Mies is for the proliferation of the glass box. Fifteen years after "Complexity and Contradiction" Venturi bemoaned the fact that nothing had really changed, *"plus ça change"* as he

above: Venturi says of the house he built for his mother, "the almost Palladian symmetry is disturbed to accommodate the particular needs of the spaces."

left: Rear façade of the Villa Pisani, Andrea Palladio (1508-80), Vicenza, Italy, 1545.

put it. He now refers to himself as a classicist whereas earlier he described himself as a mannerist.

The primary purpose of the Vanna Venturi house was to make its mark in architectural discourse rather than as actual architecture. To ignore questions of language that the house raises, therefore, is to really avoid answering the questions—what does this house mean and how has it changed things? This is important but troubling because what it "means" ultimately has nothing to do with its success as a house and everything to do with its success as an object in the language game that comprises the discourse now so much associated with architecture, a discourse that has just about worn itself out.

This might seem to draw us away from the real meaning of the house—not so. This remains all that it means and as such it is just as important. In fact the house is well designed and quite a bit less contradictory than might be imagined. One of the problems with contradiction as a stylistic gesture is once a style changes, the original gesture disappears along with it. This is also one of the traps of language—intention can no longer be experienced, it must be explained.

The color of the house is a case in point. When it was completed in 1964, Venturi painted the exterior a taupe gray. Two years later, he painted it green in response to a comment of Marcel Breuer's that green was the color of nature and therefore should never be used on buildings. The meaning of the green here is purely anecdotal. It should be pointed out that the green in question is more the green of New England meetinghouses than "the color of nature."

There is much that is mannered in the house and as such can now be looked at as the result of questions of style. Did Venturi do what he did out of necessity or simply because it broke the rules? Whatever the answer, he is still a good designer who makes quality spaces. In the end, however, it is not as a model of anything radically new that the house is important, but rather it is an emblem of change itself. The house is certainly a poke in the eye of Modernism, but what a glorious poke in the eye!

Venturi likes to contradict himself in speech as much as in his architecture: "The house is big as well as little, by which I mean that it is a little house with a big scale. Inside the elements are big: the fireplace is "too big" and the mantel "too high" for the size of the room; doors are wide, the chair rail high." "The stair, considered as an element alone . . . is bad; in relation to its position in a hierarchy of uses and spaces . . . it is good."[3]

The all-white, hard-edged geometry of the Smith House is set in opposition to the rugged Connecticut coastline.

Richard Meier considers the house his first mature building.

"It was there . . . that I was first able to develop and test a number of design issues that I had been preoccupied with. In fact, those issues still preoccupy me: the making of space, the distinction between interior and exterior space, the play of light and shadow, the different ways in which a building exists in the natural or urban world; the separation of public and private space."[1]

Almost entirely made of glass, the back wall makes the landscape part of the domestic space.

Smith House • Darien, Connecticut

The Smith House sits amid rocks and trees on one-and-a-half acres, a dense cluster of evergreens marking the entrance to the property. What greets the visitor is a flat, sheer, white, three-story high wall; except for five small windows, it is ostensibly a beautiful, blank canvas. The path extends as a kind of footbridge to the front door. There is little, if any, view beyond—the house conceals everything but the sky. From the front door, a narrow corridor of space, a slice through the house, gives us the first peak at the water and the horizon on the other side, before we step over the threshold. This momentary glimpse reveals the central meaning of the house—it is a masterful orchestration of interior and exterior spaces around a magnificent view of Long Island Sound.

The house appears in photographs to be made of concrete. In fact, it is white paint on vertical redwood siding. This is a surprise initially, but the finish seems perfectly appropriate to the setting. Photographs place it closer to its modernist relatives, whereas it's more like an American house with a European accent.

You enter at the second floor level to experience what Meier calls a "180-degree explosion." The living room, dining area, and terraces all open to the spectacular, unobstructed view of the waterfront. From this height within the house, which is already placed high upon the cliff, the vista spreads in every direction—vertically as well as horizontally. The house seems to embrace the entire landscape; what was kept out of sight at the entrance is now graciously given to us inside—as if it belonged to the house.

The dramatic view of sea and sky is framed in the trans-

Richard Meier achieved an unusual unity outside and inside the Smith House—including the simple furnishings. With the exception of paintings and a few bright accents, everything but the oak floors is crisp white. The effect is far from antiseptic, due to the constantly changing color and light from outdoors.

Fig. 3.

The Modern Cottage

It wasn't until the early 1800s that the idea of a small, but comfortable independent house with fresh air, sunlight, and greenery became an attainable goal for the average person. Once it did, it was a veritable movement. In the process a new kind of domestic literature was born; a combination of sentimental poetry and prose, it was the forerunner of today's home and style magazines. Inspirational designs were published in so-called pattern-books.

One of the most popular pattern-books, COTTAGE RESIDENCES (1842), demonstrated a concern for an original American style as well as practicality. It was written by a Hudson River Valley landscape gardener named Andrew Jackson Downing (1815-52), who foresaw a far-reaching, pastoral landscape, dotted with pleasant houses, varied but always orderly, each one set in its own extensive, well-tended garden.

Downing saw the chimney as one of the important cottage features: "The chimney-tops, in all countries where fires are used, are decidedly expressive of purpose, as they are associated with all our ideas of warmth, the cheerful fireside, and the social winter circle. The learned Bishop Hall says, 'Look to the towered chiminies, which should be the windpipes of good hospitalitie.'"

parency of the rear façade. This transparency is amplified by the sheer size of the panes of glass and the placement of the exposed, supporting steel columns. They are placed just far enough in from the outer walls that they visually, as well as physically, take the burden of weight.

Directly opposite the entry, a painted brick fireplace seems to pierce the glass as its chimney rises straight up outside into the sky. This oddly anachronistic element is so blatantly placed, as the only obstacle in an otherwise unbroken panorama, that it can't help calling attention to itself and its meaning. Frank Lloyd Wright said that "the hearth is the heart of the home," and this one is truly at the heart. It's as if the entire landscape itself were the family room.

The interior of the house is a systematic separation of its public and private spaces. The public area, where the family meets and entertains, is at the rear of the house, overlooking the water. The private side of the house, bedrooms, bathrooms, and kitchen—a series of small, closed, cellular spaces—is on the entry side, facing the land, the woods, and the road. The lower level is for dining, cooking, and laundry. The master bedroom and living room are on the main floor, with secondary bedrooms above them.

Both the living and the dining areas open directly to outdoor terraces, and the house is topped by an outdoor roofdeck. Meier adds that "all the living spaces are interconnected vertically: the living area opening up to the library and down to the dining room. They constitute the open aspect of the house and focus upon the view of the water." The view in every direction to the water is magnificent, and the house has been organized to obtain maximum benefit from it.

The Smith House is frequently compared to Le Corbusier's Villa Savoye or Rudolf Schindler's Lovell Beach House. These are, without doubt, stylistic antecedents, but the comparisons are superficial. The disposition of spaces in those houses differs from Meier's, but more important, their meaning derives from their time and place. Stylistic differences aside, the Smith House is really the next logical step in the evolution of the American suburban cottage.

above: "A suburban cottage for a small family" from Downing's *Cottage Residences,* 1842.

Downing probably would have said of the Smith House, "such a building would be distinguishable from a barn or outhouse only by the presence of chimneys and windows of larger size, and would convey to the mind no impression whatever of refinement in its occupants."

In the 1840s there began to be an emphasis on the home as a unique statement, an individualized setting for a particular family—a clearly visible means of defining themselves. "Inside" and "outside" were discussed as concepts beneficial to an individual's well-being; to be outside the city was better, for one thing. In the home itself, the flow of spaces in and out—the use of gardens, patios, porches, verandas, balconies, and other extensions of the house to the outside—meant better physical and emotional health. And, it would all be better yet if it were made visible through symbolic ornament—a meaningful style.

In their democratic wisdom the American pattern-book writers were among the first to assert that architectural forms elicit universal responses. All houses need, they argued, certain domestic symbols to articulate the feelings one associates with the home—this was called "expression of purpose." Chimneys and overhanging roofs with high gables and deep eaves evoked home, as did the welcoming entry porch and the comfortable side piazza.

Times have certainly changed. The Smith House is no mere cottage; it's more akin to what was called the cottage villa. But, aside from differences in historical context and the social class of the clients, the intentions in the Smith House are little different. The forms of the traditional house may have been turned on their head, the vocabulary may be undeniably modernist, but the Smith House is the result of the combined conscious aspirations of the clients and the architect, and their unconscious American-ness. The house has a double indentity: as one of his first published works, it distinguished the architect as a vendor of images. At the same time, it addressed the clients' desire for personal distinction.

According to Andrew Jackson Downing, who cited the English art critic John Ruskin, domestic architecture should express the owner's condition or class, his occupation and background. If overhanging eaves and gothic tracery no longer connote home, then perhaps a clean white cube, with no moldings and huge expanses of glass, will.

above: The pristine, white wall that initially greets the visitor to the Smith House.
middle: Two views of the main living area; note how the fireplace mantle extends outside.
right: Richard Meier inherited the white of Le Corbusier as his signature "color." A little recognized fact is that Le Corbusier used color (in buildings such as Unité d'Habitation). Meier follows suit here and in two or three other places on the private side of the house.

7

the

corporate

campus

General Motors Technical Center
Deere & Company Administrative Center

In the prosperity of the postwar years good design began to make good sense. Alliances were formed between museums and business where before the war they might have been considered suspect, a distasteful mingling of high culture with low. All of a sudden fine art and industrial design were being talked about in the same breath.

In 1950, Edgar Kaufmann, Jr., Director of the Department of Industrial Design at New York's Museum of Modern Art, launched a program to bring high quality modern design to the attention of the public. The *Good Design* program, as he called it, was conceived as a collaborative effort between the museum and the Merchandise Mart of Chicago.

The judges for the first *Good Design* exhibition, Meyric C. Rogers, curator of decorative arts at the Art Institute of Chicago, and Alexander Girard, a designer and architect from Detroit, selected some 250 products. Charles and Ray Eames designed the exhibition; their combination of showmanship and humor helped ease the minds of visitors, most of whom were seeing modern design for the first time. An introductory section displayed old and new products in a manner intended to show skeptics the affinities between classics of the past and potential future classics. The exhibition opened in January of 1950.

That same year Philip Johnson organized a symposium at the Museum of Modern Art on "The Esthetics of Automobile Design." When MoMA recognized

"The Good Design exhibitions mean different things to a great many people . . . . When its meaning is clear, and generally accepted, . . . it will be time to put an end to the Good Design program."[1] — Edgar Kaufmann, Jr.

Poetry in Utility

In the 1920s, J. J. Oud suggested that architecture lead to the experience of "higher things" through ruthless objectivity. The European avant-garde was always attracted to the "true" products of American culture particularly the anonymous vernacular creations of garage and factory structures. They certainly had a higher regard for the work of Albert Kahn than Americans ever did.

Before 1910 industrial buildings and factories belonged to the world of engineering rather than architectural design. By 1910, Albert Kahn (1869–1942) had created a distinctive factory idiom. In 1917 he went to work on the River Rouge plant for Ford in Detroit. In place of the traditional multi-story factories, Kahn developed open, steel-frame structures with entire walls of glass, lightweight metal and/or brick infill. Kahn sought to avoid "unnecessary ornamentation," achieve simplicity and proper respect for cost of maintenance," and to "make for a type which, though strictly utilitarian and functional, has distinct architectural merit."

Mies felt that Kahn's structures were the very essence of building, a clear display of a grammar that could be assembled into prose or elevated into poetry. Mies used a photograph of Kahn's Martin Bomber Plant as the basis for his designs for a projected concert hall. As in the case of the Glass Skyscraper, these designs would only be realized many years later.

something like the automobile, it was automatically elevated to an art form.

Public design education was not limited to the rarefied confines of the art museum, however. In the decade before the war, large corporations had already begun to see the merits of appealing to an informed public. By war's end well-known designers were being vigorously recruited in increasing numbers—Raymond Loewy at Studebaker and Greyhound, Norman Bel Geddes at Nash, Walter Dorwin Teage at Boeing, Henry Dreyfuss at Hyster and TWA—to name only a few.

With the increasing migration of corporations from urban to suburban, even rural locations, there was a growing need to bring style to citizens everywhere; a mass democratizing of taste. And, of course, this was all aided and abetted by advertising—in newspapers, magazines, radio, and now, on television.

The success of John Deere's new headquarters is an indication of the change in the climate. In the days right after the new building was completed, employees voiced concern about the daring design and the obvious expense of the project. There was fear that farmers, the primary customers for the product, would resent the outlay for the building. The fears proved quite unfounded. Farmers who had dealt with Deere all their lives, whose fathers and grandfathers had been Deere customers, were among the most enthusiastic visitors to the building. They come from all over the country to see it and identify strongly with both the building and the company. Distributors and dealers use the building as a selling point for Deere products. They bring their customers by the bus-load. Visitors are particularly interested in the exhibition in the display area—by Alexander Girard, the same architect and designer who had done many of the best of the *Good Design* shows for MoMA.

Eero Saarinen became the architect of choice to design the new corporate complexes. Saarinen was the first modern architect fortunate enough to

above: Albert Kahn and Associates, Ohio Steel Foundry Roll and Heavy Machine Shop, Lima, Ohio. 1938. Tall windows, plain stucco fascia, and light colored brick are treated as a continuous surface emphasizing the thinness and tautness of the structure.
left: Mies van der Rohe, Minerals and Metals Research Building, Illinois Institute of Technology, Chicago, 1943.

work on a titanic scale without serious budgetary restrictions. SOM would soon follow. By 1962 Saarinen's firm had completed or was finishing Bell Labs, IBM and TWA, General Motors and John Deere.

A Sleek Industrial Campus

Alfred P. Sloan, Jr., Chairman of the Board of General Motors, and "architect" of GM's decentralized organizational framework, envisioned a place where research, engineering, manufacturing, development, and styling would take place in the atmosphere of a college or university campus; or, at least the *look* of one.

"I am sure we all realize," said Sloan, "how much appearance has to do with sales. With all cars fairly good mechanically, it is a dominating proposition. And in a product such as ours, where the individual appeal is so great, it means a tremendous influence on our future prosperity."[2]

GM initially wanted another Cranbrook and might have got one from Eliel Saarinen. But, another Cranbrook wouldn't have worked for Eero, who took over the project when his father retired. He insisted on designing buildings "that would symbolize industrial achievement and look as modern tomorrow as they do today."

This sentiment probably had little appeal in an industry built upon impermanance. After all, it was General Motors who declared that "dynamic obsolescence caused by the annual model change is the lifeblood of the auto industry and a key factor in the national economy."[1] But, Saarinen was not about to give them built-in obsolescence. He convinced GM that their Technical Center should be an expression of a high-precision, mass-production metal industry. Once the corporation grasped this concept, its formidable technological resources were placed at the service of the Saarinen firm and the associated architect-engineers Smith, Hinchman & Grylls. The buildings which resulted from this fusion of serious design and technological power were to be described by *Architectural Forum* as "exalted industrial products."

above right: The dome of the Styling Auditorium of the GM Technical Center, Warren, Michigan, Eero Saarinen & Associates, 1956.

"We thank Thee , O Lord, for neoprene, sulphanilamide and nylon, and we beseech Thee now for aluminum, maganese and tin." Drawn for *Architectural Record* by Alan Dunn, c. 1947.

New Materials for Peace

The shift to a war economy had led to the construction of many new factories across the country, many expecting to be adapted to the manufacture of consumer products after the war. The National Resource Planning Board considered planning for peacetime essential to "sustain the American concept of living, for full employment, security and the pursuit of happiness."

Just 18 months after Pearl Harbor, the New York Times, in its annual report on American Industry, observed that the nation was over the hump of preparing for and serving the needs of war. The Times noted that most major companies had already established special departments and postwar planning, and predicted a boom that "will come from those three stalwarts of the First World War—railroad rehabilitation, automobiles, and housing—with added fillips from revolutionary synthetics such as nylon, rubber and plastics, the light metals, electronics, planes and new types of food."

Major manufacturers in materiel-based industries expected to have excess capacity at their disposal after the war. Many turned to prominent architects and industrial designers for assistance in conceiving and promoting new applications.

the corporate campus 183

The Future Is Here

The New York World's Fair of 1939 was conceived as a "fair of the future," and as a representation of all the interelated activities and interests of the American way of life.

The General Motors complex was four interconnected buildings. The exhibit known as "Highways and Horizons," designed by Norman Bel Geddes, was the largest presented by any individual participant at the Fair. The view above shows the enormous line waiting to enter the Futurama ride, by far the biggest hit of the entire Fair. The entrance to Futurama, a gigantic curving wall, was painted a metalic silver in imitation of an automobile finish. The appeal was obvious: technology and the machine were not a problem, but a salvation. Industrial design had turned into "scientific research" with business holding the key to a better future.

While some Americans reveled in dreams of technology, others were excluded from its promise. The social discrepancy is nowhere more incisively recorded than in Margaret Bourke-White's photograph below. African American victims of the Louisville Flood line up against a billboard advertising "The American Way."

There could be no denying the "World's Highest Standard of Living," symbolized by automobile ownership, were it not for a natural disaster drawing attention to the hardship of those already hardest hit by the economic depression of the 1930s—America's underpriviledged minorities.

Much of the manufacture of specialized parts took place on the premises. This turned out to be more than convenient. The corporation saw itself as the fourth member of a team that included architect, engineer, and contractor. Their public relations material describes their participation:

"GM's direct contributions included (a) consultation on ceramics with AC Spark Plug Division concerning glazed bricks, and (b) consultation with Inland Manufacturing Division on the Neoprene glazing frame used for solving curtain-wall problems. Likewise, the Research Staff tested many of the new materials, and the Styling Staff designed the modular, luminous ceiling for its own buildings. Even some of GM's own plants made certain special items incorporated into the buildings."

Since GM had the engineering know-how, it guaranteed technical success while logically extending the automobile aesthetic into the very fiber of the campus.

Meanwhile, Mies van der Rohe was engaged in the redesign of the campus of the Armour Institute, renamed the Illinois Institute of Technology, from 1939-1956. Coming as they did from the imagination of a modern master, IIT's factories were regarded as legitimate architecture.

Henry-Russell Hitchcock and Philip Johnson discussed the General Motors Technical Center in "The Buildings We See." In 1952 they wrote, "As has always been the case with industrial buildings, the more specialized functions of certain units provide the most interesting elements for the architect to organize visually. Thus the engine-test cell building, with its rows of round paired stacks on either side, has the most individual character and also the highest quality architecturally."

above: In addition to the *Previews of Progress* exhibit, the GM pavillion at the New York World's Fair featured an impressive, life-size, multi-leveled, futuristic "street intersection of 1960."

left: Margaret Bourke-White, The Louisville Flood. 1937.

A Harrow in the Heartland

In spite of the large sums of money often spent on corporate ventures, clients aren't necessarily any more generous or adventuresome. William A. Hewitt, President of John Deere & Company, was an exception. Both generous and adventuresome, he was a client with a vision.

Hewitt had always been interested in architecture and design. He had worked for many years with designer Henry Dreyfuss on projects for the company. Hewitt knew he wanted his new building to do two things: first, he wanted to pull the company together and improve employee working conditions. Deere employees had been scattered around downtown Moline in several different buildings—some quite old—and clearly there was a need to integrate departments.

Then, he wanted a building that would help the company attract and hold superior personnel. This is of crucial importance to an international business located in a small Midwestern city. To improve the company's image in the world at large and raise the architectural standards of the local community, Hewitt knew that the building had to be esthetically outstanding.

After intensive research and a thorough search for an architect, Hewitt met Eero Saarinen and knew he was the right person for the job. Hewitt describes his first meeting:

"I said to him, 'Well, Eero, I'm glad that you're going to do the job, and I recognize the fact that you are the professional, the expert, and I've heard a lot of horror stories about how clients have ruined the work of good architects by interjecting too much of their own opinion, too many views that are unacceptable to the architect. So I'm not going to breathe down your neck. You go ahead and do it the way you think best.'

"At that point Eero, who was a great pipe smoker, puffed his pipe and said, 'Well, Bill, maybe you *should* breathe down my neck.'"[3]

General Motors Technical Center

World Through a Windshield

At the General Motors Technical Center the car is the measure of all things. Eero Saarinen used automotive materials and technology throughout. He also used the car as a way to measure time and space. He said, "The Center was designed at automobile scale and the changing vistas were conceived to be seen as one drove around the project.

"It has been said that in these buildings I was very much influenced by Mies. But this architecture really carries forward the tradition of American factory buildings which had its roots in the Middle West in the early automobile factories of Albert Kahn . . . the design is based on steel—the metal of the automobile. Like the automobile itself, the buildings are essentially put together, as on an assembly line, out of mass-produced units."

Saarinen was criticized for giving over the spaces of the Technical Center to the automobile.

You can't sense the buildings and the grounds from any one place at Versailles either, so the criticism seems oddly misplaced.

the corporate campus 185

top: Raised walkways link the buildings of the Research Department, GM Technical Center.

above: A postcard gives a sense of the mammoth size of the General Motors campus.

right: Everything about the Technical Center is "automobile," from its scale to its materials.

General Motors Technical Center • Warren, Michigan

General Motors was Eero
Saarinen's coming of age.
Kevin Roche, who had joined
the design team just when the
commission was getting underway, spoke later about
Saarinen's approach:
"Eero brought to [GM] the
humanist tradition of his father,
his own observation of the
architecture of the past, his
Beaux Arts training, and a very
penetrating, very investigative
mind. He brought to it also the
kind of experience he and
Charles Eames had gained
together in exploring the application of new materials and
production techniques to furniture design—all brought with
tremendous ambition. It was
clear that Eero was going to
be a great architect. He was
going to explore everything on
every level. He was not someone who was focusing on a
narrow aspect of architecture,
but on every aspect—master
planning, social implications,
political implications, materials
technology, function, structure,
and decoration."[1]

At the close of World War II the Saarinen firm, father and son, was approached by General Motors Corporation with a proposition—to design what they called a "corporate campus," an idyllic setting for their engineers to dream up the dream cars of average Americans. Though Eero later praised the firm for its generosity and wisdom, in a letter to a friend at this point he seems more than a little skeptical about the pending project, especially the role of the automobile:

> "I am working very hard—the group is the so-called G.M. Engineering Center . . . They are enormous inhuman buildings—the total numbers of cars that have to be parked is 8,000[2]—it is a very tough job . . . so the end result will be not so very good—we will see."[2]

Two years later GM called upon Eero to re-design; his father had stepped down due to failing health. Eero grasped the problem with both hands. Now the automobile played a clear and prominent role in his vision. In another letter to the same friend, Eero says,

> "We have a terrifying amount of work to do. The most interesting of our different projects and also the biggest is a Research Center for General Motors I may have told you a bit about it earlier. We were working on it earlier but the project was discontinued about two years ago—now three months ago they have decided to go ahead again but with a new plan entirely. It is very seldom that one gets a chance to redesign a thing that big and get a chance to correct all one's mistakes and make a whole new set of mistakes. Actually I am

From the very start of the project the architects discussed the need for an elevated water tank and how, since such tanks are usually ugly structures, they are typically relegated to the background. In this instance, it was felt that the tank could be brought out in the open and assigned a place of prominence as a symbol and a design feature. Eero writes "water tanks can be very handsome. We shall make a feature of this tank instead of trying to hide it."

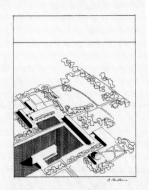

quite enthusiastic about the new plan I think it will be really good—and as you know I don't often praise our own work, the buildings are going to be very very simple the whole thing will look like a small city of factory buildings in a park and in the middle of the park is a large man made lake, the whole group will when built cost about 25 to 30 million dollars what is that in crowns must be something like 140,000,000 crowns—it is about 1/2 of the United Nations that Harrison is doing. When you come the next time to this part of the world I will show you the real thing."[3]

The GM complex would turn out to be one of the first triumphs of the new, postwar corporate-industrial architecture in the United States; it would, in fact, cost over 100 million dollars. Nowhere else, at that point, could one see industrial technology brought to bear so imaginatively on so many emerging problems of contemporary design. As Saarinen put it: "Our intention was threefold: to provide the best possible facilities for industrial research; to create a unified, beautiful, and human environment; and to find an appropriate architectural expression."

The General Motors Technical Center, as it was finally called, occupies the central 320 acres of an approximately 900-acre site. It consists of 25 buildings clustered in five separate organizational constellations—Research, Process Development, Engineering, Styling, and a Service Center.

"Some sort of campus plan seemed right," said Saarinen, "but we were concerned with the problem of achieving an architectural unity with these horizontal buildings. The earlier scheme we made in 1945 had its great terrace and covered walk which unified the buildings into one great enterprise, but these had proved expensive and impractical. In the new scheme, developed when General Motors came back in 1948, we depended on simpler visual devices."[4]

Chief among these devices is a twenty-two-acre pool—a great, man-made rectangular lake about a third of a mile long. Teeming with fish and waterfowl, the lake has four islands planted with weeping willows. It also contains an impressive fountain in the form

left: Sketches by delineator Glen Paulsen for the July 1949 cover of ARCHITECTURAL FORUM. Shown here but never realized is the office building in the pool. The article claimed, in advance, that the Center will "serve as a standing refutation to those who conceive so highly industrialized an operation as being in its nature 'purely mechanical' and 'anti-human.' In all essentials it depends on qualities of perception, of insight, of human spirit."

of a 115-foot-long, 50-foot-high wall of moving water. And, at the northeast corner, perched upon its tripod, stands the signature 250,000-gallon, 138-foot high, stainless steel water tank. The tower rises above the surface of the water as if it were Eero's machine-age version of the sculptures at Cranbrook. It's not for nothing that *Architectural Forum* called the Technical Center "GM's Industrial Versailles."

Without exception every project of Eero's has a large body of water attached to it. Water and trees were connections to the family home Hvitträsk, the pastoral idyll of his boyhood in Finland. At a another level, Eero thought of these and the single dominant vertical element as necessary primal symbols. Kevin Roche tells of flying with Eero to see the IBM site; Saarinen silently smoked his pipe the entire way. When the plane landed, Saarinen turned to Roche and said, "Architecture consists of placing something between earth and sky."

The elegantly calibrated buildings, distributed in five main groups on three sides of the water are unified, and differentiated by another device. Their long rhythmical façades of glass and metal are terminated at each end by brightly colored glazed brick—placards of glowing color—red, orange, yellow, tangerine, a deeper red, light blue, and dark blue.

The structures are an assemblage of alternating bright and neutral planes, which cannot be taken in at a single glance, but compel one, as Saarinen intended, to tour the site by car; after all, this is the world of the automobile.

The third unifying device is the surrounding forest of 13,000 trees. It provides a green belt that gives the complex the effect of being at the edge of a large glen; you wouldn't know you were in Detroit.

The trees were also planted to mask the parking which is placed at the periphery of the campus. Saarinen may have used automobile technology and the car as his unit of measure, but he didn't want us to look at seas of parked vehicles. People are upset nowadays when they can't reach meetings in time because they have to find the time to park. Out of laziness they now park along the main roads, which were

Saarinen used bright color on the machinery inside the mechanical facilities to avoid what he called the "slumlike" appearance of factory buildings. In the case of the Dynamometer building, the blue, which signifies air in engineering standards, continues outside to the large, tubular exhaust vents (top and page 184).

He also tiled the ends of each of the mechanical buildings with custom-fabricated, glazed brick. Seen behind the trees and at the ends of streets, the color demarcates the functions of buildings and breaks up different kinds of activity. The color is both functional and aesthetically expressive. When lit by the sun the walls are quite spectacular.

Saarinen said, "The use of color in an overall sense was devised, not only for its pleasing aspects, but also to help bind the project together. By an overall sense, I mean that color is not used in small ways on the exterior. The brilliant blues, reds, yellow, orange, black are on the great big end walls of buildings. Some of these are about forty feet high and each is of one color, so they are rather like cards of color in space. Then all the glass and metal walls have certain standardized neutral colors."

Saarinen said he wanted touches of color "like autumn leaves." He carefully chose each hue and had kilns set up to glaze the tiles on the premises of the Technical Center. He was such a perfectionist that when the blue glaze (pictured above) failed he had the bricks removed and a new glaze formulated. The AC Spark Plug Division were consultants on the glazing process.

Heavenly Stairways

In keeping with emblematically showing off the idea of progress, two unique stairways were conceived as distinctive, yet functional, sculptural objects. One is a spiral stair in the Research and Design Building (above), designed by Kevin Roche. The treads of green Norwegian granite, each weighing 1,500 pounds, seem to float upwards in the space suspended by two conical sprays of stainless steel tension rods.

In the lobby of the Technical Center Administration Building is a spinal-beam stair of inch-thick travertine treads (below). It also seems to float free, kept away from the enclosing walls, suspended by stainless steel rods.

Saarinen freely conceded the influence of Mies throughout his scheme. But, exuberant touches such as the fountains, the color, and the staircases, are anything but Miesian. Two great, often conflicting traditions of the new architecture met at the Technical Center: the dominant objectivist philosophy, and a richly diversified, and therefore less easily categorized, romantic subjectivity. This meeting place characterizes the work of Saarinen as a whole.

strictly meant to be thoroughfares. Clearly, the concessions that were made to the auto in 1948 were nomimal by today's standards.

The trees that surround the Styling Auditorium are regularly pruned—a very European effect. This keeps them from blocking our view of the dome, but it also gives a sense of scale and a magisterial quality to the adjacent brick-walled garden. The dome of the Auditorium, covered in steel plate, constantly changes with the sky. The single space inside was designed so that diffused, indirect lighting eliminates all reflections on the curved surfaces of the autos on display. The bright even light, and absence of shadows, permits better evaluation of proposed designs.

Saarinen had full-sized mockups made of exterior wall sections to test materials. These were erected close to trees in order to judge the buildings proportions against the foliage.

He decided on a 5-foot module as the suitable proportion inside and out. This caused some difficulty; since the standard module is 4 feet, manufacture of everything needed to be modified. Even fluorescent tubes had to be specially manufactured in 5-foot lengths. Companies had to be found that could retool and GM had to incur extra expense.

A thin laminated panel was designed—porcelain-enameled metal over a fireproof core—as part of a prefabricated system for both exterior and interior walls. The first of their kind, these spandrels are only two and half inches thick, but provide good insulation, and are free of the rippling that previously marred such surfaces.

One of the more interesting developments was a neoprene gasket weather seal, which holds fixed glass and metal panels to their aluminum frames. It is windproof and waterproof and allows the glass or panels to be removed whenever a building's use changes. The windows look very much like automobile windshields. All these developments inspired by the auto industry technology are now part of the building trade and a common part of the language of modern architecture.

Attention to interior detail is pronounced everywhere, from

Saarinen said, "Each of the staff organizations prides itself on its own individuality and its range of activities. Each wanted its own "personality." We tried to answer this desire architecturally in the main lobby of each of the five groups. In four of these, the visual climax to the lobby is the main staircase. These staircases are deliberately made into ornamental elements, like large-scale technological sculptures."

the lighting fixtures to the pressed wood ceiling panels, from office furniture to the stainless steel tie-rods that hold the granite steps.

The floor of the Administration building is travertine. The pool of running water under the staircase has terrazzo designs, since covered by gravel. The walls are black-glazed brick; windows are floor to ceiling glass in their original gaskets. Chairs in the waiting area were designed by Saarinen.

The interiors—for the most part column-free—are completely modular. The ceilings in the drafting rooms are the first developed completely luminous ceilings using special modular plastic pans. Ceilings, like walls and floors, and with them air-conditioning, illumination and other mechanical equipment, are integrated in a multi-dimensional, rigorously consistent structural system which creates large areas of "universal" space that may be easily adapted to new or changing use. Some of the spaces at GM were purportedly reorganized 500 percent within the first decade.

"Like the automobile itself," said Saarinen, "the buildings are essentially put together, as on an assembly line, out of mass-produced units. And, down to the smallest detail, we tried to give the architecture the precise, well-made look which is a proud characteristic of industrial America. The architecture attempts to find its eloquence out of a consistent and logical development of its industrial character.

"Every time I go to the Tech Center, I think what a great client General Motors was. The buildings are perfectly maintained. And they prove that in the long run good materials pay. The Engineering group is eight years old, but it looks as if it had been finished yesterday."[5]

The General Motors Technical Center is now over 50 years old and it still looks as good, in every way, "as if it had been finished yesterday."

New Forms, New Art

Many of the artworks, especially commissioned for the Technical Center, reflect automotive technology in some way. "Lines in Motion," a sculpture by the Russian Constructivist Antoine Pevsner (1886-1962) stands outside the Administration Building.

Harry Bertoia (1915-1978) is best know for his wire-frame chair which he developed for Knoll in 1951. Trained in sculpure at Cranbrook, he later established the metalworking studio there. Later he worked with Charles and Ray Eames developing techniques for molding plywood. As a sculptor he made a number of metal screens as large-scale commissions for open spaces such as the one shown above.

American abstract painter Charles Sheeler (1883-1965), like many artists, writers, and intellectuals of his generation, regarded the machine as the premier symbol of his era.

Sheeler's best-publicized and most lucrative commission was the painting he produced for the board room of the GM Technical Center. One of the largest paintings Sheeler ever produced, it was to express "the spirit of research." Sheeler, who revered Eero Saarinen, was enthusiastic about the opportunity and boastful about his design: "I have decided the canvas will be my Masterpiece."

Charles Sheeler visited the labs in 1955 and later spoke of Saarinen's architecture itself as his inspiration. The design of the spiral stairway in the Research and Design Building was the focus of his painting. It is accompanied by two other inventions in which the lab took great pride: the Helmholz Coil, a device designed to increase the accuracy of studies of magnetism, and the Dodrill-GMR mechanical heart, which greatly facilitated open heart surgery.

"Conveying significant meaning is part of the inspirational purpose of architecture and therefore, for me, it is a fundamental principle of our art.

"Deere & Company is proud of its mid-western farm-belt location and of its strong, handsome farm machinery. The proper character for its headquarters' architecture would reflect the big, forceful, functional character of its products. Its architecture should not be a slick, precise, glittering glass and spindly metal building, but a building which is bold and direct, using metal in a strong, basic way.

"These convictions about the character of Deere & Company influenced our decisions about the structural system, the search for the special steel, the site plan and every aspect of the design."[1]

— *Eero Saarinen*

Deere & Co. Administrative Center • Moline, Illinois

The Deere & Company building was every bit as much the vision of its president, William A. Hewitt, as it was its architect. Working closely with Eero Saarinen for seven years, Hewitt was the project's driving force from inception to realization. The importance of the Hewitt-Saarinen rapport—the enormous amount of thought and insight that each man brought to the planning process—cannot be overestimated.

"In 1955 when I became president of the company, one of the things we needed was a new headquarters office in Moline and at that time we made two decisions: first, to build outside the city in rural surroundings, and even more radically after 120 years, to consider using an independent architect. No one in the company had much experience with architects other than our own, so it was more or less up to me to pick a firm."[2]

Hewitt favored modern architecture; at the same time he wanted a building that would be appropriate for a farm-machinery business. "Among the many buildings I visited was the General Motors Technical Center near Detroit, then just completed. Afterwards I went by to meet the architect and talk with him . . . . Then and there I decided Eero Saarinen was the man for the job."[3]

Saarinen's firm was large enough to undertake a big job, yet small enough for him and Hewitt to work together. Their interaction was unusually productive: that rare combination of a client with ample resources and unusually high standards, collaborating with a remarkably gifted and perceptive architect. Together they worked for overall excellence in every phase of design and execution.

The man-made lake looks beautiful; it also serves a practical function. In the summer, water heated by the air conditioning system is sprayed into the air, cooled, and then recirculated. In the winter, warm water is returned to the lake so it doesn't freeze, at least in the middle. The water right around the building does freeze, but the company aerates it near the supporting piers, which allows the fish to survive the winter months.

Classical Vistas
While Eero Sarrinen's response to the land was a combination of intuition, inspiration, and experience, he also drew upon the many years he studied with his family and his father Eliel.

From the time he was a boy in his native Finland, to the time he worked with Eliel in their Cranbrook office, Eero developed a classical vision of the meaning of the relationship of architecture and landscape. Every one of his projects included sweeping dramatic views; man-made bodies of water with fountains; rationally designed plazas, steps, paths, and sculpture; and incomparable plantings—often acres of forest.

Compare Eliel's concept (above) with Eero's (below).

Hewitt explained what he was looking for in a letter to Saarinen in 1957:

"First, let me say that I have no preconceived ideas as to the specific design of our new buildings. I believe creation of the forms and relationships of these buildings is basically your responsibility.

"At the same time, I believe it is our responsibility at Deere & Company to do all we can to help you create buildings which will be in harmony with our functions and traditions, and also be indicative of the objectives and progress we envision for the future.

"In thinking of our traditions and our future, and in thinking of the people who will work in or visit our new headquarters, I believe it should be thoroughly modern in concept, but at the same time, be down to earth and rugged."[4]

Soon after he was engaged, Saarinen participated in the selection of the land, which was purchased especially for the building, and he spent days in Moline tramping over the property until he was thoroughly familiar with it.

He presented preliminary designs for the building in 1958 about which he said:

"We had three major intentions in planning designing of these buildings. First, to provide functional, efficient space which would take care of future expansion inflexible ways. Second, to create the kind of pleasant and appropriate environment for employees which is part of Twentieth Century thinking. And third, to express in architecture the special character of Deere & Company."[5]

Saarinen's first design was an inverted pyramidal structure situated on top of a hill. The company rejected this design because they felt it didn't suit their organization—too lofty and commanding a presence on the land—nor did it provide them with the flexibility they needed.

In Saarinen's next design he placed a more horizontal,

Father and son create the same event under the porticoes of their respective buildings.
above: Cranbrook Academy of Art, Bloomfield Hills, Michigan, 1943, Eliel Saarinen.
left: Deere & Company Administrative Center, Moline, Illinois, 1963, Eero Saarinen.
At Cranbrook, Eliel was assisted by the Swedish born Carl Milles (1875-1955), who collaborated in the water design of the mall (above), and who did all the sculpture there.

land-hugging structure astride a stream, down in a ravine. This was the design the company chose to build, the one they could identify with. In Saarinen's words:

"The 600-acre site consists both of high table land and low river land, its edges broken by wooded ravines. One of the broad ravines seemed the finest, most pleasant and most human site for the building complex, In such a tree-studded site, where it would be intimately connected with nature, a strong, dark building seemed appropriate.

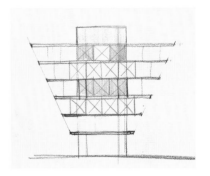

"The eight-storey administration building is placed crosswise on the floor of the valley. At its fourth floor level, glass-enclosed flying bridges stretch out to the laboratory and the exhibition buildings on the high slopes of the ravine. The complex is approached from the valley below. We planned the roads carefully, keeping in mind how the building would be seen as one drove along the man-made lake up to the parking lot behind the building and to the entrance.

"Having selected a site because of the beauty of nature, we were especially anxious to take full advantage of views from the offices. To avoid curtains or venetian blinds, which would obscure the views, we worked out a system of sun-shading with metal louvers and specified reflective glass to prevent glare . . . .

"Besides functioning as an efficient sun-shading device, the steel louvers dramatize the character of the building, which is one where we have tried to use steel to express strength."[6]

It's not possible to see this building without being impressed, even deeply moved. Nestled in a valley amid acres of woods, the strength of its design is immediately apparent; its rust-red steel frame stands forward from the shimmering glass underneath, as it contrasts with the surrounding greenery.

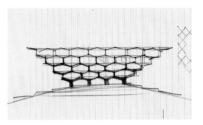

The integration of the building into the environment is faultless. The way the building effortlessly spans the

These characteristic rough sketches in pencil on tracing paper show the evolution of Saarinen's thinking. The inverted ziggurat was too lordly a form for the corporation, however the structural steel-work begins to be the primary feature right away. Saarinen finished the working drawings of his building, but he did not live to see it completed. He died the week after construction began.

ravine—the stream running under it, the way it rises out of the valley, the way the trees have grown around and embraced it, the way its material has weathered—all these things contribute to the sensation that the building naturally grew from its surroundings.

The grounds are immaculately manicured, constantly mowed by roving John Deere tractors. Trees are extremely important in the design scheme. Since some will periodically die back, the corporation adds from 500 to 1,000 trees and shrubs a year to maintain a full array. There are waterfowl and an elegant aerating fountain in the sculpted lagoons. The fountain has a function which seems well in advance of the time in which the building was built—it acts as a means of heating or cooling the building.

The Deere Headquarters is divided in three: a public entry/exhibition hall for Deere products with an adjacent auditorium, a detached administrative block, and the West Office Building, originally planned, but not added until 1978 by Roche and Dinkeloo. The beautiful, wood-lined auditorium seats 400 people and boasts perfect acoustics. The mammoth enclosed display area can accommodate Deere's brightly colored, behemoth-size tractors and farm machines. As visitors enter they look down on the product display area and then cross a glass enclosed bridge that connects to the main building at the fourth floor level. The bridge provides a sense of participation with nature as one walks across at tree top level in the midst of an outdoor panorama; the stream runs below.

An outrigging of weathering steel louvers surrounds and projects from the building; four suspended vanes shield the offices from the sun without interfering with the view. Open grill decking, also of weathering steel, projects out to provide balconies for window washing and additional protection from the sun. The upper five floors of the building are given over to general office space, while directly beneath is the executive floor, with private offices lining the periphery, and largely open secretarial spaces down the middle. The ground floor is devoted to building services and an executive dining

above: David B. Gamble House, Pasadena, California, 1908, Greene & Greene, architects.

The house achieves its low, sensitive relationship to the rolling site through use of strong horizontals expressed in cantilevers, roof lines, broad bands of casement windows, sleeping porches, outdoor terraces, and wide stairways.

room, lounge, and gallery almost projecting into the lake.

The interior spaces were designed with great care to maximize views. Each department has a large open area situated next to the outside glass wall (with the exception of the Executive Floor). Private offices are atypically located in the center of the building so that the average employee has an outside view. Outside walls are glass with bronze-colored vaporized metal sealed between two laminated plate sheets. This glass reflects outside light and glare without affecting visibility from the inside, and in the summer it helps reduce the load on the air-conditioning system. A combination of metal-louvered sun screens and glare resistant glass is very effective in keeping the building comfortable without having to use shades which would block the views.

Efficiency and functionalism are evident throughout the building. The partitions that form the spaces for offices in each department are movable; this means the building is responsive to the changes that are inevitable as the organization grows. These are, in fact, changed and rearranged from time to time.

It was Saarinen's feeling that people would add the color in this building and that the out-of-doors would become part of the interior, hence a low-key, almost colorless, color scheme. The central halls don't necessarily afford a clear view to the outside, but every time you pass a corridor and can see past the office spaces, there is a clear sense of the outside always on the inside.

People add color to this building in more ways than one. It may be hard to imagine a work place that is exhilarating, where people dress up to go to work. When employees are interviewed about working in this building, the most widely shared feeling is pride. It is a major tourist attraction and the people who work here love to show it off. The beautiful setting is the number one reason people enjoy working in what one employee called "our crystal palace."

right: The Kagawa Prefectural Government Office, Kagawa, Japan, 1955-58, Kenzo Tange, architect. Tange was the preeminent post-war Japanese modernist. Most influenced by Le Corbusier, he also admired Saarinen as an architect and as a friend.

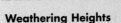

Weathering Heights

It was Eero Saarinen Associates who first specified and completed a building using weathering steel. Until that time painted or stainless steel-clad structural steel epitomized the product's application.

"Having decided to use steel, we wanted to make a steel building that was really a steel building (most so-called steel buildings seem to me to be, more glass buildings than steel buildings, really not one thing or the other). We sought for an appropriate material—economical, maintenance free, bold in character, dark in color. We located a certain high tensile steel, which has a peculiar characteristic: if this steel is left unpainted, a rust coating forms which becomes a protective skin over the steel.

"This rust coating—which does not develop beyond a certain point—is a cinnamon brown color which makes a beautiful dark surface on the steel. We built a full-size mock-up section of the façade on the site to make sure the steel would act as we had anticipated. It has. I predict other architects will use it widely."[7]

Saarinen's associates, Kevin Roche and John Dinkeloo, subsequently made Cor-ten their signature material.

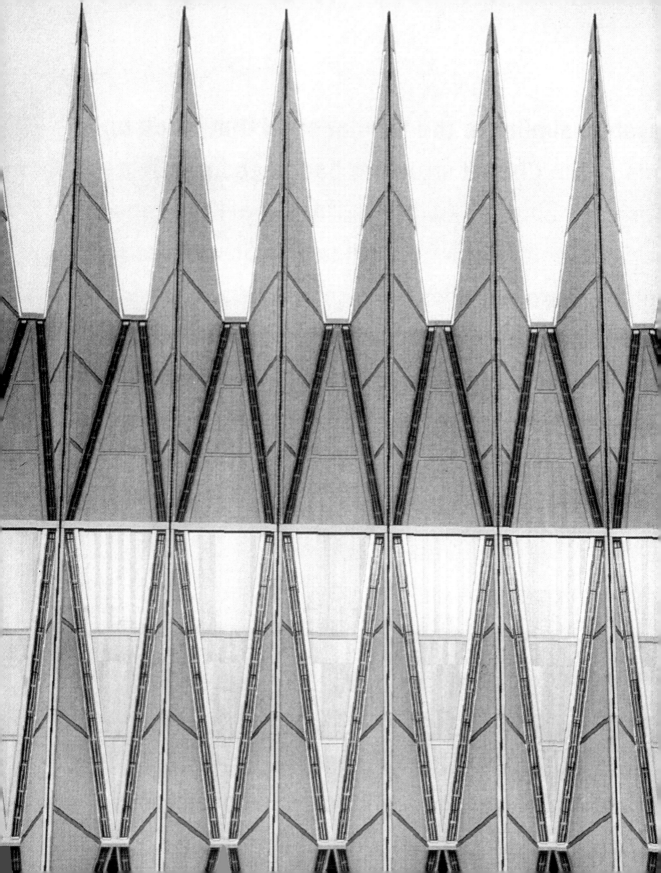

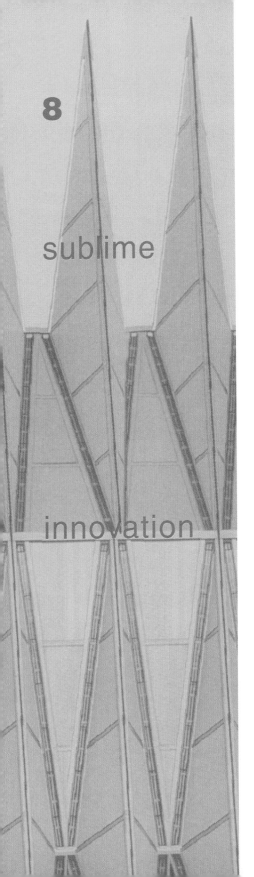

8

sublime

innovation

Solomon R. Guggenheim Museum
Gateway Arch
U.S. Airforce Academy Chapel
John Hancock Center
Kimbell Art Museum

Ostentation in building projects, as well as just about everything else we humans do, has always been a clear indication of power and success —as well as where, and on what, we place value. The only thing that changes over time is where the emphases are placed; where is the power? What are the measures of success? What is valuable? The 2,000-year old inscription on the marble basin in the Roman bath pictured at the bottom of page 201 boasts that it cost no less than 5,250 *sesterces*. Our guidebooks will tell us that the Gateway Arch required nearly 900 tons of stainless steel to build.

Innovation is simply the introduction of something for the first time. Since quantity can be measured, such as size for instance, it follows that what is measureable is of greatest significance, or at least is something that we can easily discuss and judge. The sheer scale of most architectural undertakings, coupled with a frequent need for special engineering and developing technologies, would make it appear that whatever is new or done for the first time has the most merit.

But is this where real, lasting value resides? What is merely new doesn't remain so for very long. Everything is surpassed by something newer, larger, more expensive. Will the Gateway Arch be any less beautiful if a larger one is built elsewhere—one that requires 1,000 tons of stainless steel?

"Are we to believe that because one is an engineer, one is not preoccupied by beauty in one's constructions, or that one does not seek to create elegance as well as solidity and durability? Is it not true that the very conditions which give strength also conform to the hidden rules of harmony?" — Gustave Eiffel

Each of the undertakings in this section is a successful collaboration between engineering and architecture. But, more important, each is a melding of inspiration with the language of execution—whereby form is not only inseparable from function—they are indistiguishable each from the other. In the process it is possible to say, along with Gustave Eiffel, that in each project there is "elegance as well as solidity and durability." They are the result of sublime innovation.

Abstract Objective

The two most important material advances of the 20th Century were steel and reinforced concrete. The Guggenheim uses more than its share of both, particularly the latter. Frank Lloyd Wright was an old hand at concrete; his first poured-in-place structure was the Unity Temple in 1904. As for the Guggenheim, Wright, with his characteristic wit, exclaimed, "When the first atomic bomb lands on New York [the museum] will not be destroyed. It may be blown a few miles up into the air, but when it comes down it will bounce!"[1]

But is it their use of concrete that makes Unity Temple or the Guggenheim important? Or is there something else?

As little as they would appear to have in common at first, the Unity Temple (page 87), the Larkin Building (1904, page 32), Johnson Wax (1939, page 36), and the Guggenheim Museum (1959, page 202) share the same Wrightian conviction that a building's purpose is to be revealed in its interior. Until the Larkin Building a structure was essentially a container or box. Wright said:

> "I think I first consciously tried to beat the box in the Larkin Building—1904. I found a natural opening to the liberation I sought when (after a great struggle) I finally pushed the staircase towers out from the corners of the main building, made them free-standing individual features."[2]

He took this concept even further with the Johnson Administrative Building, bringing the car and its very shape into the curving forms of the building. With the Guggenheim, whose first scheme was to have automobile access as well, Wright's exterior and interior are melded into one great, single form—a spiral ramp.

All of these buildings, and many more Wright did in between,

above: Bruce Goff's vision for a "Crystal Chapel" designed in 1949 for the University of Oklahoma at Norman. Unbuilt, the chapel is shown here in model form.

left: Concordia Senior College, Fort Wayne, Indiana, Eero Saarinen, 1953-1958.

have multi-storied interior courts with balconies and natural light. But, more important, their insides open to reveal their meaning.

The Guggenheim succeeds most fundamentally, as do all of Wright's best buildings, because it has forever changed the way we look at a building. It's not the form that should be imitated, but how it redefines the workings of a structure, in this case a museum. There hasn't been a museum built since that hasn't been informed in its purpose by the advances made in the Guggenheim Museum.

Fearful Symmetry

The Gateway Arch has more than an element of the mysterious about it; by all rights it shouldn't even be standing. It almost defies explanation.

Eero Saarinen worked for eight years to refine the shape of the Arch: hanging chains, weighting them, making drawings and models, and calculating agonizingly complicated mathematical formulas. He felt strongly that if it were to affirm our belief in the nobility of our existence, it had to soar into the sky with a grace that made it seem more a force of nature than a piece of architecture. It had to achieve perfection.

Saarinen conceived of the Arch as an exaltation of pure geometric form. "The mathematical precision seemed to enhance the timelessness of the form," he said, "but at the same time its dynamic quality seemed to link it to our own time." This is why he felt it needed no architectural extras where the legs meet the ground; no ornamentation, no surface texture, no paint.

A complete marriage of architecture, engineering, and sculpture, the Arch plays with the changing light and color of the sky; it is truly transcendental to behold.

Just as understanding the physics of refraction won't steal the magic we see in the rainbow, all the knowledge of the Arch's fabrication can't dispel its mystery.

Divine Engineering

Engineers are often the great, unsung heroes of architecture. For one thing, because architects have admired and borrowed from them. For another, because little built in this past century would work without their help. They are often called upon to carry out flights of fancy and make them real. None of the projects in this book would have happened without them, particularly those in this chapter.

There are three engineers who bear mentioning here. Eugene Freyssinet designed record-length bridges in France. He designed two immense barrel-vaulted hangers for airships at Orly. He patented prestressed concrete in 1928.

Swiss Engineer Robert Maillart (1872-1940) demonstrated new forms for making elegant concrete structures such as the Saliginatobel Bridge opened in 1930. Maillart also invented new floor and roof forms.

Trained as a chemical engineer, A. Gustave Eiffel (1832-1923) worked as a railway bridge designer. He considered calculation essential in an era when trial and error was the order of the day. His Garabit Viaduct set a record for the longest arch span, his famous tower in Paris set one for height. He designed the internal frame for the Statue of Liberty.

14 July 1888

above: A concrete skin covers the bridge-like arches of the Orly dirigible hangars by Freyssinet and Limousin, 1924. This photo appears in "Towards a New Architecture" with penciled-in arc completed by Le Corbusier.

right: Gustave Eiffel's famous tower in Paris. Note the similarity in construction methods between both structures on this page and the Gateway Arch on page 215.

Strutting Its Stuff

The Statue of Liberty (1886-88) appears to have been the first American structure, other than a bridge, to be systematically wind-braced throughout its frame with a complex of iron diagonal braces and struts.

At 16 stories the Monadnock Building (above) was briefly the world's tallest office building. Its brick walls were load-bearing and were consequently 6 feet thick of necessity at street level; the building tapered in above the first story.

Contemporary critics saw it as rational, honest, and exemplary of what a commercial building should be. Montgomery Schuyler called it "the thing itself," a masterpiece of bold simplicity.

A noteworthy technical feature of the Monadnock Building is the presence of iron I-beam wind-bracing embedded in its structure.

Heavenward Glances

The combination of aeronautical forms rendered in aluminum, with a somewhat more traditional use of stained glass, exposed an uneasy tension between the military and religion inherent in the design of the U.S. Air Force Academy Cadet Chapel. Promoted as emblematic of "Air Age Gothic," it was clearly the militaristic, rather than the architectural associations, that stood out. The sharp upward-thrusting spires, combined with the geometry of the tetrahedrons and metal skin, are more suggestive of upended fighter planes than they are the forms of Chartres Cathedral.

Ironically, the Chapel's architect, Walter Netsch was able to please religious leaders and users of the chapel long before he pleased Senators and Congressmen who were on the government's budgetary committee. Controversy touches a sore spot for sure—but, it's usually an important one—a place where people deeply care. Netsch wasn't so much interested in the controversy as he was in serving a community; and, he served it well.

The Chapel draws more than a million visitors every year to Colorado Springs. The controversy has faded, but the issues regarding tradition, symbolism, and cultural values persist. The Chapel remains a reminder of a time when architects were optimistic about proposing answers to these questions.

Bracing Honesty

Bruce Graham remained a steadfast proponent of structural rationalism even as architects began turning away from Modernism and the principles they had previously revered. When presented with Graham's compelling plans, the developer was swayed by the logic of an efficient and cost-effective structure, an unusual and striking aesthetic, and the prestige afforded by a hundred-story tower. Even the conservative insurance firm, who was brought in to underwrite the development, concurred with the scale and the pioneering aspects of the design.

As Graham described the approach to designing the John Hancock Center: "The search for a new kind of structure which would accommodate multiple uses and also express the scale and grandeur of a one-hundred-story tower, lead Dr. [Fazlur] Khan and me to the diagonal tube. It was as essential to us to expose the

above: Monadnock Building, Chicago, 1891, Burnham & Root, architects.
left: John Hancock Center, Chicago, 1970, SOM, architects.
These two buildings have much in common besides being Chicago landmarks.
They both have exterior load-bearing walls and structural wind-bracing.
John Hancock revolutionized skyscaper design with its steel exo-skeleton which it proudly displays.

structure of this mammoth as it is to perceive the structure of the Eiffel Tower, for in Chicago, honesty of structure has become a tradition."[3]

The bracing so clearly visible on the exterior of "Big John,"—designed to stabilize the tower in high winds—may have worked just as well embedded in the walls of the tower; no one would be the wiser. Instead they proudly exhibit themselves. The building declares—"This is what I am."

Essentially Illuminated

The principal influence of an architect is not just through the buildings they design but, more significantly, through the ideas the buildings represent. Among contemporary architects Louis I. Kahn was perhaps the most insistent on giving primacy to an architecture infused by an idea, by an intellectual and emotional position which was their necessary spark.

The great contribution that Kahn made to the architectural ideas of the second half of the century was to show the possibilities of an architecture that had mass and permanence —that had the timeless qualities of classical forms—but was nevertheless unmistakably of our time. His is not a derivative architecture that quotes the superfice of past style. It is not that his architecture even made deeper historical references, so much as it partook of the same archetypal sources of the works of the past.

In Louis Kahn's Kimbell Museum, the works of art and the building are in absolute sympathy with each other. Paintings and sculpture of different periods and different cultures are shown to advantage in spaces that have something of the character of a room but are not at all box-like enclosures.

The museum's spaces are made by rooms and defined enclosures; they are also made by light. Spaces are connected but nevertheless have defined boundaries. Light enters and is controlled in these spaces and makes them come alive. These qualities, so characteristic of Kahn's architecture, are important to the success of museums.

Nowhere was he more successful than in the Kimbell.

Let There Be Light

Charles Moore said, "Space and form are understood in light. Light can clarify them, as the ancient Greeks knew, or it can extend and enhance mysterious distances . . . . Light can sparkle or dapple or slide across a surface or even flash from a neon tube."

Architects fashion light as if it were another material. In the 20th Century the combination of artificial and natural light has been a critical consideration. Louis Kahn was a master of light and used its changeability as a plastic element in all his work.

The vaulted shapes of ancient Roman architecture were another love of Kahn's. He used the vault to no better effect than in the Kimbell Art Museum. He said, "My mind is full of Roman greatness and the vault so etched itself in my mind that . . . it's there always ready. . . . And I realized that the light must come from a high point where the light is best in its zenith."

above: The central west porch of the Kimbell Art Museum, Louis I. Kahn.

right: Caldarium, men's bath, Pompeii, First Century A.D.

Wright surveys his work with contractor George N. Cohen without whom the Guggenheim Museum would never have been built. Cohen's name is inscribed with Wright's at the Museum's entrance.

The ramp is the Museum, the works are hung on the spiraling walls. Wright's rationale was that a slow descent would help visitors avoid "museum fatigue," that the outward-slanting walls resembled easels and thus permitted a more faithful presentation of paintings than would vertical walls.

" . . . with supreme respect for Wright, this is unmitigated nonsense," said Peter Blake. "The fact is, quite simply, that Wright just had to build one great, wonderful spiral before be died, and he managed to sell the Guggenheim Foundation on the idea that it would make a good museum."[1]

Blake has also referred to the Guggenheim as "one of the most beautiful spaces created in this century."[2]

Solomon R. Guggenheim Museum • New York City

In early June 1943, Frank Lloyd Wright received a note from the Baroness Hilla Rebay von Ehrenweisen asking him to seriously consider designing a museum for Solomon R. Guggenheim's collection of 20th Century non-objective art. In it, she said, "I feel that each of these great masterpieces should be organized into space and only you so it seems to me would test the possibilities to do so . . . . I need a fighter, a lover of space, an originator, a tester and a wise man . . . . I want a temple of spirit, a monument!" She ended by saying, "May this wish be blessed." You don't have to be Frank Lloyd Wright to be flattered by a plea such as this.

"I appreciate your appreciation," Wright wrote back, "I would like to do something such as you suggest for your worthy foundation." Wright was then 74 years old.

In another letter to the Baroness from January 20, 1944, Wright shows he has already formed a clear concept:

". . . If non-objective painting is to have any great future it must be related to environment in due proportion as it pretty much is already, not to the high ceiling. . . . A museum should have above all a clear atmosphere of light and sympathetic surface. Frames were always an expedient that segregated and masked the paintings off from the environment to its own loss of relationship and proportion, etc. etc.

"A museum should be one extended expansive well proportioned floor space from bottom to top—a wheel chair going around and up and down, throughout. No stops anywhere and such screened divisions of the space gloriously lit within from above as would deal appropriately with every group of paintings or individ-

Frank Lloyd Wright spoke of his Museum as one giant frame for painting: " . . . faced slightly upward to the viewer and to the light in accord with the upward sweep of the spiral the paintings themselves are emphasized as features in themselves and are not hung "square" but gracefully yield to movement as set up by these slightly curving massive walls. In a great upward sweep of movement the picture is seen framed as a feature of Architecture."

The Great Spiral

Wright claimed, "I never sit down to a drawing board—and this has been a lifelong practice of mine—until I have the whole thing in my mind. I may alter it substantially, I may throw it all away, I may find I'm up a blind alley; but unless I have the idea of the thing pretty well in shape, you won't see me at a drawing board with it."

This is, of course, a classic rendering of genius—where the vision in the mind's eye is everything. We have seen, however, that Wright often had something on that drawing board—in fact, for many years.

Knowing what we know of the present Guggenheim Museum, it would seem Wright's image of the ideal museum in his letter to Baroness Rebay, particularly its spiral form, was already clearly established, if not on paper, at least in his mind's eye. A spiral would be the next, and as it turns out last, logical step in Wright's architecture.

One of the first spiral structures he proposed was a planetarium project for Gordon Strong, in 1924. Strong had come to Wright wanting nothing more than a place from which to gaze at the skies; when Wright was finished, he had redesigned all of Sugar Loaf Mountain, Maryland, turning its entire top into a spiral automobile approach to the planetarium at the summit.

From the planetarium project on, Wright kept coming back to the idea of the spiral until, during the later war years, he developed two projects in which the spiral ramp became the central theme: the San Francisco store for V. C. Morris, and New York's Guggenheim Museum.

ual paintings as you might want them classified.

"The atmosphere of the whole should be luminous from bright to dark—anywhere desired; a great calm and breadth pervading the whole place, etc. . . .

"The whole thing will either throw you off your guard entirely or be just about what you have been dreaming about."

It would take another sixteen years for the great spiraling "expansive well proportioned floor space," "with no stops anywhere," to materialize as the Guggenheim Museum. Construction didn't start until 1956; the building remained unfinished at Wright's death, three years later at the age of 89. His last building, it would open to acclaim—and attack—just after he died.

No sooner did the trustees announce that Wright's project would be built than a group of New York artists petitioned against it. They disliked the obtrusiveness of the architecture, especially the tilts of wall and floor planes. They were especially disgruntled that Wright should have anything to do with a museum when he had repeatedly complained that pictures spoil architecture—a comment no doubt deriving from his instinct for the publicity to be gained from making shocking statements.

It's true that Wright's enthusiasm for primitive and exotic arts did not extend to the most progressive work going on around him. He was also particularly suspicious of painting, regarding it as incidental to, yet competing with, architecture, and tending in both respects to disturb the integrated design he sought in his interiors.

But, when Wright began his designs,

top: All his life Wright was enamored of The Great Mosque of Samarra in Iraq. Built in the 9th Century, the spiral-ramped minaret is the oldest in Islam.
above: One of Wright's drawings for the Gordon Strong Automobile Objective (unbuilt), Sugarloaf Mountain, Maryland, 1924.

the official name of the institution was *The Museum of Non-Objective Art*. The Baroness had encouraged Solomon Guggenheim to adopt the collecting and exhibiting of such art as its policy.[3] Wright sincerely considered his "new kind of museum" as especially appropriate for "non-objective" painting. He later wrote:

> "The building was intended by Solomon R. Guggenheim to make a suitable place for the exhibition of an advanced form of painting wherein line, color and form are a language in themselves. . . . independent of reproduction of objects animate or inanimate, thus placing painting in a realm hitherto enjoyed by music alone.
>
> "This advanced painting has seldom been presented in other than the incongruous rooms of old static architecture. Here in the harmonious fluid quiet created by this building interior the new painting will be seen for itself under favorable conditions."[4]

Wright may have been converting fancy into the kind of logic that convinces clients to back a scheme and foot the bill. But, even allowing for Wright's customary rationalization for what he wanted to realize, we needn't doubt that he had at least convinced himself that his new kind of museum was appropriate for non-objective painting.

When the Museum opened its doors to the public, a *New Yorks Times* front-page headline read, "Wright V.s. Art,"[5] But, there was great praise, also. *Interiors* magazine cautioned us that, " . . . perhaps Wright's triumph, in the face of the serious reservations of the informed as well as the uninformed, is a cue for the re-examination of our criteria."[6]

The Guggenheim Museum takes up the entire end of a city block with no other structures immediately against it. There are tall buildings behind it and on the blocks on either side. It faces Central Park. As we approach, and bits of the building are revealed, it holds its own against the scale of the detail of adjacent apartment houses which bulk larger than the Museum and wall it in. It looms largest as we approach

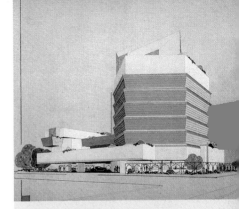

Painterly Ideas

On some of his early drawings for the Guggenheim, Wright penciled in the Mesopotamian word "ziggurat," meaning "to build high." Since the ramp of the building would expand as it rose, he referred to it as the "optimistic ziggurat."

Wright's Guggenheim drawings are more lavish than most he produced. Painted more than drawn, they are perhaps in keeping with the concept of a museum for painting.

"When [Guggenheim] saw the first sketches I made," said Wright, "he went over them several times without saying a word or looking up. Finally when he did look up there were tears in his eyes, 'Mr. Wright, he said, 'I knew you would do it. This is it.'"[1]

Wright's early schemes show the building in poured cement covered with a white, deep rose, or beige veneer of marble.

In the first design scheme for the Museum (above), a glassed-in hexagonal spiral ascends uniformly.

In the second design scheme (below), the spiral gets smaller as it ascends, not unlike the drawing for the Automobile Objective (opposite).

The third scheme is the one we have today, with the spiral growing larger as it climbs to the top.

above: A perspective of the first scheme, 1943. Daylight enters through clerestories made of glass tubes not unlike those at Johnson Wax.

above: A perspective of the second scheme, 1944. The building is clad in rose-colored marble. Note the car pulling in to the front entrance in both schemes.

Complex Forms

The design of the Guggenheim posed a large number of complex difficulties in construction. How does one build a curvilinear structure with a technology designed for a rectilinear world? Even things as basic as measuring had to be handled differently.

Wright said the building was "more like an egg shell" than "a criss-cross structure . . . . The structural calculations are thus those of the cantilever and continuity rather than the post and beam. All is as one and as near indestructible as it is possible for science to make a building."

Forms, or molds, are usually made of flat wood, are uniform, and can be reused. Wright's plans called for large, individually shaped forms with continually changing dimensions, to be bent in at least two directions; too labor intensive and expensive.

The forms that were finally used, far easier to construct, were made by piecing together strips of straight lumber and had only one bend.

Depending on the light, the resulting angularity that makes up each curve is clearly evident—more perceptible on the exterior due to weathering over time.

from the downtown side. From this angle we can't measure it against windows, bricks, ornaments, balustrades, or any of the other familiar devices that the eye uses as a scale for judging the size of something else. On the other hand, viewed diagonally from the uptown side, the building tends to appear smaller than it is.

Part of this is that we have nothing in our experience against which to compare this building. The form expresses its conceptual metaphors in other than a known architectonic sense. Structures with free forms frequently bring unwanted images that play games with our perception; unfortunate comparisions are made to animals, gas tanks, space ships.

There's another problem with the building's unfamiliarity: until we know what it is inside that is being telegraphed to the outside, the exterior makes little sense. A car ramp is obviously a ramp for cars—this structure is a ramp, for what? However, since the building became an icon almost instantly—known the world over for simply what it is—wondering what the outside tells us about the inside becomes irrelevant—we all know, don't we? In any case, the real experience of the Guggenheim awaits us inside.

One enters the building between the great spiral and the smaller side-structure Wright called "the monitor." We pass under a horizontal single-story-high concrete soffit that runs the length of the street front. As in all of Wright's works, the space of this entrance is both low and dark.

The entrance takes us to where the original open loggia would have been. The plan was later changed, but as with the Johnson Wax Buildings, this is where cars would have entered and dropped off passengers. The loggia has since been glassed in, and the original drive-through and sculpture garden behind have been enclosed to accommodate a bookstore. Through a circular glass vestibule projecting from the right, we move under a low ceiling and out to the floor of the main gallery.

Once again Wright has brought us through a series of small, low, dark spaces and released us into a large, high, bright interior volume. This last is a true world unto itself,

above: Construction of the main rotunda, circa. 1957. Reinforcing rods for the rotunda floor are laid in preparation for the concrete to be poured.

left: Construction of the main rotunda, circa 1958. With the ramp completed, formwork is erected for the structural members of the skylight.

defined by its own astonishing spiral geometry—its means of support invisible—growing up from the ground in one continuous curve.

While we recall from the exterior that the spiral expands as it rises, inside we find that the space diminishes as it ascends (this is because the ramp is widening as it nears the top of the building). This creates a perspectival effect that makes the central space seem even taller than it actually is. The skylight, circular in plan and divided into twelve segments, allows copious amounts of light to cascade into the space from above.

This is the full, glorious experience of the building. There is truly nothing like it anywhere—nothing can compare with it. It must be seen to be believed.

Many of those who were initially distracted by the experience of going around the ramp have found (to their surprise) that repeated visits to the Museum so accustom them to the experience that it somewhat recedes from consciousness, permitting the works of art to reassert themselves. Repeated exposure to the Museum reveals the unimportance of the element of novelty in the experience.

Debates over the museum's success or failure as a museum are by no means trivial; one is never clear as to whether the building is "friendly" to art or not. As architectural space has become more extravagantly sculptural, painting and sculpture have changed with it. Contrariwise, modern painting and sculpture have transformed architecture.

Long before the Museum was finished Lewis Mumford praised it. Though he was a champion of Wright's "greatness and originality," he brought enough balance in his depiction of the architect to somehow predict what difficulties there might be:

"Each building by Wright stands in self-imposed isolation—a monument to his own greatness, towering defiantly above the works of his contemporaries. Though it dazzles us by its brilliance, it sometimes fails to invite our love, because it offers no halfway place between rejection and abject surrender."[7]

Wright believed that painting should be frameless, mounted off the wall or suspended, and angled upwards to catch the light. Maybe he was talking about sculpture. He said:

"All this has been so carefully considered in this building that the whole interior would add up to a reposeful place in which the paintings would be seen to better advantage than they ever have been seen."

The neon works of Dan Flavin filled the spaces of the Guggenheim to mark the occasion of the 125th anniversary of Wright's birth and the re-opening of the Museum after its restoration in the summer of 1992—a perfect marriage between site-specific sculpture and a museum for non-objective art.

top: The domed skylight went through many variations before Wright settled with something that reflects his earliest explorations of stained glass.
above: The Museum was featured with Wright on a stamp just three years after it opened.
middle: Framed by the architecture: an installation of the work of Dan Flavin, 1992.
right: The iconic facade right after the Museum opened.

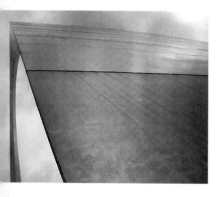

Constructing the Gateway Arch wasn't like building a pyramid, a dome, an obelisk, or even the world's tallest office building. Eero Saarinen had taken a catenary curve—the arc of a chain suspended from two points—turned it upside down, and left it to an army of engineers and workmen to figure out. The Arch had to be invented twice; first in Saarinen's imagination, then for real beside the Mississippi River.

More than a decade later, project engineers led by John Dinkeloo, who had worked with Saarinen, devised a new engineering plan based on a single hollow curving tube with a triangular base. They looked to new building materials and deep foundations to stabilize the form. The resulting structure supports itself.

Gateway Arch • St. Louis

The idea of a monument to America's westward expansion was born in 1933, the brainchild of Luther Ely Smith, a St. Louis lawyer and civic leader. Smith was a persuasive and persistent man, but it took 14 years of perseverance before Smith's vision initiated a national architectural competition to give form to the monument.

After an executive order was signed in 1935 by Franklin Delano Roosevelt, the old St. Louis riverfront was chosen as a site. An area of some 40 city blocks was purchased and all buildings were cleared, but due to the Second World War further progress on the Memorial was halted. In 1947 the Jefferson National Expansion Memorial Association, a group of public-spirited citizens, held a nationwide competition to obtain a fitting design for a monument.

Eliel and Eero Saarinen, though still partners, entered separately and worked on their designs in the same Cranbrook studio, divided by a partition. Something more was going on than simply one firm taking two shots at the same prestigious commission. Eero's daughter Susan later explained, "My father was . . . dying to break out and do his own thing."[1] When the five finalists were chosen, the competition jury, in error, notified Eliel. The Saarinens broke out the champagne. Three days later came an embarrassed clarification: Eero was actually the finalist. That called for more champagne, and— as history would later confirm—more rightful rejoicing.

Eero Saarinen's proposal won over 171 other entries; the competition jury called it "a work of genius." Some of the other competitors were Louis I. Kahn; Harry Weese; Harrison & Abramovitz; Skidmore, Owings & Merrill; Hugh Stubbins, Jr.; Edward Durell Stone; Charles Eames, Ray Eames & John

Both the Arch and the 91-acre Jefferson National Expansion Memorial in which it stands pay tribute to the thousands of pioneers who journeyed westward from St. Louis.

Eero Saarinen said, "We believed that what downtown needed was a tree-covered park. We wanted to have the most nature possible toward the City."

Gateway to the Wilderness

The Jefferson National Expansion Memorial is not just the Gateway Arch, it's also 91 acres of landscape designed by Eero Saarinen and Dan Kiley between 1948 and 1964 and constructed in phases between 1971 and 1981.

Kiley, who served as a member of the original design team in 1947-48, worked closely with Saarinen over the next 16 years. Many versions of the site plan were developed during this time. The design changed from the original concept of a symbolic, forested wilderness, to the more open lawn areas with reflecting pools that characterize today's site.

Kiley had originally specified the planting of tulip poplars because, "I wanted something that soared up, cathedral-like with big, high trunks . . . . I thought the scale of the Arch being 600 feet, an 80-foot tree would be in good scale and give an elevating feeling, too . . . a classic, spiritual feeling." He was "appalled" to hear later that white ash had been planted, a tree he considers most "uninteresting."[2]

Beginning in the early 1990s, the National Park Service began a sensitive and rigorous restoration, rightfully working from the hypothesis that the Memorial landscape has the same significance as its more prominent centerpiece.

Enteza; to name but a few.

It had taken 15 years to get from the conception to the prize, but serious problems would delay the start of construction for yet another 14 years. The Korean War diverted federal funding. The elevated railroad tracks along the river had to be relocated. Eero Saarinen and his associates spent eight years engineering the structure and refining the form. He felt the original flat leg didn't look quite right and the Arch might not even stand properly. He changed the leg to a triangular one for extra stability. The final design follows the shape of a hanging chain whose links vary in size just as the tapering of the arch suggests. This catenary curve, as it is called, was a subtle adjustment, and an excruciating one to calculate, but it gave the Arch the visual inevitability of a force of nature.

Saarinen finally completed the plans for what might be called his greatest achievment, indeed one of the greatest achievements of any architect. But he would not live to see it realized, just as he would not live to see John Deere or Dulles Airport finished. In August of 1961, in the midst of his creative prime and greatest popular acclaim, Saarinen's physicians found he had a brain tumor, and only two weeks later he was dead.

In St. Louis, ten months after Saarinen had passed away, on June 27, 1962, the first several tons of concrete were poured into foundation forms 45 feet below ground.

The Gateway Arch is an incredible piece of architecture; it is also an incredible feat of engineering. It spans 630 feet between the outer faces of its legs at ground level, and its top soars 630 feet into the sky: it's as wide as it is high. The complex engineering, design, and construction is completely hidden from view. All that can be seen is its stainless steel outer skin, which combined with an inner skin of carbon steel, carries the gravity and wind loads to the ground. The Arch has no real structural skeleton.

Each leg is an equilateral triangle with a side of 54 feet at

above: Looking west, the 630-foot-high arch frames much of downtown St. Louis including the Old Courthouse (1839) where the slave Dred Scott sued for his freedom in 1847. The exposed roof of the visitor center can be seen between the legs of the arch.

left: Curving walks, allees of trees, and lagoons are clearly visible from the top of the Arch.

ground level, tapering to 17 feet at the top. The double walls of steel are 3 feet apart at ground level and about 8 inches apart above the 400-foot level. Up to the 300-foot mark the space between the walls is filled with reinforced concrete. Beyond that point steel stiffeners are used. The triangular sections were placed one on top of another and then welded inside and out to build the legs of the Arch.

Structural engineers Severud, Elstad, Krueger and Associates report that under a wind load of 55 pounds per square foot (equivalent to a 150-mile-per-hour wind), the Arch will deflect at the top only 18 inches in the east-west direction. Its legs are oriented on a north-south line.

Stainless steel was chosen for its tensile strength, non-corrosiveness, and beauty. High-strength steel bolts connect the inner and outer layers. Concrete, bolstered by steel tensioning rods, fills the space between the plates. By tightening the bolts and rods, the steel skin was stretched tight.

Cranes could reach only the first 72 feet of each leg. The MacDonald Construction Co. of St. Louis devised a way to hoist the gigantic sections into place, and then provide a secure place for workmen to pour concrete and weld the outer seams. Temporary tracks were bolted to each leg of the Arch, and an 80-ton creeper derrick tugged itself up as work progressed.

The biggest concern was the one that occurred to every St. Louisan watching the work progress from the sidewalks below: What if the two pieces don't meet at the top? A mistake of one-sixty-fourth inch at the base would cause too large a variation at 630 feet for the tusks to be torqued into their appointment. To keep the alignment within tolerance, surveyors on the ground sighted on lights at night when the sun wasn't heating and expanding the Arch.

There were less obvious problems involving the human equation. As the Arch curled skyward, several electricians quit, citing claustrophobia and a "tilting sensation" inside the triangular tube. Other workmen complained about the heat, which in summer reached 115 degrees inside; the National Park Service scrambled to find funds for an air-conditioning

Creeper Cranes

The construction team lifted the first six triangular steel sections into place, up to a height of 72 feet, with standard ground-based cranes. Above that height, two special cranes placed on mobile platforms, each weighing 80 tons, were used to raise the 12-foot high, 50-ton sections into place. As work progressed, each crane climbed higher on a track system attached directly to the leg. Once each section of the arch was raised, it was bolted into place.

The derricks pulled themselves up the curved legs of the Arch; their adjustable supports kept them level regardless of the height and curvature. Because the height made it impracticable for workmen to climb to and from the work area, the derrick platforms were reached by a passenger elevator and were equipped with a tool shed for workmen, sanitary facilities, and communications equipment. Two vertical tracks held the sled that supported the derrick and platform.

The entire derrick crept up after it had placed four sections of the Arch. Lifting an Arch section into place took only about one-half hour. The last step was to put the final "keystone" section into place to complete the Arch.

All survey work was done at night to eliminate the distortion caused by the sun's rays heating one side of the Arch while the other two sides were in shadow.

above: October 28, 1965, workers dropping the keystone section into place. Plate-glass port holes provide panoramic views of St Louis to the West and Illinois to the East.
right: Until the legs reached 530 feet, their strength was in equilibrium, but beyond that, the construction load made the structure top-heavy. At the very end, a 58-ton stabilizing strut—held by jacks and a steel harness—allowed the weight to be transmitted to the foundations.

Monumental Criticism

When renderings of the Saarinen proposal first appeared in the press, they provoked a range of commentary on the project. The New York Times called the Arch "a modern monument, fitting, beautiful and impressive." The architectural press also reacted positively. By contrast, many locals referred to the Arch as a "stupendous hairpin and a stainless steel hitching post."

Nonetheless, the most volatile criticism came from Gilmore D. Clarke, a landscape architect and Chairman of the National Commission of Fine Arts. In a letter to jury Chairman William Wurster, Clarke charged that Saarinen's design for the Arch too closely resembled one approved by Italian Dictator Benito Mussolini for a Fascist exhibition in Rome in 1942. For this reason, he felt that the Arch could not symbolize Jeffersonian Democracy.

The Clarke controversy attracted national attention. While Saarinen thought the objections ridiculous, Wurster took the charges quite seriously and with other members of the jury drafted a rebuttal which finally ended the controversy. Their reply stressed the historic and modern usage of the arch as an architectural form, and that it was clearly not a fascist invention. In reference to Saarinen's Arch, they reiterated the suitability of its symbolism as the Gateway to the West.

For his part, Saarinen claimed that his Arch was based on mathematical principles. "It's just preposterous to think that a basic form, based on a completely natural figure, should have any ideological connection."

system. In 1964, civil rights activists protested the fact that no African-American workers were employed in the skilled trades on the construction project, and a federal investigation ensued.

A certain uneasiness mingled with anticipation in the autumn air over St. Louis as the days of October 1965 ticked away. The Gateway Arch stood one section from completion, two colossal tusks poised to touch 630 feet in the sky. The gap between them was an arm's length, two and a-half feet. The section that had to fit into it was eight feet long. Hydraulic jacks, exerting 625,000 pounds of force, would have to pry the arcs farther apart. Such a thing had never been done before. On October 28, 1965, as jacks pushed the two legs apart, workers dropped the keystone section into place. Almost three years since the ground-breaking, the Arch was complete.

The Jefferson National Expansion Memorial broke ground in architecture, engineering, and landscape architecture. Saarinen always considered landscape to be an essential and integral part of his designs. "I see architecture not as the building alone, but the building in relation to its surroundings."

Saarinen played an active role in developing the site plan. The site originally had a railroad trestle running along the Mississippi levee. The first proposal shows the monument on a level with the waterfront behind the trestle. Years of wrangling with the railroad resulted in the present scheme; Saarinen designed a cut for the rail line to run in and he raised the Arch and the park. With the park at a higher level, lagoons could be added. Saarinen also designed all the walks and steps around the Arch and throughout the park; they reflect the catenary curve of the monument. Dan Kiley developed the planting plan which reinforced the curves of the walks.

Over time the site plan became more spare and simplified. Saarinen's most radical decision was to do away with the

above: An early presentation drawing by Jay Henderson Barr shows the arch with "flat" legs viewed from the Mississippi with the Eads Bridge (1874) overhead. Barr made about 100 sketches to demonstrate the design's impact from different viewpoints.
left: Saarinen poses for a newspaper photographer contemplating various catenary models, a hanging chain or rope and drawings of famous monuments on the wall behind.

intended buildings, the frontier village, the symbolic Oregon and Santa Fe trails, the tea house and restaurant. The only structure—the visitors center—was relegated to its present place underground. The architect decided that there would be no structures to compete with the Arch.

The entrance to the Arch is from the underground visitor center. Visitors are carried from the lobby level below to the observation platform at the top of the Arch by a unique conveyance system—a 40-passenger train made up of eight five-passenger capsules in each leg.

It was Saarinen's method to envision and then count on others to extrapolate and execute his ideas. Recognition must go to the many people who carried out the construction of this monument with care and precision—the structural workers, electricians, steamfitters, sheet metal journeymen, and others who risked life and limb, using their skills to meld the components together into a lasting monument for the inspiration of future generations. It was estimated that 13 workers might lose their lives; there were no fatalities. The dedication and determination of those involved echoed the pioneer spirit of those it commemorates, the people who explored and settled the American West.

The Arch has helped spark a renaissance in the downtown area of St. Louis, with new buildings, a new stadium, new shops, and new apartments filled with people proud to move back to the city from the suburbs.

It is unfortunate that Eero Saarinen did not survive to see his most magnificent achievement realized. His vision, however, remains alive, an inspiration—and an admonition—to all of us who make buildings or commission them or work in them or live in them. In an interview with Time magazine in 1956, he said, "Our architecture is too humble. It should be prouder, more aggressive, much richer and larger than we see it today. I would like to do my part in expanding that richness."

Within weeks of designing the ingenious Gateway Arch tram system (above), its inventor, Dick Bowser, received a two-year contract. As it turned out, the job lasted six years, until 1967. Bowser stayed on with the Park Service maintenance staff at the Arch until 1972.

Cabins in the Sky

The tram system that takes visitors to the summit of the arch is as unique and special as the monument it services. It was the vision of a creative and special man, one of the heroes in the story of the construction of the Gateway Arch.

The entire system is a one-of-a-kind invention, conceived in just two short weeks by Dick Bowser. He and his father had developed, manufactured, and installed Bowser Parking System elevator equipment. These elevators could travel horizontally & diagonally through a structure as well as the normal vertical travel.

The Bowser company was called by Eero Saarinen's office, while it was looking for a firm to take on a "transporter" project for the Gateway Arch. "There were two of Saarinen's partners on the line. Their first question was 'did an elevator have to travel vertically?' I said I didn't think so."

Bowser worked day and night at home in his basement for the next two weeks to complete his plans.

"The first drawing that I got [from them] had an outline of the Arch, and down at the bottom was a square that said 'elevator' that's all there was."

One by one, standard elevators, escalators, and ferris wheel cars were ruled out. Bowser describes the tram system he invented:

"The eight small capsules, used in each of the two Arch trains, are similar to the barrels used in cement mixers. Each train capsule has a 5-foot diameter barrel that is open on the front and closed on the back. The back has a center pivot shaft, and surrounding the open front there is a frame with rollers, so the barrel can rotate within the frame that is supported by wheels running in the channel-shaped tracks. There are 5 seats in each barrel, so the weight of the passengers helps keep [the capsule] in an upright position. "I told my wife, 'I can't believe I was involved in all this and I don't believe I have the guts to do such a thing again.'"[3]

The United States Air Force Academy presides over one of the most breathtaking sites of any major building group in the country, with the Rampart Range of the Rocky Mountains as a backdrop and the Academy itself sharply etched on a podium atop hills which rumble and fade into the plains to the east.

While the chapel fills spiritual needs, it also provides the architectural rationale for the campus, its heaven-thrusting spires—like the folded plane wings on the flight deck of an aircraft carrier—dramatically relieving the horizontality of its neighbors. Without its serrated verticality mobilizing the group, its unity would be diminished.

The chapel was the last major building finished at the Academy, and though it is not the church everyone wants, it is remarkable.

U.S. Air Force Academy Chapel • Colorado Springs

The first thing one sees when approaching the United States Air Force Academy is the glistening file of spires of the Cadet Chapel, and it remains the dominant visual force for as long as one stays. Looming dramatically over the flat parade grounds and the squat structures of the surrounding campus, the bristling tips of the Chapel's spires seem to brush the sky.

No one can remain indifferent to the Chapel; to some it has an awesome grace, to others a forbidding inhumanity. It's a structure that almost didn't happen, mired as it was in delays and controversy. But, controversy suited the architect Walter A. Netsch just fine. "I would rather people have some reaction to it," he said, "than have the cadets merely shrug and say, 'And that's the chapel.'"[1]

The Academy Chapel commission was touchy from the beginning since it required the approval of Congress as the first major government-supported marriage of religion and modern architecture in the U.S. When the final plan was submitted, Virginia's Senator A. Willis Robertson said it looked like "an assembly of wigwams," and Congressman Errett P. Scrivner demanded to know why Congress should appropriate more than $3,000,000 for so many spires when one spire per church had been sufficient in the past. The budget-conscious won a modest victory: the 19 spires in the original design were reduced to 17.

Netsch began working on the chapel in 1954 when Skidmore, Owings & Merrill received the original commission to design the Academy itself. Netsch's task was to build a place of worship for the cadets and to create a national monument—no mean feat. Furthermore, his building would

As controversial as the Chapel design was among congressmen it was looked upon favorably by religious leaders who praised it enthusiastically.

Each of the many thousands of pieces of glass were hand-struck with hammers to make facets that create the endless, shimmering variations in the light.

Frame of Reference

Replacing the folded plate construction of the original design was a space frame of tetrahedrons made of tube steel and enclosed with aluminum panels.

"In the meantime," Netsch recalls, "I had gotten this idea here in Chicago, working with my engineer, of the tetrahedrons and compiling the tetrahedrons together—you know, piling them up so they inverted."[2]

The 100 tetrahedrons are each 75 feet long; have a structural skeleton of steel pipe; and are clad with aluminum sheets outside, while their interior finish is plaster on precast panels held in aluminum surrounds. The primary members are 6-inch pipe; secondary crossbraces are 4-inch pipe. Pipes were mitered at intersections, welded into units off the site and shipped by rail and truck. Cranes lifted the tetrahedron units into place; bolting was used for field erection; the structural assembly was then welded. Steel angle frames support the skin; aluminum frames carry the interior finish and sash.

The orientation of the tetrahedrons alternated from the base to the pinnacle to produce a complex effect with a simple form. The tetrahedrons were spaced a foot apart to allow light to flow through a narrow band of stained glass, which marked their juncture. From a series of granite abutments the Chapel's spires rose to a height of 150 feet.

have to serve Protestants, Catholics and Jews. A single-spire motif would imply one religion, and a three-spire motif would make no sense. The problem was how to produce a building that would be unmistakably a house of worship, without benefit of using, on the exterior at least, any of the traditional hallmarks of any one faith.

According to the myth surrounding the project, a piece of folded paper resembling Japanese origami was used, under pressure of the deadline, to temporarily stand in as a religious structure on the model. When SOM made its initial presentation of the master plan in May 1955, the Chapel immediately came under attack. When controversy over the design threatened to throw the whole project off course, the Air Force insisted that the chapel be removed from the model. Nathaniel A. Owings waffled about the firm's intent regarding the initial design and suggested that it was only a symbol. But, a reporter for a local paper taking note of the intricacy of the model questioned the reasoning, stating that it "took more than a little folding to do."

Netsch's account of that presentation clearly shows the depth of his involvement in the Chapel design as well as the generous encouragement and support that Owings gave him. Netsch says,

> "At the end of that presentation, everything had been going along so well, and all of a sudden the senator from South Carolina said, 'Everything looks fine, except that chapel. I don't hear the rustle of angels' wings.' And some senator from North Dakota said, 'It looks like a bunch of tepees to me.' All of a sudden the earth fell in on that poor little chapel design. I was in tears in the back of the room, and Nat [Owings] came back and said, 'What's wrong with you? Everything is approved but the chapel, and you can always do another one'—that sort of thinking.
>
> "Nat said, 'You're going to have to go to Europe, because you've never been to Europe, and you must design another chapel.'"[3]

above: A single 75-foot-long tube-steel tetrahedron on route from Missouri, where it was fabricated.

left: The space-frame under construction is remarkable in its own right.

It was decided to go ahead with the Academy, wait until a suitable chapel design could be resolved and things simmered down. Construction began on the Academy and Netsch went off to Europe.

"Sainte-Chapelle made a tremendous impression on me being flooded with colored light, and the fact that it had a chapel on two floors. I also saw St. Francis of Assisi when I got to Italy, and Gordon remembers it as his inspiration on his having decided that the chapel at the Academy should be on two levels. I can remember Gordon and I discussing both buildings.

"I can remember to this day of seeing Chartres arise over the wheat fields. As I approached it. It was sense of place—you know, the Air Force Academy out in the middle of nowhere—the idea of the sense of place that it had.

"I came home with this tremendous feeling of how can I in this modern age of technology create something that will be as inspiring and aspiring as Chartres, and with the light of Sainte-Chapelle and the light of Chartres."[4]

Even after the European trip Netsch's design retained its controversial elements. The complex geometric nature of the original design was not one that could easily be adjusted to respond to criticism; any significant change would have been drastic. Although SOM was ordered by the Air Force to produce four or five alternatives, it's not clear whether the firm ever had any intention of significantly departing from the original design proposal.

Netsch tore up eight false starts before the final design came to him in the form of an inspired doodle. He had drawn a series of near-vertical connected lines that looked a bit like the tracing of a seismograph. Then the idea of using tetrahedrons came to him—100 four-sided structures of steel tubing serving as the building blocks of a whole series of spires that would reach upwards and still flow logically from the design. "By literally placing the tetrahedrons on top of

All the People, All the Time
The plan for the Academy Chapel was to put three faiths under one roof with the Protestant Chapel on the upper level and the Catholic and Jewish chapels below.

Some critics were incredulous that such essentially divergent religious viewpoints could be reconciled in one structure to begin with, especially since "Protestantism, by its very nature, is in contradiction to Catholicism, and Judaism is in contradiction to both." Then, there's the incontrovertible fact that even sects of Protestantism have very real differences.

Aware of the problems of meeting the unique requirements of the different Protestant denominations within one chapel, the chaplains requested early in the design process that they be closely involved in the development of liturgical furnishings and appointments.

At one point, when the Air Force appeared insistent on a cruciform shape for the building, the chaplains protested that the "Jewish Welfare Board and other Jewish agencies would strenuously object to worshiping in a building which was deliberately constructed as a cruciform."

Where optimists saw the Chapel as a "unifying symbol appropriate for our democracy in a world of conflict" (this was the Cold War, after all), others perceived grave danger in the smoothing over of differences.

right: The United States Military Academy Cadet Chapel at West Point, Cram, Goodhue & Ferguson, West Point, New York, 1910.
Things were probably a great deal easier for Ralph Adams Cram (1863-1942) since Gothic was the only vocabulary used in churches and chapels when the military commissioned this, and it was assumed that everyone was a Protestant of one kind or another.

Code of Silence

In an interview with Betty J. Blum, Walter Netsch talked about the notoriety of the Chapel and how it broke the silence around who the designers were at SOM:

Netsch: Nat [Owings] had been a firm believer in anonymity. Everything was SOM, and it wasn't until I did this controversial building—really controversial building . . .

Blum: The chapel?

Netsch: The chapel, that some of the partners were very happy to have it named Walter's work. So it's Netsch's chapel, and that's what broke the hold of it. You'll find that Gordon's buildings got identified as Gordon's buildings after that.

Blum: So why be anonymous?

Netsch: For two reasons—one, Nat wanted it that way because none of them would be an Owings building.

Blum: He wanted this crew of anonymous medieval workmen-craftsmen—that idea?

Netsch: That's right. That's what he wanted. The partners, like Walter Severinghaus and Bill Brown, already labored under a difficult cloud because they were Gordon Bunshaft's project managers, but they were co-equals. They were partners as Gordon was a partner. There were touchy times when very emotional things would occur out of the blue—"But Gordon, what I'm doing is just as important as what you do. You wouldn't be able to get Connecticut General built if it weren't for me!" It was also to keep egos happy that this thing—and I say, it wasn't until contretemps, until we had a building that some people didn't want to be identified with, that the designer got named. Isn't that funny? I never expected to be the cause of it all."[5]

one another," says Netsch, "I made an enclosure that embodies the concept of light and space—and that is the dominant part of church architecture."[6]

On seeing the revised plans, Congressional critics complained bitterly that "three years later they have come up with substantially the same appearing building that they had in the first instance." Other critics claimed that they had been intentionally misled to believe that the revised Chapel would be more conservative, but instead found it "worse than the old one."

The interior was another controversy—this time with the clergy. From the very beginning, Netsch had ruled out what he calls "a supermarket cathedral"—a single chapel that can change faith at will, using gimmicks such as revolving altars. Each religion would have a chapel of its own. The Protestants, being in the majority, got the largest, and since the academy service is fairly formal, the chapel was endowed with lofty grandeur. The Roman Catholic chapel and the Jewish place of worship are underneath, which caused one Catholic chaplain to observe: "The Protestants are nearer to Heaven, but they need the head start." The Catholic chapel, with its gentle arches and stonework, suggests the architecture and masonry of the Romanesque cathedral. The Jewish chapel is housed within a round wooden screen from which all structural elements have been eliminated. This, says Netsch, goes back to the ancient tents of the wandering Tribes of Israel, for each tent created, in architect talk, a "non-structural space."

The most striking feature of the Cadet Chapel is its magnificent stained glass. Netsch's commitment to it's luminous color as a primary expressive power was reinforced by his European trip. Things weren't made any easier by budgetary restrictions, but once again his tenacity is remarkable. He personally designed the color and placement of each and every fragment, of which there are thousands, according to a scheme that he devised and scrupulously charted.

"So we had the system of how to do it, and I wanted

above: The SOM team working on the Academy model in the Chicago office, Walter Netsch at right, c.1955.
Netsch became public spokesperson and defender of the Chapel design. Carrying a large model of the Chapel, complete with lights, he toured the country and appeared before architectural and religious organizations to engender support.

the windows to, in a sense, start from Genesis, being dark colors, and go to gold over the altar and the other. Since I had a mile of this glass to do, I then had a pallet of blues and purples and reds and greens and then yellows. I would sit in my living room . . . with little chips of colored pencil and a drawing of a facade of the building. I would make that blue and that red and that purple and so forth and so on, and as the window went up towards the apex it would get lighter so you would see this transition of color horizontally and vertically. Since the tetrahedrons crossed, they would meet and come back again."[7]

The stained glass is as beautiful when seen from the outside at night as it is inside the Chapel during the day.

The building miraculously survived the controversy of its origins. Indeed, its difficult history plays a positive role in the outcome since the design evolved and the Chapel grew into a better structure. Capitulating to the pressure could have resulted in a form without any meaning. Everyone would have been pleased—but would they? Netsch would have given the Air Force a "supermarket cathedral" and the cadets would have shrugged and said, "And that's the Chapel."

Instead the building soars as much through its strength of resolve as it does through it design elements. It is a fusion of opposites that uses the tension of difference as a positive force, as a means of expression.

For Netsch the community was the main thing: the fusion of the gothic and the space age makes perfect sense in the middle of the deserts of Colorado on the campus of an Air Force Academy. It seems quite natural that the spires should also suggest giant wings, and even the hangar-like quality of the Protestant chapel interior seems in its own way just right. The building's metallic majesty, visible across the countryside like the church spires of rural Europe, is in perfect harmony with the spirit of the Academy. Its materials and basic forms are largely those of an airplane, and its spires do not merely point, they soar.

above: The colored glass strips are composed of 24 hues (no greens), and range in general tonality from violet at the narthex through blues and reds to a golden glow at the reredos and altar. The gable ends and triangular base windows are glazed with a luminated, tempered, amber glass containing a reflective layer of antique silver which reduces both radiant heat and glare.

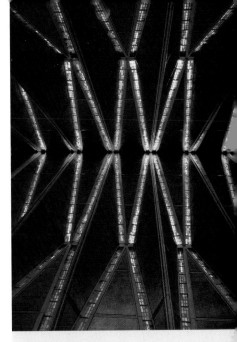

Celestial Light

The fastidious attention paid by Walter Netsch to the choice of color and to the fabrication of the stained glass windows is remarkable. It finds its parallel in the craftsmanship in the European cathedrals he so very much admired.

"Robertson Ward and I talked about what we were going to do, and Bob came up with some samples by talking to different glaziers of how you could glue things on glass and everything, and I had done some research on it. I then tried to see if they would hire somebody, and the answer was, 'Absolutely, no. You've gotten us into this, you get us out of it'—that sort of attitude. I talked to Robertson, and Robertson came up with a very practical idea of inventing a window frame one foot wide and, say, three feet long, divided into panes. Then he said, 'Well, you know, Walter, we can do the dalles'—that's a thick glass that we were going to use—'and this would fit in the frame,' and then there would be another one, and then you would have another dalles. This is where his genius comes in. He said, 'Walter, don't worry. We'll have the workmen just sit around with their hammers and chip this off.'

" . . . so the light as it filtered would do all of these wonderful things."[8]

The John Hancock Center is the world's tallest mixed-use skyscraper, combining offices, stores, and private apartments. On the 44th floor is a grocery, fitness center, and the highest swimming pool above street level, anywhere.

From the very beginning Chicagoans were attracted to the bold image of the new high-rise, which they christened "Big John." Even before the project's formal announcement, rumors had leaked that SOM was designing a 100-story structure near the lake, and by March 1965 requests flooded in requesting advance space in the building.

One newspaper reported how a resident, having left a home in the suburbs for the tower, had taken an interest in nature after his move to the city. Now, with his expansive view of lake and sky, he could watch the sun rise over the lake, the stars and moon in the sky, and the annual migration of birds.

John Hancock Center • Chicago

With the hopes of attracting investment to the area, the neighborhood around Chicago's North Michigan Avenue was dubbed the "Magnificent Mile" in 1947. By the 1960s, corporations and large retailers still wouldn't budge from the city's central business district where they'd been since the 19th Century.

All that changed in 1964, when Skidmore, Owings, and Merrill presented builder-developer Jerry Wolman with a choice between two potentially successful building schemes for the area: a double-tower plan, and a mixed-use, single-tower alternative. The single-tower plan offered certain advantages: the building would cover less of the site, leaving more open space for pedestrians; blocked views between the two buildings would be avoided; and putting apartments above the office space would remove them from the hustle and bustle of the street. In addition, the "world's highest" residences, with their spectacular views of the city and the lake, would command the greatest profit for the developer. There was only one problem—the wind.

The skyscaper was born in Chicago over a century ago when the cast-iron skeleton was introduced into construction for the first time. It was almost immediately recognized that outer walls are no longer needed to hold up a building. And, since the walls were now just a skin, the building's bones could rise infinitely—almost. For SOM to build near the lake—to create a structure that could tolerate occassional gale-force winds—would require re-thinking the skyscraper and making a complete about-face on 80 years of its evolution. A completely new kind of skyscraper was about to be born—in Chicago once again.

The tapered form of "Big John" suggests the nobility and monumentality of an obelisk as it looms gracefully behind the Chicago Water Tower, 1869.

One of the few buildings to survive the Great Fire of 1871, the water tower has become a symbol of the Chicagoans' tenacious will to succeed.

Teamwork

The John Hancock Center was designed collaboratively by architect Bruce J. Graham and structural engineer Fazlur R. Khan, both of Skidmore, Owings & Merrill. The two formed an easy partnership, the engineer proposing structural concepts that the architect would craft into architectural space.

Khan had the rare ability to describe complex engineering ideas in a way that made them both comprehensible and exciting; Graham's receptiveness nourished Khan's creativity.

Referring to the achievement of the Hancock Center, Khan stressed that "a structural solution or a breakthrough is only as good as an equivalent and complementary architecture." For his part, Graham averred that it was in "the gutsy, masculine, industrial tradition of Chicago, where structure is of the essence."

In 1969, the two collaborated on another record-breaking project that would mark the Chicago skyline—the Sears Tower. It remained the world's tallest building for over 20 years.

By the 1960s computers began to allow for the investigation of new and different structural systems. This, combined with the development of high grade steel and fusion-welded sections, made it possible to design structures that could resist the sideward force of the wind and the downward pull of gravity more effectively. But, how much steel is reasonable?

If a tall structure's resistance to wind depends on the width of its core, then the strongest structure will be the widest. With the necessary extra bracing, the result would be a prohibitively expensive building that is all structure and no space. The next logical step, if SOM were to proceed, was to get rid of the core and put the load back on the exterior walls—the building, in effect, becomes a tube. The width gained in this fashion should give greater height to the design.

The solution is in John Hancock's structural system as conceived by the late Fazlur Khan, pioneer and engineering luminary of tall building construction. His revolutionary idea can be understood just by looking at Hancock's façade—it's completely revealed on the surface of the structure. The diagonal X-bracing is continuous from face to face and is connected to the columns, allowing the load to be transferred from bracing to column and back again. The bracing is fused at the building's corners, thereby arresting motion in every direction. Meanwhile, this intersecting of cross bracing and columns gives the façade a dynamic visual force.

The final form of the building was derived from a combination of functional and structural requirements. Office, commercial, and garage uses require large, unobstructed floor areas. Residential use requires smaller floor areas and core to exterior wall dimensions. By combining these uses in one unified structure, certain advantages accrue in locating the residences at the top of the building. All apartments become prime units high above street noise with spectacular views unobstructed by adjacent buildings; elevator requirements are simplified making it possible to share shafts; and the dimensions of the building are reduced where wind loads are maximum. The tapered form that evolved satisfies these requirements functionally and esthetically. Structurally, it is a more stable structure than a conventional rectilinear volume of equivalent area for its height. Esthetically, the shape is elegant as well as distinc-

above: Presentation of John Hancock model by Fazlur Khan, far left, and Bruce Graham next to him.
left: By placing most of the steel on the outside of the structure, where it acts as a wind brace, the Hancock's innovative engineering system was also economical; it required half the steel of a building with traditional internal columns. Less than 30 pounds of steel per square foot of floor area was used in the building, equaling that of a 40- to 50–story traditional tower.

tive—the building is now an inseparable part of the Chicago skyline.

The end result is an extremely simple and highly efficient system for a structure of this magnitude and height. Floors are virtually free of interior columns beyond the central core and provide a variety of depth and sizes to accommodate the requirements of the different occupancies.

The inward-leaning sides reduce a 47,000-square-foot floor plan at the base to 17,000 square feet at the roof. While seeking a compelling building aesthetic and spatial arrangement, the designers had to account for the structural requirements of the trussed-tube system. As a result, office and apartment floor-to-floor heights vary, as do the slopes of the cross-bracing diagonal columns.

In addition to serving the building program, this unique shape lowered wind pressures on the tower as well. The building's sway, a big problem with tall buildings, is kept to a minimum of 5 to 8 inches in 60-mile-per-hour winds. The structure can withstand winds up to 132 miles-per-hour. On a clear day one can see Illinois, Indiana, Michigan, and Wisconsin from the 94th floor observatory.

All the exterior steel is clad in black aluminum accented with tinted bronze, glare-reducing glass, and bronze-colored aluminum window frames. The plaza at ground level, recessed court, and the first floor base upon which the structure rests are covered in travertine marble.

It is only fitting that Bruce Graham and Fazlur Khan—a team that personified form and function——would blaze the trail for the next phase of megastructures in Louis Sullivan's home town. The John Hancock Center's clear integration of structural form and architectural space reflects the vital spirit with which Chicagoans—architects, engineers, developers and residents—have embraced the challenges posed by the modern scale of urban tall-building development. Gracefully celebrating the city's crucial role in twentieth-century architecture, the soaring tower is still, 35 years after its design, a symbol of innovative and collaborative achievement between architect and engineer.

John Hancock Center's lower five floors are devoted to commercial use, followed by seven floors of in-building parking. The next 28 floors are approximately one million square feet of virtually column-free office space. The 42nd and 43rd floors are devoted to mechanical equipment.

The Sky Lobby of the upper living portion occupies the 44th and 45th floors and serves as the upper terminal for the high speed express elevators originating at the apartment street lobby. The next 48 floors are approximately one million square feet of flexible apartment space—about 700 apartments.

Originally the Hancock had a poor relationship to the street; the plaza was buffeted with traffic noise, inclement weather, and gusting winds.

However, a revitalization of the plaza was completed in 1995. A successful new design includes improved lighting, a 12 high waterfall to muffle street sounds, and the re-circulation of office and retail pedestrian traffic.

above: The X-bracing shows in some of the apartments and might be considered an obtrusive feature. Not so for the Chicagoans who bought them—they were all the first to be sold. Apparently, for many, the bracing signals the building's significance.
middle: The Sky Lobby on the 44th floor.
right: The Michigan Avenue entrance and sunken public plaza.

The appointment of Richard Fargo Brown as director of the Kimbell at the end of 1965 turned out to be crucial for the development of the museum, especially as it made for a successful collaboration between client and architect.

Brown was more than enthusiastic on completion of the building; he thought of the Kimbell as "what every museum man has been looking for ever since museums came into existence."

As notoriously self-critical as Louis Kahn was, he felt that the Kimbell was one of his most successful buildings.

Fondly referred to as the villa in the park, the Kimbell is the last building that Kahn designed and saw completed.

Kimbell Art Museum • Fort Worth, Texas

Louis Kahn had two driving passions his whole life through: managing the subtle variables of light, and reviving archetypal forms—massive, primal forms—that reflected his interest in ancient cultures. These passions intersect and overlap in all his projects, but in none so successfully as the Kimbell Art Museum. Here they are so inexorably bound as to be a single phenomenon—light carves out form, form gives light a place to be. At the Kimbell one is forced to agree with Kahn—the "sun never knew how great it was until it struck the side of a building."[1]

Kahn often repeated and grouped his forms—used them as modules—then connected them all inside. The Kimbell is no exception—the single module that is repeated is a long, vaulted structure that is grouped end to end and side by side. In the initial scheme, units were left out to form interior gardens. In the final version, the missing modules are staggered in from the edges allowing park space to enter the museum complex.

The buildings are actually small; Kahn thought of the museum as "a friendly home." Three full-length, un-walled bays form long porches that serve as entrance/shelters, but also inform us as to the building's structure. Without walls to get in the way the form of the building is made completely clear before you go inside. Kahn used to say, "Space is not space unless you can see the evidence of how it was made."[2]

Each of the marvelous structures measures 104 feet long, 23 feet wide, and its walls are 4 inches thick. The vaults, which rest on supports only at their ends, are separated laterally by 7-foot-wide concrete alleys which contain air-conditioning and electrical service. The travertine walls at the

Before Kahn began the project, Richard Brown prepared a statement of purpose that read: "The creative strength of such a building lies in simplicity and directness of approach to the uses of the building, clarity of the disposition of parts, honesty in the relationship between visible form and means of construction, taste in the proportions of those forms, quality of materials, and exquisite craftsmanship in putting the materials together.

Past, Present, and Future

Frequent travel and constantly inspired sketching fueled Louis Kahn's passion for archetypal form. His projects were often linked to a specific place that fired his imagination: the Richards Medical Center and San Gimignano; Salk and Asissi; Ahmedabad and Ostia.

Many of the forms of the Kimbell were inspired by Kahn's trip to the temple of Ammon at Karnak in Egypt.

In the sketches he produced during his travels in France, Italy, and Egypt there is a continuous preoccupation with the elemental forms of masonry and the play of light and shade on these. The columns of the temple of Karnak, the brick walls of Ostia, or the towers of the cathedral at Ailbi were recorded with great vigor and became part of the mental background that must have affected the selection of beginnings. It did so because of the respect which was accorded to these forms.

Louis Kahn was in Venice at the end of February 1971 when the shuttering for the Kimbell shells was being put into place. Having been shown the roofs of the Ducal Palace, he said: "The roofs of Venice are nothing short of fantastic. When you climb them as I did and take a tour of the roofs it is a sea of lead which you see in front of you, and lead is an undeniable material for roofs. This lead is thick and has turned the right color, the roofs look like snow in this spring weather. How much of a lesson this is to us: the importance of finishing our buildings and giving the ground on which the building is built back to the roof, which is really the reflection of the ground which is occupied below."

ends of each gallery are non-load-bearing; they are essentially infill which is why there can be a gap between wall and roof.

Kahn chose the same kind of concrete finish he used at the Salk Institute (though ultimately a different aggregate was used) and the travertine came from the same quarry in Italy. The vaults were cast onsite. The interior surface of the concrete is only washed, and otherwise left rough. The cutting marks from the quarry have also been left untreated on the travertine surfaces.

The roofs were covered in lead, a material that continued the tonal palette of the concrete and travertine. Lead also gives a feeling of permanence which was so essential to Kahn's timeless design.

Inside the museum, there is no other source of light other than the daylight that enters a slot at the top of each vault and runs along its entire length (technically these are not vaults since the slot means the cast shells on either side don't meet anywhere along the summit). At this point the light is controlled with careful precision. A portion of daylight filters through the perforated aluminum diffusers that Kahn called "natural light fixtures"; the rest bounces up off the vault and washes down the polished concrete to the space below (there is artificial back-up lighting in the diffusers). The effect is of a vault hovering over the darker space of the gallery. Diffusing the light practically solves the needs of a museum where natural light can be dangerous; meanwhile, it helps raise the ceiling in a space that is otherwise diminutive. The light succeeds in lessening the gallery's materiality while aggrandizing the space.

When he lectured specifically on the Kimbell lighting system, Kahn said, "An architecture must have the religion of light. A sense of light as the giver of all presences. Every building, every room must be in natural light because natural light gives the mood of the day. The season of the year is brought into a room. When a light enters a room, it is your light and nobody else's. It belongs to that room. The Kimbell Art Museum uses all natural light."[3]

above: The Kimbell's south garden court with sculpture by Isamu Noguchi.

left: Dummy (roomless) chapels along the wall around the Step Pyramid built by King Zoser. Saqqara, Egypt c. 2600 B.C. The façades imitate timber-framing in limestone.

The thin arc of glass at the ends of the galleries, where the walls ought to meet the ceilings, further serves to lift the vault while it conveys a sense of continuation—the sensation that the gallery doesn't come to a halt at the end walls. At first this gap was to be constant in width, but Kahn decided to make the contour of the wall part of a circle so that the opening varies in width, widening from the top to the bottom. The geometry of the vault, which is cycloidal, suddenly becomes visible and clear. There is something provocative about these two shapes in tandem.

The reflective quality of pale concrete and travertine is an essential factor in the luminosity of the interior. Positioning water next to the open vault on the west side produced reflected light on the underside of the shell and sand-blasting the stainless steel provided a metal that avoided highlights. Everywhere within the spaces of the museum the light glows with a soft, silvery intensity.

One of Kahn's best buildings, the Kimbell is silent, but never mute. It speaks volumes through its light and its forms. It partakes of the order of classical structures, but without mimicry; there is nothing nostalgic about Kahn's forms. They look as if they were always there, yet they look as if they will always be new. They have a presence that connects them to a past brought forward to the present. They are authentically monumental—timeless.

Kahn's special gift was that he could manage the variables of light, that he could revive archetypal forms, and that he could put them together in a transcendental experience. But, he was able to bring all that to a building that does its job well. In the end he built a museum of art—one of the finest in the world.

When Thomas Messer, who was then Director of the Guggenheim Museum in New York, visited the Kimbell after it opened, he said, "A museum is not all that complicated a mechanism. The important thing that an architect can contribute is a noble, monumental, or intimate space—whatever is required of him—where works of art come alive. And I certainly feel that this has been done."[4]

Every decision of Kahn's has a twofold purpose; it is beautiful and it is practical.
above: The light gap also serves as an expansion joint.
middle: Mezzanine library. A typical gallery with original furniture.
right: Passageway between buildings. Full-height wall of glass to the right provides light to the offices below.

A RCHITECTURAL RECORD celebrates its 110th anniversary with a gift. The book that you hold represents a new venture, a series of books published by McGraw-Hill that bears our name. However, our magazine, ARCHITECTURAL RECORD, reaches a professional audience while architecture affects us all. This series can help bridge the gap, widening public appreciation and understanding by demystifying this fundamental art.

Everyone, from children to learned practitioners, can sense architecture's power: it surrounds us, enfolds us, covers us, and protects us. Whether or not we are able to name the components or mathematically analyze the forces at play, we can describe the feelings and moods great buildings conjure up from compressed urban pathways to intimate private spaces. Our knowledge is 3-dimensional, derived from binocular and peripheral vision, the immediate memory of what lies behind, and even the events of the past. How much richer the mix can become.

That is what Roger Shepherd, who inaugurates the series, prepares us for. He enriches our potential experiences by telling us more. Page after page he elucidates what had been in shadow—naming the parts without resorting to pedantry, telling the stories of how a building came to be without overt historicism. He explains and explicates, both breaking these complex assemblages down into their simpler components, and demonstrating that no project remains static. Every building takes on the life of the people that actually use it, evolving through time in an almost organic way, changing into a changeling.

This book, and the series, then acts like a friend. The layout appears accessible and variable, from the text on the major projects that changed our lives, to the smaller sidebars that describe the events, people, and special interests that made the projects unique. Other such books lie within our own plans. As you read, learn and love more deeply: the built world demands your attention. This is our gift, and our charge, to you.

Robert Ivy, FAIA
Editor in Chief
Architectural Record

(page viii) 1. Mies van der Rohe quoted in Blaser, *Werner, Mies van der Rohe: The Art of Structure* (London: Thanes & Hudson, 1965), prologue.

Preface

1. The 1971 Weyerhaeuser Headquarters in Tacoma, Washington was selected as the 2001 recipient of the A.I.A. 25-five Year Award. The five-story, 358,000-square-foot head-quarters for a natural resources company, on a 230-acre wooded campus, was designed by Charles Bassett (Skidmore, Owings & Merrill) with landscape architect Peter Walker.

Introduction

1. Sullivan, Louis H., "Ornament in Architecture," *The Engineering Magazine*, August 1892.

2. I'm writing this just as two terrorist airplanes crash into each of the two World Trade Center Towers, and destroy them; another plane crashes into the Pentagon.

3. Wright, Frank Lloyd, "A New Reality: Glass," from *An Autobiography* (New York: Duell, Stone and Pearce, 1943), pp. 337-49.

4. Drexler, Arthur, "Post-war Architecture," from *Built in USA: Post-war Architecture* (New York: Museum of Modern Art, 1952), p. 20.

5. Welch, Philip B., ed., "Advancing Architecture," *Goff on Goff: Conversations and Lectures* (Norman: University of Oklahoma Press, 1996), p. 320.

6. Hitchcock, Henry-Russell, "Introduction," from *Built in USA: Post-war Architecture* (New York: Museum of Modern Art, 1952), p. 15.

7. Pick, Grant, "A School Fit for Children," *The Chicago Reader*, March 1, 1991.

8. Schulze, Franz, *Mies van der Rohe: A Critical Biography* (Chicago: The University of Chicago, 1985), p. 270.

9. Sullivan, Louis H., *The Autobiography of an Idea* (New York: Dover Publications, Inc., 1956), pp. 257-58.

10. Sullivan, Louis H., "Ornament in Architecture," *The Engineering Magazine*, August 1892.

12–15. Pick, Grant, "A School Fit for Children," *The Chicago Reader*, March 1, 1991.

15. "Principle One" from Keim, Kevin P., *An Architectural Life: Memoirs and Memories of Charles W. Moore*, (New York: Little, Brown and Company, 1996), page 280.

16. IBID., p. 281 ("Principle Two").

17-20. Moore, Charles and Lyndon, Donlyn, *Chambers For a Memory Palace* (Boston: MIT Press), 1994, pp. 257-259.

21. Giedion, Sigfried, *Space, Time and Architecture: The Growth of a New Tradition* (Cambridge: Harvard University Press, 1941), p. 748. Gideon by no means invented the notion of a "slab." He notes that the *WPA New York City Guide* (1939) mentions that observers were impelled to nick-name the RCA Building "the Slab."

22. Mumford, Lewis, "The Sky Line: Rockefeller Center Revisited," *The New Yorker*, May 4, 1940.

23. Giedion, Sigfried, *Space, Time and Architecture: The Growth of a New Tradition* (Cambridge: Harvard University Press, 1941), p. 753–755. Although published in 1941, *Space-Time and Architecture* was delivered as talks in the Charles Eliot Norton series of 1938-39. Consequently,

Mumford may have been aware of their content when he wrote "The Sky Line" in note 22 above.

24. Reinhard, L. Andrew, "What is the Rockefeller Radio City?," *Architectural Record* 69:4 (April 1931): 277-81.

25. Moore, Charles and Lyndon, Donlyn, *Chambers For a Memory Palace* (Boston: MIT Press, 1994), p. 48.

1 The Garden in the City

1. Bauer, Catherine, *Modern Housing* (New York: Houghton Mifflin Company, 1934), p. 214.

2. Dal Co, Francesco, "Kevin Roche on Design and Building: Conversation with Francesco Dal Co," *Kevin Roche* (New York: Rizzoli, 1985), p. 20.

3. Cram, Ralph Adams, Radio City-And After," *American Mercury* 13 (July 1931): 291-96.

4. Reinhard, L. Andrew, "What is the Rockefeller Radio City?," *Architectural Record* 69:4 (April 1931): 277-81.

5. An Associate of New York's *Commonwealth Fund*, Geddes Smith (1890–1953) wrote pamphlets for its *Institute of Child Guidance* for almost three decades.

6. Federal Writers' Project, *New York Panorama*, 230.

7. Mumford, Lewis, "The Sky Line: The American Tradition," *The New Yorker*, March 11, 1939, pp. 37–39.

8. Bauer, Catherine, *Modern Housing* (New York: Houghton Mifflin Company, 1934), p. 239.

9. "Robert Alexander returns to Baldwin Hills," *LA Architect*, June 1990, p. 5

Rockefeller Center

1. Reinhard, L. Andrew, "Organization for Co-operation," *Architectural Forum* 56 (january 1932): pp. 77–80.

2. Address given at the opening of the Rockefeller Center Gymnasium, September 20, 1939, quoted in Fosdick, *Rockefeller*, 264.

3. IBID.

4. Corbett, Harvey Wiley, quoted in "Coming City of Set-Back Skyscrapers," *The New York Times Magazine*, April 29, 1923, p.5.

5–6. Hood, Raymond, "The Design of Rockefeller City," *Architectural Forum*, January 1932, pp. 1–12.

7. Hood, Raymond, "Rockefeller Center," *Society of Beaux-Arts Architects Yearbook*, p. 70.

8. Cram, Ralph Adams, Radio City-And After," *American Mercury* 13 (July 1931): 291-96.

9. Mumford, Lewis, "Notes on Modern Architecture," New Republic 66 (March 18, 1931): pp. 119-122.

10. Hood, Raymond, "Rockefeller Center," *Society of Beaux-Arts Architects Yearbook*, p. 70.

11. "Le Corbusier Scans Gotham's Towers," *The New York Times Magazine*, November 3, 1935, p. 10.

12. Hamlin, Talbot, "Architecture," in *New International Yearbook* (New York: Funk and Wagnalls, 1932): 52-58.

13. Jacobs, Jane, *The Death and Life of Great American Cities* (New York: Random House, 1961), p. 181–183.

14. Giedion, Sigfried, *Space, Time and Architecture: The Growth of a New Tradition* (Cambridge: Harvard University Press, 1941), p. 643.

15. Mumford, Lewis, "The Sky Line: The American Tradition,"

The New Yorker, March 11, 1939, pp. 37–39.

Baldwin Hills Village

1. Mumford, Lewis, Introduction to Clarence Stein's *Toward New Towns for America* (Cambridge: MIT Press, 1957), p. 17.

2. Bauer, Catherine, "Baldwin Hills Village," *Pencil Points* 25 (September 1944), pp.46–60.

3. Stein, Clarence, *Toward New Towns for America* (Cambridge: MIT Press, 1957), p. 190. All other quotes by Clarence Stein are from *Toward New Towns for America.*

4. Mumford, Lewis, "Baldwin Hills Village," *Pencil Points* 25 (September 1944), p. 44.

2 Elevating the User Experience

1. Wells, Herbert George, *The Outline of History*, (New York: Macmillan, 1920), p. 215.

2. Kahn, Louis, *Writings, Lectures, Interviews*, New York, 1991, p.118.

3. The financial editor of the *Milwaukee Journal* quoted in "New Frank Lloyd Wright Office Building Shows Shape of Things to Come," *LIFE* 6:19 (May 8, 1939): p. 15.

SC Johnson & Son Administration Building

1. Letter from Frank Lloyd Wright to Herbert F. Johnson dated March 2, 1939, published in *Frank Lloyd Wright: Letters to Clients* (Fresno: California State University Press, 1986) pp. 156–57.

2. "New Frank Lloyd Wright Office Building Shows Shape of Things to Come," *LIFE* 6:19 (May 8, 1939): p. 15.

3. This is no longer true; visitors now park in large open lots away from the building and walk to the front entrance.

4. The concept underlying Johnson Wax was first developed in the plans for the Capital Journal Office Building (1931) and the National Insurance Company Building before that (1924). This "recycling" occurs again with Price Tower and the Guggenheim Museum.

5. Since Wright hated what he called "tyrannical super-building in cities," he convinced the company to move from Racine proper out to the country. Meanwhile, he created a building in a park setting that has no views of the outside world.

6. Wright, Frank Lloyd, "In the Cause of Architecture: Part VI, The Meaning of Materials—Glass," *Architectural Record*, July 1928.

Salk Institute for Biological Studies

1. PIA, April 1961.

2. Kahn, Louis, "Remarks," Lecture at Yale University, October 30, 1963, *Perspecta*, No. 9/10: p. 305.

3. Kahn, Louis, "Silence," *VIA 1* (1968): 88–89.

Ford Foundation Headquarters

1. Dal Co, Francesco, "Kevin Roche on Design and Building: Conversation with Francesco Dal Co," *Kevin Roche* (New York: Rizzoli, 1985), p. 37.

2. Roche speaking in the A.I.A. video, "Accent on Architecture 1995: A Video Tribute to the 1995 Gold Medal and Twenty-Five Year Award of the American Institute of Architects."

3. Kiley, Dan and Amidon, Jane, *The Complete Works of America's Master Landscape Architect* (New York: Little Brown and Company, 1999), pp. 66-67.

4-5. Barnett, Jonathon, "Innovation and Symbolism on 42nd Street," Architectural Record, February 1968.

Philips Exeter Academy Library

1. Letters, Rodney Armstrong to Louis Kahn, July 14 and September 3, 1965, Kahn Collection (see note 3 below).

2. Ackerman, James S., *The Architecture of Michelangelo* (London: A. Zwemmer, Ltd., 1961), pp.111-112

3. Rodney Armstrong (Exeter librarian), tape-recorded interview with David Carris, April, 1982, Louis I. Kahn Collection, University of Pennsylvania and Pennsylvania Historical and Museum Commission, Philadelphia.

3 Where Nature and the Built World Meet

1. Ruskin, John, *The Elements of Drawing*, Letter III, section 215.

2. Moore, Charles; Allen, Gerald; Lyndon, Donlyn, *The Place of Houses* (New York: Henry Holt and Company), 1974, p. 43.

3. Wright, Frank Lloyd, "A New Reality: Glass," from *An Autobiography* (New York: Duell, Stone and Pearce, 1943), pp. 333.

4. Welch, Philip B., ed., "The Continuous Present in Architecture," *Goff on Goff: Conversations and Lectures* (Norman: University of Oklahoma Press, 1996), p. 222.

5. IBID., p. 199.

6. IBID., p. 197.

7. "Architect Ed Barnes: Toward Simpler Details, Simpler Forms, and Greater Unity," *Architectural Forum* 119:8 (August 1973): pp. 74–79.

8. Moore, Charles; Allen, Gerald; Lyndon, Donlyn, *The Place of Houses* (New York: Henry Holt and Company), 1974, p. 47–48.

9. IBID., p. 269.

Taliesin West

1. Wright, Frank Lloyd, "A New Reality: Glass," from *An Autobiography* (New York: Duell, Stone and Pearce, 1943), pp. 339.

2. IBID., p. 331.

3. Tafel, Edgar, *Apprentice to Genius* (New York: McGraw-Hill, 1979), p. 195–96.

4. Wright, Frank Lloyd, *Frank Lloyd Wright on Architecture*, edited by Frederick Gutheim (New York: Duell, Stone and Pearce, 1941), p 248.

5. Peter, John, *The Oral History of Modern Architecture*, (New York: Harry N. Abrams, Inc., 1994) p. 40. When asked in a1955 interview to choose three great works Johnson said, "I would pick . . . the Marseilles apartments of Le Corbusier, Taliesin West of Wright, and the 860 Lake Shore Drive towers of Mies van der Rohe."

Bavinger House

1. Heyer, Paul, *Architects on Architecture: New Directions in America* (New York: Walker and Company, 1966), p. 70.

2. Goff, Bruce, "Forty-Four Architectural Realizations," The Art Institute of Chicago Goff Archives, Manuscripts.

3. Welch, Philip B., ed., "The New Geometry in Architecture," *Goff on Goff: Conversations and Lectures* (Norman: University of Oklahoma Press, 1996), p. 303.

4. Welch, Philip B., ed., "The Continuous Present in Architecture," *Goff on Goff: Conversations and Lectures* (Norman: University of Oklahoma Press, 1996), p. 192–3.

5. Heyer, Paul, *Architects on Architecture: New Directions in America* (New York: Walker and Company, 1966), p. 71.

6. Welch, Philip B., ed., "The Continuous Present in Architecture," *Goff on Goff: Conversations and Lectures* (Norman: University of Oklahoma Press, 1996), p. 193.

7. Fowler, Orson Squire, *A Home for All*, or *The Gravel Wall and Octagon Mode of Building*, 1853 (New York: Dover Publications, Inc., 1973), p. 82.

Haystack Mountain School of Crafts

1–2. Barnes, Edward Larrabee, *Edward Larrabee Barnes: Architect* (New York: Rizzoli International Publications, 1994), p. 70.

3. "Archirect Ed Barnes: Toward Simpler Details, Simpler Forms, and Greater Unity," *Architectural Forum* 119:8 (August 1973): pp. 74–79.

4, 5, 6. Barnes, Edward Larrabee, *Edward Larrabee Barnes: Architect* (New York: Rizzoli International Publications, 1994), p. 70.

Sea Ranch Condominium I

1. Moore, Charles; Allen, Gerald; Lyndon, Donlyn, *The Place of Houses* (New York: Henry Holt and Company), 1974, p. 34.

2. IBID., p. 31.

3. IBID., p. 48.

4. IBID., p. 32.

5. IBID., p. 47.

4 The Essense of Style

1. Saarinen, Eliel, *Search For Form: A Fundamental Approach to Art* (New York: Reinhold Publishing Company, 1948), p. 186.

2. IBID., p. 188.

3. In 1960 Eero referred to his father's earlier advice when he said, "We should stop thinking of our individual buildings. We should take the advice my father gave me, 'Always look at the next larger thing.' When the problem is a building, we should look at the spaces and relationships that that building creates with others . . . In the process [the architect] will gradually formulate strong convictions about outdoor space—the beauty of the space between the buildings—and if he does, he will carry his conviction on to his most important challenge—how to build cities." From Temko, Alan, *Eero Saarinen*, (New York: George Braziller, 1965), p. 26.

4. Peter, John, *The Oral History of Modern Architecture*, (New York: Harry N. Abrams, Inc., 1994) p. 66.

5. Saarinen, Eliel, *Search For Form*.

6. Wright, Frank Lloyd Wright, "Notes on the Building of the H. C. Price Company," April, 1953.

7. From "A Conversation," an NBC telecast interview between Frank Lloyd Wright and Hugh Downs, May 17th, 1953.

8. Saarinen, Aline (ed.), *Eero Saarinen on His Work* (New Haven: Yale, 1962), pp.92.

9. "Art form of man is something which is within man, which is strong when man is strong, and which declines when man declines." From Saarinen, Eliel, *Search For Form*, p. 347

10. *See note 1, above.*

11. Saarinen, Aline (ed.), *Eero Saarinen on His Work* (New Haven: Yale, 1962), pp.94.

Crow Island School

1. Washburne, Carleton, "The Winnetka Plan," *Strategy of the Winnetka School District*, 1937.

2. From "An Oral History of Lawrence Bradford Perkins," an interview with Betty J. Blum in November 1985, compiled under the auspices of the Chicago Architects Oral History Project, The Ernest R. Graham Study Center for Architectural Drawings Department of Architecture, The Art Institute of Chicago, ©1997-2000, The Art Institute of Chicago.

3. Washburne, Carleton, "Notes on Planning," *Architectural Forum* 75:2 (August, 1941): p. 80.

3. Mock, Elizabeth B., "Schools are for Children: Observations on Elementary School Design," 1943. This article was based on a traveling exhibition, *Modern Architecture for the Modern School*, produced by Mock and the Museum of Modern Art in New York and "recommended for communities which plan post-war school construction." The rental fee for 3 weeks was $40.

5. Hudnut, Joseph, "Crow Island School, Winnetka, Ill.," *Architectural Forum* 75:2 (August, 1941): pp. 83–91.

Christ Church Lutheran

1. *See Essence of Style, note 3, above.*

2–3. The Reverend William A. Buege quoted in Christ-Janer, Albert, *Eliel Saarinen: Finnish American Architect and Educator* (Chicago: University of Chicago Press, 1948), p. 118.

4. IBID., 121.

5. IBID., 118.

Yale University Art Gallery

1. "Kahn, Louis, *Writings, Lectures, Interviews*, New York, 1991, p.104.

Price Tower

1. Harold Price interviewed by Sue Lacy for the Landmarks Preservation Commission of Bartlesville, Oklahoma, February 24, 1990.

2. Wright, Frank Lloyd, *Frank Lloyd Wright on Architecture,* edited by Frederick Gutheim (New York: Duell, Stone and Pearce, 1941), p 523.

3. Welch, Philip B., ed., "Advancing Architecture," *Goff on Goff: Conversations and Lectures* (Norman: University of Oklahoma Press, 1996), p. 323.

4. Wright, Frank Lloyd, *Sixty Years of Living With Architecture*, series 9, (Chicago 1956), n.p.

Dulles International Airport

1. "Sensitivity & Crust," *TIME*, September 8, 1961, p. 69.

2–3. Saarinen, Aline (ed.), *Eero Saarinen on His Work* (New Haven: Yale, 1962), pp.92-103.

4. From Kevin Roche's letter to the Jury of Institute Honors, American Institute of Architects, nominating Dulles International Airport for the 25-Year Award, August 26, 1986.

5. Heyer, Paul, *Architects on Architecture: New Directions in America* (New York: Walker and Company, 1966), p. 352.

6. Kiley, Dan and Amidon, Jane, *The Complete Works of America's Master Landscape Architect* (Little Brown and Company, New York, 1999), pp. 40-41.

7. Heyer, Paul, *Architects on Architecture: New Directions in America* (New York: Walker and Company, 1966), p. 353.

5 A Sense of Proportion

1. Hitchcock, Henry-Russell, "The International Style Twenty Years After," *Architectural Record*, August, 1951, pp. 89–97.

2. Rowe, Colin, and Koetter, Fred, Collage City (Cambridge: MIT Press, 1978), p. 7.

3. "Frank Lloyd Wright Ridicules Architectural Schools as Waste," *The New York Times*, June 26, 1952, p. 47.

4. Quoted in Schulze, Franz, *Philip Johnson: Life and Work*, (New York: Alfred A. Knopf, 1994) p. 270.

5. Peter, John, *The Oral History of Modern Architecture*, (New York: Harry N. Abrams, Inc., 1994) p. 201.

6. Vincent Scully, "The Death of the Street," Symposium at the Museum of Modern Art, New York, November 16, 1952.

7. Roth, Richard, quoted in "Architectural League Bewails Boom," *Interiors* 121 (December 1961): p. 69.

8. Mumford, Lewis, "Sky Line: Crystal Lantern," *The New Yorker*, November 13, 1954, pp. 149-56.

9. Louchheim, Aline, "Newest Building in the New Style," *New York Times*, April 27, 1952.

10. Mumford, Lewis, "Sky Line: House of Glass," *The New Yorker*, August 9, 1952, pp. 48–50.

11. "Emergence of a Master Architect," *LIFE* 42:11 (March 18, 1957): p. 64.

Equitable Savings and Loan

1. Peter, John, *The Oral History of Modern Architecture*, (New York: Harry N. Abrams, Inc., 1994) p. 40.

2. Belluschi, Pietro "Notes on the New Equitable Building," typescript, 10 January 1946, (Belluschi files).

3. A 13th story was added later.

860-880 Lake Shore Drive Apartments

1. Mies van der Rohe, "Foreword" to the official catalogue of the Stuttgart Werkbund exhibition *Die Wohnung*, 1927.

2. Quoted in Blake, Peter, *The Master Builders: Le Corbusier, Mies van der Rohe, Frank Lloyd Wright* (New York: Alfred A. Knopf, 1960), pp. 244–245.

3. From an untitled text on the Friedrichstrasse skyscraper project, Frülicht, 1922, quoted in Johnson, Philip, *Mies van der Rohe*, (New York: Museum of Modern Art, 1953), p. 182.

4. Neutra, Richard, *Architectural Record*, August, 1956, pp. 174–77.

Lever House

1. *LIFE*, June 2, 1952.

Business Week praised Lever House as "spacious, efficient, and washable," a building that had "gone a long way toward making a work of art out of office space." "Lever House:

Spacious, Efficient and Washable," *Business Week*, May 3, 1952, pp. 76-77.

Jacobus, John M., "Skidmore, Owings and Merrill," *Encyclopedia of Modern Architecture*, (New York: Harry N. Abrams, Inc., 1964), p. 261.

2. Mumford, Lewis, "The Sky Line: House of Glass," *The New Yorker*, August 9, 1952, pp. 48-50.

3. Louchheim, Aline, "Newest Building in the New Style," *The New York Times*, April 27, 1952.

4. Mumford, Lewis, "Sky Line: Crystal Lantern," *The New Yorker*, November 13, 1954, pp. 149-56.

5. "Miniature Skyscraper of Blue Glass and Metal Challenges Postwar Craze for Overbuilding City Lots," *Architectural Forum*, June 1950, pp. 85-86.

6. Louchheim, Aline, "Newest Building in the New Style," *The New York Times*, April 27, 1952.

7. Mumford, Lewis, "The Sky Line: House of Glass," *The New Yorker*, August 9, 1952, pp. 48-50.

8. "The Talk of the Town: Clean," *The New Yorker*, April 26, 1952, pp. 27-28.

Seagram Building

1. Lambert, Phyllis, letter to Eve Borsook, December 1, 1954, quoted in "How a Building Gets Built," *Vassar Alumni Magazine*, February 1959, p. 17.

2. Mumford, Lewis, "Sky Line: The Lesson of the Master," *The New Yorker*, September 13, 1958, pp. 141-148.

3. Corbett, Harvey Wiley, quoted in "Coming City of Set-Back Skyscrapers," *The New York Times Magazine*, April 29, 1923, p.5.

4. Phyllis Lambert quoted in "Monument in Bronze," *TIME*, March 3, 1958, p. 52.

5. Mies quoted in Carter, Peter, *Mies van der Rohe at Work* (New York: Praeger, 1974), pp. 61–62.

6 The Way We Live

1. Cleaveland, Henry William, *Village and Farm Cottages*,1854. A pattern-book designer, Cleaveland believed that a well-designed home was within reach of every virtuous Christian family at very little cost.

2. From an interview with Ray Eames conducted by Ruth Bowen, July-August, 1980, Venice, California, The California Oral History Project, Archives of American Art, Smithsonian Institution, p. 13

3. Blake, Peter, *The Master Builders: Le Corbusier, Mies van der Rohe, Frank Lloyd Wright* (New York: Alfred A. Knopf, 1960), pp. 230-31.

4. Venturi, Robert, *Complexity and Contradiction* (New York: Museum of Modern Art, 1977), p. 118.

5. Remarks made by Richard Meier upon receiving the 25-Year Award at the National Building Museum, Washington, D.C., January 2000.

Eames House

1. "Case Study Houses 8 and 9 by Charles Eames and Eero Saarinen, Architects," *Arts & Architecture*, December 1945.

2. Eames, Charles and Entenza, John, "What is a House?," *Arts & Architecture*, July, 1944

3. From an interview with Ray Eames conducted by Ruth

Bowen, July-August, 1980, Venice, California, The California Oral History Project, Archives of American Art, Smithsonian Institution, pp. 12-13

Philip Johnson Residence [the Glass House]

1. Philip Johnson, "House at New Canaan, Connecticut," *Architectural Review* 108:645 (September 1950): pp. 152-59.

2. Giovannini, Joseph, "Johnson and His Glass House: Reflections," *The New York Times,* July 16, 1987.

3. Drexler, Arthur, "Architecture Opaque and Transparent," *Interiors & Industrial Design,* October 1949.

Farnsworth House

1. Quoted in Neumeyer, Fritz, *The Artless Word: Mies van der Rohe on the Building Art* (Cambridge: MIT Press, 1991), p. 74.

2. Blake, Peter, *The Master Builders: Le Corbusier, Mies van der Rohe, Frank Lloyd Wright* (New York: Alfred A. Knopf, 1960), pp. 228-229.

Vanna Venturi House

1. Venturi, Robert, "Diversity, Relevance and Representation in Historicism, or Plus Ça Change. . ." *Arcitectural Record,* June 1982, p. 114.

2. IBID, p. 118.

3. Venturi, Robert, *Complexity and Contradiction* (New York: Museum of Modern Art, 1977), p. 118.

Smith House

1. Remarks made by Richard Meier upon receiving the 25-Year Award at the National Building Museum, Washington, D.C., January 2000.

7 The Corporate Campus

1. Kaufman, Edgar, Jr., *Interiors,* March 1951, p. 100.

2. From "Styling-The Auto Industry's Cinderella," General Motors paper, 1958, p.1.

3. Hewitt, William A., "The Genesis of a Great Building—and of an Unusual Friendship," [Hewitt's address to the A.I.A. College of Fellows Convocation dinner in San Diego, California, June 6, 1977] *Journal of the A.I.A.,* August 1977, p. 36.

General Motors Technical Center.

1. Dal Co, Francesco, "Kevin Roche on Design and Building: Conversation with Francesco Dal Co," *Kevin Roche* (New York: Rizzoli, 1985), p. 22.

2. Letter from Eero Saarinen to Astrid Sampe, dated January 9, 1953, Cranbrook Archives.

3. Letter from Eero Saarinen to Astrid Sampe, no date, Cranbrook Archives.

4. Saarinen, Aline (ed.), *Eero Saarinen on His Work* (New Haven: Yale, 1962), p 24.

5. Saarinen, Aline (ed.), *Eero Saarinen on His Work* (New Haven: Yale, 1962), p 28.

Deere & Company Administrative Center

1. From "Challenge to an Architect: Deere & Company Administration Center," statements by Eero Saarinen edited by Aline Saarinen, published as a public relations brochure, c. 1965.

2-3. Hewitt, William A., "The Genesis of a Great Building

—and of an Unusual Friendship," *Journal of the A.I.A.,* August 1977, p. 36.

4. Letter from William A. Hewitt to Eero Saarinen dated August 23, 1957.

5. From a live radio interview with William A. Hewitt and Eero Saarinen, broadcast June 11, 1958.

6. Saarinen, Aline (ed.), *Eero Saarinen on His Work* (New Haven: Yale, 1962), p 82.

8 Sublime Innovation

Solomon R. Guggenheim Museum

1. Blake, Peter, *The Master Builders: Le Corbusier, Mies van der Rohe, Frank Lloyd Wright* (New York: Alfred A. Knopf, 1960), pp. 377–8.

2. Blake, Peter, "The Guggenheim: Museum or Monument?," *Architectural Forum,* December 1959, pp. 86–92.

3. Once James Johnson Sweeney became director, how-ever, he promptly enlarged the museum's purview, and with this expansion of interest, its name became what it is today, a memorial to its founder.

4. Wright, Frank Lloyd Wright, "The Solomon R. Guggenheim Memorial Museum: An Experiment in the Third-Dimension," May 16, 1958, p. 17.

5. Canaday, John, "Wright V.s. Painting," *The New York Times,* October 21, 1959, p.1.

6. "Frank Lloyd Wright's Sole Legacy to New York," *Interiors,* December 1959, pp. 89–95.

7. Mumford, Lewis, "Sky Line: Fujiyama of Architecture," *The New Yorker,* 1953.

Gateway Arch

1. Cheek, Lawrence W., "Eero Saarinen: Architect, Sculptor, Visionary," Jefferson National Expansion Historical Association, 1998.

2. Dan Kiley, interview with Bob Moore, July 23, 1993, The Office of Dan Kiley, Charlotte, Vermont, quoted in "Preserving Modern Landscape Architecture: Papers from the Wave Hill-National Park Service Conference," May 1999.

3. France, Bob, "Gateway to Midwest Takes Visitors to Top," *Flagler/Palm Coast News-Tribune,* September 3, 1997, p. 5.

U.S. Air Force Academy Cadet Chapel

1. "Spires That Soar," *TIME* 80:4 (July 27, 1962): p. 64.

2-8. From "An Oral History of Walter Netsch," an interview with Betty J. Blum in June 1995, compiled under the auspices of the Chicago Architects Oral History Project, The Ernest R. Graham Study Center for Architectural Drawings Department of Architecture, The Art Institute of Chicago, ©1997-2000, The Art Institute of Chicago.

Kimbell Art Museum

1. Kahn, Louis, *Writings, Lectures, Interviews,* New York, 1991, p. 277.

2. Quoted in "Louis Kahn," *Conversations with Architects,* ed. John W. Cook and Heinrich Klotz (New York: Praeger, 1973), 212.

3. Wurman, R.S., *What Will Be Has Always Been: The Words of Louis Kahn* (Cambridge: MIT Press, 1973), p. 216.

4. Drysdale, Susan, "Fort Worth Museum," *Houston Post,* November 9, 1972.

l. = left; r. = right; t. = top; c. = center; b. = bottom

Roman face denotes reference in text.
Italic denotes reference in a sidebar.
Bold denotes a photograph.